990 Handbook

A Line-by-Line Approach

Jody Blazek

JOHN WILEY & SONS, INC.

New York • Chichester • Weinheim • Brisbane • Singapore • Toronto

WILEY NONPROFIT LAW, FINANCE, AND MANAGEMENT SERIES

The Art of Planned Giving: Understanding Donors and the Culture of Giving by Douglas E. White
Beyond Fund Raising: New Strategies for Nonprofit Investment and Innovation by Kay Grace
Budgeting for Not-for-Profit Organizations by David Maddox
Charity, Advocacy, and the Law by Bruce R. Hopkins
The Complete Guide to Fund Raising Management by Stanley Weinstein
The Complete Guide to Nonprofit Management by Smith, Bucklin & Associates
Critical Issues in Fund Raising edited by Dwight Burlingame
Developing Affordable Housing: A Practical Guide for Nonprofit Organizations, Second Edition by Bennett L. Hecht
Faith-Based Management: Leading Organizations that are Based on More than Just Mission by Peter Brinckerhoff
Financial and Accounting Guide for Not-for-Profit Organizations, Sixth Edition by Malvern J. Gross, Jr., Richard F. Larkin, Roger S. Bruttomesso, John J. McNally, PricewaterhouseCoopers LLP
Financial Empowerment: More Money for More Mission by Peter Brinckerhoff
Financial Management for Nonprofit Organizations by Jo Ann Hankin, Alan Seidner and John Zietlow
Financial Planning for Nonprofit Organizations by Jody Blazek
The First Legal Answer Book for Fund-Raisers by Bruce R. Hopkins
The Fund Raiser's Guide to the Internet by Michael Johnston
Fund-Raising: Evaluating and Managing the Fund Development Process, Second Edition by James M. Greenfield
Fund-Raising Fundamentals: A Guide to Annual Giving for Professionals and Volunteers by James M. Greenfield
Fundraising Cost Effectiveness: A Self-Assessment Workbook by James M. Greenfield
Fund-Raising Regulation: A State-by-State Handbook of Registration Forms, Requirements, and Procedures by Seth Perlman and Betsy Hills Bush
Grantseeker's Budget Toolkit by James A. Quick and Cheryl S. New
Grantseeker's Toolkit: A Comprehensive Guide to Finding Funding by Cheryl S. New and James A. Quick
Grant Winner's Toolkit: Project Management and Evaluation by James A. Quick and Cheryl S. New
High Impact Philanthropy: How Donors, Boards, and Nonprofit Organizations can Transform Nonprofit Communities by Kay Sprinkel Grace and Alan L. Wendroff
High Performance Nonprofit Organizations: Managing Upstream for Greater Impact by Christine Letts, William Ryan, and Allen Grossman
Improving the Economy, Efficiency, and Effectiveness of Nonprofits: Conducting Operational Reviews by Rob Reider
Intermediate Sanctions: Curbing Nonprofit Abuse by Bruce R. Hopkins and D. Benson Tesdahl
International Fund Raising for Nonprofits by Thomas Harris
International Guide to Nonprofit Law by Lester A. Salamon and Stefan Toepler & Associates
Joint Ventures Involving Tax-Exempt Organizations, Second Edition by Michael I. Sanders
The Law of Fund-Raising, Second Edition by Bruce R. Hopkins
The Law of Tax-Exempt Healthcare Organizations, Second Edition by Thomas K. Hyatt and Bruce R. Hopkins
The Law of Tax-Exempt Organizations, Seventh Edition by Bruce R. Hopkins
The Legal Answer Book for Nonprofit Organizations by Bruce R. Hopkins
A Legal Guide to Starting and Managing a Nonprofit Organization, Third Edition by Bruce R. Hopkins
The Legislative Laberynth: A Map for Not-for-Profits, edited by Walter Pidgeon
Managing Affordable Housing: A Practical Guide to Creating Stable Communities by Bennett L. Hecht, Local Initiatives Support Corporation, and James Stockard
Managing Upstream: Creating High-Performance Nonprofit Organizations by Christine W. Letts, William P. Ryan, and Allan Grossman
Mission-Based Management: Leading Your Not-for-Profit In the 21st Century, Second Edition by Peter Brinckerhoff
Mission-Based Management: Leading Your Not-for-Profit In the 21st Century, Second Edition: An Organizational Development Workbook by Peter Brinckerhoff
Mission-Based Marketing: How Your Not-for-Profit Can Succeed in a More Competitive World by Peter Brinckerhoff
Nonprofit Boards: Roles, Responsibilities, and Performance by Diane J. Duca
Nonprofit Compensation and Benefits Practices by Applied Research and Development Institute International, Inc.
The Nonprofit Counsel by Bruce R. Hopkins
The Nonprofit Guide to the Internet, Second Edition by Michael Johnston
Nonprofit Investment Policies: A Practical Guide to Creation and Implementation by Robert Fry, Jr.

The Nonprofit Law Dictionary by Bruce R. Hopkins
Nonprofit Compensation, Benefits, and Employment Law by David G. Samuels and Howard Pianko
Nonprofit Litigation: A Practical Guide with Forms and Checklists by Steve Bachmann
The Nonprofit Handbook, Third Edition: Management by Tracy Daniel Connors
The Nonprofit Handbook, Third Edition: Fund Raising by James M. Greenfield
The Nonprofit Manager's Resource Dictionary by Ronald A. Landskroner
Nonprofit Organizations' Business Forms: Disk Edition by John Wiley & Sons, Inc.
Planned Giving: Management, Marketing, and Law, Second Edition by Ronald R. Jordan and Katelyn L. Quynn
Private Foundations: Tax Law and Compliance by Bruce R. Hopkins and Jody Blazek
Program Related Investments: A Technical Manual for Foundations by Christie I. Baxter
Reengineering Your Nonprofit Organization: A Guide to StrategicTransformation by Alceste T. Pappas
Reinventing the University: Managing and Financing Institutions of Higher Education by Sandra L. Johnson and Sean C. Rush, PricewaterhouseCoopers LLP
The Second Legal Answer Book for Nonprofit Organizations by Bruce R. Hopkins
The Second Legal Answer Book for Fund Raisers by Bruce R. Hopkins
Social Entrepreneurship: The Art of Mission-Based Venture Development by Peter Brinckerhoff
Special Events: Proven Strategies for Nonprofit Fund Raising by Alan Wendroff
Starting and Managing a Nonprofit Organization: A Legal Guide, Third Edition by Bruce R. Hopkins
Strategic Communications for Nonprofit Organizations: Seven Steps to Creating a Successful Plan by Janel Radtke
Strategic Planning for Nonprofit Organizations: A Practical Guide and Workbook by Michael Allison and Jude Kaye, Support Center for Nonprofit Management
Streetsmart Financial Basics for Nonprofit Managers by Thomas A. McLaughlin
A Streetsmart Guide to Nonprofit Mergers and Networks by Thomas A. McLaughlin
Successful Marketing Strategies for Nonprofit Organizations by Barry J. McLeish
Successful Corporate Fund Raising: Effective Strategies for Today's Nonprofits by Scott Sheldon
The Tax Law of Charitable Giving, Second Edition by Bruce R. Hopkins
The Tax Law of Colleges and Universities by Bertrand M. Harding
Tax Planning and Compliance for Tax-Exempt Organizations: Forms, Checklists, Procedures, Third Edition by Jody Blazek
The Universal Benefits of Volunteering: A Practical Workbook for Nonprofit Organizations, Volunteers, and Corporations by Walter P. Pidgeon, Jr.
The Volunteer Management Handbook by Tracy Daniel Connors
Trade Secrets for Nonprofit Managers by Thomas A. McLaughlin
Values-Based Estate Planning: A Step-by-Step Approach to Wealth Transfers for Professional Advisors by Scott Fithian

This book is printed on acid-free paper. ♾

Published simultaneously in Canada.

ISBN 0-471-41781-5
Printed in the United States of America.
10 9 8 7 6 5 4 3 2 1

Contents

Preface

The Forms 990 have entered the 21st century on the Internet courtesy of Guidestar.org. It's critical these annual federal returns be prepared, not only as financial documents, but also as a tool for communicating an organization's mission and accomplishment to the public. Forms 990 provide a wealth of financial and programmatic information to enable government regulators, funders, journalists, and the interested public to measure a nonprofit's performance. A copy of the forms must be provided to anyone that asks and for charities, they are now posted on the Internet. These forms are the most widely used tool for evaluating tax-exempt organizations. Schools, health and welfare organizations, business leagues, civic associations, museums, parent groups, garden clubs, private foundations, and the myriad of other nonprofit organizations recognized under section 501 and political organizations exempt under section 527 of the federal tax code must file this form annually. Clear, correct, and concise preparation of Forms 990-EZ, 990, 990-PF, and 990-T is critically important to nonprofit organizations.

My goal for this handbook is to demystify the Forms 990 for financial professionals and nonprofessionals alike—to make it easy for a nonprofit organization to achieve the best possible presentation of their financial activity and mission accomplishments for all to see. The reason why information is requested is briefly explained to give the preparer a context for presenting the information. The criteria applied to determine, for example, whether to report a government grant as a donation on line 1 rather than program services revenue on line 2 of part I of the Form 990 is presented. Secondarily, readers will find out how the choice impacts the public support test. The few circumstances in which the tax reporting rules differ from reporting according to the accounting standards are presented. Hopefully, complicated concepts are translated into understandable language to explain the why and how Forms 990 can be optimally prepared. Among the tools that are provided are:

- Tips on the order in which the returns should be prepared—front to back in sequential order is inefficient and, in the case of a private foundation, is impossible.
- Instructions on how to prepare the Part VII analysis of revenues can be vital in avoiding unnecessary IRS scrutiny of earned income
- Explanation of consequences of answers that can have several interpretations
- Suggestions for reporting changes in fiscal year, accounting method, and activities to the IRS and deciding when to seek overt IRS approval as an organization grows and changes
- Methods for maximizing deductions in calculating tax due on unrelated business income with good cost accounting records that identify applicable deductions on Form 990-T
- Tips for successful navigation of the interactive parts of Form 990-PF and reducing excise tax

Issues that are key to maintaining exempt status are highlighted in this handbook to alert readers to questions that deserve close attention. Footnotes provide references to the tax code and to the 3rd edition of my *Tax Planning and Compliance for Tax-Exempt Organizations, Forms, Checklists, and Procedures* book where extensive discussions of criteria for obtaining and maintaining tax-exempt status can be found. The often-arduous process of completing and getting approval for Forms 1023 and 1024, Applications for Recognition of Tax-Exempt Status, is considered in the tax book. The issues that Form 990 preparers should be particularly sensitive to are highlighted in the handbook with references to book chapters. Specifically the type of transactions that can endanger a nonprofit's tax-exempt status and/or result in an unexpected tax liability are explained. The parameters for doing business with an organization's insiders, for establishing reasonable compensation levels, for identifying activities that produce income incident to accomplishing the exempt purposes versus unrelated business income that might be taxed, for complying with employment tax issues, and a myriad of other issues are given special consideration.

This 990 Handbook begins with an explanation of the filing requirements and continues to explain completion of Form 990, Schedule A, Form 990-PF, and Form 990-T line-by-line. The relevance of the information requested is discussed. A synopsis of applicable tax rules is provided to give a context to the many choices a return preparer must make in completing these complex government forms. The last chapter makes suggestions for communicating with the Internal Revenue Service as the organization evolves. When and how to inform the IRS Exempt Organization division of changes in activities, structure, public charity status, and more is considered. The IRS Exempt Organization repesentatives are customarily well trained and helpful. Folks in my office call 1-877-829-5500 to get an IRS opinion on filing matters for which we can't find a ready answer or simply want to know their view. During 2001, readers should expect to see the results of their new public education effort designed to publish "plain language" publications to explain the rules applicable to tax-exempt nonprofits. As the IRS itself says on page 3, "Form 990 is available for public inspection and, for some people, serves as the primary or sole source of information about a particular organization. How the public perceives an organization in such cases may be determined by the information presented on its return." I hope this handbook provides a useful tool to enhance public information reporting by nonprofit organizations.

Jody Blazek
February 2001
Houston, Texas

Acknowledgments

First and foremost I acknowledge and thank my brilliant assistant, Gabriele Schweigart, whose invaluable help made this book possible. I am deeply grateful for the talent she applied to editing the text, dreaming up filled-in forms, and questioning my explanations. I am also indebted to my tax associate, Lois Yager, for her creativity in reviewing the forms. Next I thank all the folks at John Wiley & Sons that make the Wiley Nonprofit Series of books an invaluable collection of reference books for the nonprofit sector. Lastly I treasure all those who have joined me in serving the Texas Accountants and Lawyers for the Arts, the AICPA Tax-Exempt Organizations Resource Panel, the Volunteer Services Committee of the Houston Chapter of CPAs, and the Management Assistance Program of the United Way of the Texas Gulf Coast over the years. Together we have enhanced the body of knowledge available to the nonprofit sector and improved the resulting delivery of valuable services to the constituents those nonprofits serve.

This book is dedicated to all the tireless volunteers who serve nonprofit organizations.

About the Author

Jody Blazek is a partner in Blazek & Vetterling LLP, a Houston, Texas CPA firm focusing on tax and financial planning for exempt organizations and the individuals who create, fund, and work with them. BV serves over 250 nonprofit organizations providing financial attestation services and tax compliance and planning services.

Jody began her professional career at KPMG, then Peat, Marwick, Mitchell & Co. Her concentration on exempt organizations began in 1969 when she was assigned to study the Tax Reform Act that completely revamped the taxation of charities and created private foundations. From 1972 to 1981, she gained nonprofit management experience as treasurer of the Menil Interests where she worked with John and Dominique de Menil to plan the Menil Collection, The Rothko Chapel, and other projects of the Menil Foundation. She reentered public practice in 1981 to found the firm she now serves.

She is the author of three other books in the Wiley Nonprofit Series: *Tax Planning and Compliance for Tax-Exempt Organizations, 3rd Edition* (1999), *Financial Planning for Nonprofit Organizations* (1996), and *Private Foundations: Tax Law and Compliance* (1998) coauthored with Bruce R. Hopkins.

Jody is the vice-chair of the American Institute of Certified Public Accountants' Tax-Exempt Organizations Resource Panel and chair of its Internet Services Task Force. She serves on the national editorial board of Tax Analysts' *The Exempt Organization Tax Review* and the Community Service Committee of the Houston Chapter of Certified Public Accountants. She is a founding director and program chair for the Texas Accountants and Lawyers for the Arts and a member of the board of the Anchorage Foundations, Houston Artists Fund, Main Street Foundation, and the River Pierce Foundation. She is a frequent speaker at nonprofit symposia, including AICPA Not-for-Profit Industry Conference, The University of Texas School of Law Nonprofit Organizations

Institute, the Institute for Board Development, and Nonprofit Resource Center's Nonprofit Legal and Accounting Institute, among others.

Blazek received her BBA from University of Texas at Austin 1964 and attended South Texas School of Law. She and her husband, David Crossley, nurture two sons, Austin and Jay Blazek Crossley.

CHAPTER ONE

Tools, Concepts, Filing, and Reporting Requirements

Forms 990, 990-EZ, and 990-PF are designed to accomplish many purposes that go far beyond simply reporting to the Internal Revenue Service (referred to in this book as the IRS). The forms present a myriad of financial and programmatic information that allows Federal and state regulators to scrutinize the activities of organizations qualifying for tax-exemption as public and private charities, civic and business leagues, labor unions, social clubs, and many other types of nonprofit organizations. Those that financially support nonprofits with their time and money, as well as those journalists and scholars who record and scrutinize their performance and impact on society, use the forms to gather information. It is, therefore, crucial that these annual returns be prepared, not only as a financial document, but also as a tool for communicating an organization's mission and accomplishment to the public.

Accurate and complete preparation of the forms should be given top priority as the forms enter the electronic age accessible to one and all on the Internet. A copy of the forms must also be provided to anyone that asks and is willing to pay a modest fee. A nonprofit organization's public reporting responsibilities have entered another dimension and deserve careful attention. Chapters 2, 3, and 4 lead the reader through the forms line-by-line and give instructions and suggestions for preparing the forms. Even though they are classified as a tax-exempt organization, some nonprofits receive business income subject to the normal income tax. Chapter 5 considers the preparation of form 990-T required to be filed to report business income and presents ideas for maximizing deductions and minimizing the resulting tax liability. Lastly Chapter 6 reviews procedures and choices for informing the IRS of changes in an organization's activities and structure as it evolves and changes over the years.

In March 1997, the IRS contracted with the Urban Institute of Washington, D.C., to receive and place the forms for the years 1996 through 2001 on CD-ROM with the hope that Forms 990s would be made available on the Internet. In a coordinated effort, Philanthropic Resources, Inc. began in 1998 to digitize the information so that it can be sorted and searched. Information from prior 990s of some 40,000 public charities was originally entered (www.guidestar.org). The Guidestar site provides an abstract of information they glean from the forms and also posts the complete form.[1] The IRS is also studying an electronic filing system for 990s to eliminate the paperwork altogether and allow them to more effectively monitor exempts in a statistical and focused fashion.

In essence, and now in fact, the Forms 990 are public documents. Yet another reason for a tax-exempt organization to pay careful attention to completion of the forms is the requirement that copies of the three most recent years' returns must be given upon request to those who pay a modest fee. Between 1984 and 1997, an organization had to allow anyone who knocked on its door a look at its Forms 990 and 1023 or 1024 in its office. Since June 8, 1999, a copy of the forms must also be furnished to anyone willing to pay a fee as discussed in §1.2(a). Forms 990 are also used for a wide variety of state and local reporting purposes. In many states, an exempt organization can satisfy its annual filing requirement by furnishing a copy of Form 990 to the appropriate state authority. Many grant-making foundations request a copy of Form 990 in addition to or in lieu of audited financial statements, to verify an organization's fiscal activity. The open-records standards applicable in many states also require all financial reports and records be open to the public.

The Forms 990 illustrated in the appendices to chapters 2 through 5 provide a wealth of information. An organization's basic financial information—revenues, expenses, assets, and liabilities—are classified into meaningful categories to allow the IRS to evaluate a nonprofit's ongoing qualification for federal tax exemption under Internal Revenue Code (IRC) §501 (hereinafter code section numbers are simply identified with the symbol "§"). The returns are also used by funders, state and federal regulators, journalists, and many other persons to evaluate the scope and type of a nonprofit's activity. Information pertaining to the accomplishment of the organization's mission is presented—how many persons are served, papers researched, reports completed, students enrolled, and the like. Extensive details are furnished for grants paid to support other organizations and disbursed as aid to the poor, sick, students, and others in need. For leagues, details regarding payments to members are provided. Details are furnished to reflect overall compensation for services, sales of assets, and loans (if any) to or from persons who run and control the organization. The program accomplishment reports should particularly be prepared with a view to presenting the organization to funders and other supporters. Some use the information to compare nonprofit organizations statistically.

A comprehensive survey of the federal tax rules pertaining to the tax-exempt organizations of all sorts—charitable, business, social, and civic organizations—are contained in another of the author's book in the Wiley Nonprofit Series, *Tax Planning and Compliance for Tax-Exempt Organizations,* now in its third edition and supplemented annually for current development and new forms. Citations to the *Tax Planning and Compliance* book can be found throughout this book for readers who want to study the issues in more depth.

A long list of questions on Forms 990 and 990-PF fish for failures to comply with the federal and, to some extent, state requirements for donor and member disclosures, mandatory payout, political and lobbying activity, transactions with nonexempt organizations, insider transactions, and more. In sum, the returns are designed to show that a nonprofit organization is entitled to maintain its tax-exempt status and also to provide a wealth of other information of interest to funders, constituents, and regulators. Readers might also find the annual tax compliance checklists for preparation of Forms 90, 990-PF, and 990-T found in the *Tax Planning and Compliance* volume useful. They are designed to make survey a wide range of tax issues, including state and payroll reporting requirements, satisfaction of the disclosure rules, and many other issues. The type of questions that can be answered with information on the forms follow:

- Do Parts III and VII of Form 990 and Parts IX-A, IX-B, and XV of Form 990-PF indicate the organization's activities focus on an exempt purpose?
- Do the fund-raising costs shown on Part I, line 15, and detailed in column (d) of Part II, Form 990, equal too high a percentage of the total expenses, indicating that the nonprofit fails the commensurate test?[2]
- Does column (b) of Part VII of Form 990 and Part XVI-A of Form 990-PF show a high percentage of unrelated business revenues in relation to the total revenues, indicating that the organization is devoted to business interests rather than exempt purposes?[3]
- Do payments in Part II, lines 24 through 30, and Part V of Form 990 and Part I, lines 13 through 16, and Part VIII of Form 990-PF reflect high compensation payments to private individuals?[4]

- Is the amount a public charity reported on Schedule A, Part VI-A or B for lobbying expenditures excessive (private foundations can spend none and some nonprofits exempt in categories other than 501(c)(3) can spend an unlimited amount)?[5]
- Do a public charity's sources of support shown in Part IV of Schedule A indicate it receives 33⅓ percent of its support from the public so it continues to be classified as a public charity under 509(a)(1) or (a)(2)?[6]

It is extremely important by way of introduction to remind readers that tax-exempt organizations are taxpayers. Though certain types of revenues they collect may not be subject to income tax under §501(c), they are subject to all of the sections contained in the Internal Revenue Code and the tax rules imposed by the states in which they operate. Many of the problems nonprofits ask the author to solve stem from lack of awareness of this fact. Matters that deserve attention include federal payroll taxes, gift and estate taxes, donor and dues deductibility rules that impact persons who provide the revenues, and other federal issues, such as labor laws and employee retirement plans (Employee Retirement Income Security Act [ERISA] rules). Throughout this handbook, references to the author's *Tax Compliance* book are tied to points about which readers may benefit by a more thorough discussion.

Finally, representatives of federally tax-exempt organizations must also inform themselves of the wide variety of state and local tax compliance and filing requirements beyond the scope of this handbook to which the nonprofit may be subject. Due to the increasing globalization of activity fostered by the Internet, readers must pay close attention for new developments in this regard. Professional help should be sought; certified public accountant (CPA) and bar association referral services are available to recommend persons with nonprofit organization experience. For those organizations that cannot afford to pay, a nonprofit management assistance program can be found. Many civic-minded CPAs, lawyers, and businesspeople volunteer their time through local bar and CPA societies, the United Way, retired executive groups, and the like.

1.1 FIND OUT WHY THE NONPROFIT QUALIFIES FOR TAX EXEMPTION

Either Form 1023 or 1024 is filed to seek IRS recognition of tax exemption. Ideally, this application is filed before a Form 990 is due at the end of a newly created organization's first fiscal year closing. A nonprofit seeking to be classified under IRC §501(c)(3) as a charity does not qualify until it files Form 1023 for recognition. Once the IRS determines exemption is permitted, qualification is granted retroactive to date of formation. For other categories of tax-exempt organization, Form 1024 is filed. Submitting Form 990 for an organization that has not yet sought recognition of exemption will bring an IRS request that Form 1023 or 1024 be filed. The author recommends that tax return preparers review the application and any IRS correspondence pertaining to a nonprofit's qualification. For many reasons, it is important to know why the IRS granted exempt status. Forms 990, 990-EZ, and 990-PF ask each year, "Did the organization engage in any activity not previously reported to the IRS?" To identify revenues as related or unrelated to the nonprofit's mission necessitates an understanding of an entity's exempt functions. The starting point for evaluating whether a proposed program might in any way endanger the organization's exempt status is the rationale for their original qualification.

The world of tax-exempt organizations includes a broad range of nonprofit institutions: churches, schools, charities, business leagues, political parties, schools, country clubs, and united giving campaigns conducting a wide variety of pursuits intended to serve the public good. All exempt organizations share the common attribute of being organized for the advancement of a group of persons, rather than particular individuals or businesses. Most exempt organizations are afforded special tax and legal status precisely because of the unselfish motivation behind their formation. The common thread running through the various types of exempt organizations is the lack of private ownership and profit motive. A broad definition of an *exempt organization* is "a nonprofit entity operated without self-interest to serve a societal or group mission that pays none of the income or profit to private individuals."

Federal and state governments view nonprofits as relieving their burdens and performing certain functions of government. Thus, many nonprofits are exempted from the levies that finance government, including income, sales, ad valorem, and other local property taxes. This special status recognizes the work they perform essentially on behalf of the government. In addition, for charitable nonprofits, labor unions, business leagues, and other types of exempt organizations, the tax deductibility of dues and donations paid to them further evidences the government's willingness to forgo money in their favor. At the same time, deductibility provides a major fund-raising tool. For complex reasons, some of which are not readily apparent, all nonprofits are not equal for tax deduction purposes, and not all "donations" are deductible.[7]

On the federal level, IRC §501 exempts 28 specific types of nonprofit organizations, as well as pension plans (IRC §401) from income tax. Although exempt organizations are often perceived as charitable, many other types of nonprofits are classified as tax-exempt under the federal income tax code. Labor unions, business leagues, community associations, cemeteries, employee benefit societies, social clubs, and many other types of organizations are listed in IRC §501. For purposes of federal tax exemption, each category has its own distinct set of criteria for qualification.[8]

1.2 FILING FORMS 990

The annual Forms 990 are submitted to a processing center devoted exclusively to exempt return filings. In 1997, the IRS centralized the filing of Forms 990EZ, 990-PF, 990-T, 1041-A, 4720, 5227, 5578, and 5768 in the Ogden, Utah, Service Center. The centralization was planned to improve the speed and accuracy of return processing through a consolidation of expertise on exempt organization matters. In a similar fashion, the applications for recognition of initial qualification for tax-exempt status, Forms 1023 and 1024, are all filed with the Cincinnati, Ohio, Key District Office.[9] Examination of exempt organizations is the responsibility of the Dallas, Texas, Key District; technical advice and ruling continue to be issued by the Washington office.

The forms have evolved slowly over the years through cooperative efforts between the IRS, nonprofit organizations, the American Institute of Certified Public Accountants (AICPA), the American Bar Association (ABA), and state officials. Page 6 of Form 990, added by Congressional mandate, reveals the related and unrelated nature of an organization's revenues.[10] Part IV-A and B was added in response to Financial Accounting Standards Board (FASB) pronouncements in 1995. Although no major changes are expected in the near future, readers should always consult the current supplement to this book for new versions. The author has suggested redesign of Schedule A to contain one summary page that prompts attachment of detailed attachments only by those public charities to which they apply. Presently, a complete filing must contain all six pages, at least three of which are almost always inapplicable.

(a) Who Is Required to File What

The numerous categories of organizations exempt from income tax are reflected in the different types of returns to be filed. Not all organizations are required to file annual reports with the IRS. Churches, their affiliated organizations, and divisions of states or municipalities, in a manner similar to the Form 1023 rules, do not file Form 990, except for 990-T. Modest-sized organizations may also be excused from filing. The different types of exempt organization annual reports and their basic requirements are as follows:

- *No Form Filed.* Organizations with gross annual receipts "normally" under $25,000, churches and certain of their affiliates, and other types of organizations listed in §1.2(d) need not file; but see why to file below.

- *Form 990-EZ.* All exempt organizations, except for private foundations, whose gross annual receipts equal between $25,000 and $100,000 and whose total assets are less than $250,000 file Form 990EZ.[11] (See Appendix 2A.)
- *Form 990.* All exempt organizations, except private foundations, whose gross annual receipts are more than $100,000 or that have assets of more than $250,000 must file Form 990. (See Appendix 2B.) Section 501(c)(3) organizations that are public charities also file Schedule A. (See Appendix 3A.)
- *Form 990-PF.* All private foundations (PFs) file Form 990-PF annually, regardless of annual receipts or asset levels (yes, even if the PF has no gross receipts). (See Appendix 4A.)
- *Form 990-T.* Any organization exempt under §501(a), including churches, state colleges and universities,[12] and §401 pension plans (including individual retirement accounts) with $1,000 or more gross income from an unrelated trade or business must file Form 990-T. (See Appendix 5A.)
- *Form 990-BL.* Black lung trusts, §501(c)(21), file an annual Information and Initial Excise Tax Return for Black Lung Benefit Trusts and Certain Related Persons.
- *Form 4720.* Form 4720 is filed to report excise taxes and to claim abatement of such taxes imposed on §501(c)(3) charities and their insiders for conducting prohibited activities. (See Appendix 4B.)
- *Form 5500.* One of several Forms 5500 may be due to be filed annually by pension, profit sharing, and other employee welfare plans. Form 5500EZ is filed for one-participant pension benefit plans.
- *Form 5768.* The form filed to elect or revoke an election by a public charity to measure its permissible lobbying expenditures under §501(h).[13]
- *Forms 941, 1099, W-2, W-3, and other federal and state compensation reporting forms* are filed to report payments to workers that perform personal services for tax-exempt organizations.[14]

(b) Federal Filing Not Required

The list of organizations not required to file is reproduced each year in the instructions to Form 990. The most recent version should be consulted if there is any question about filing requirements. The instructions for 2000 list the following organizations as being excused from filing:

- Churches and their affiliates, a convention or association of churches, an integrated auxiliary of a church (such as a men's or women's society, religious school, mission society, or youth group) or an internally supported, church-controlled organization[15]
- Church-affiliated organizations that are exclusively engaged in managing funds or maintaining retirement programs and are described in Rev. Proc. 96-11, 1996-1 C.B. 577
- Schools below college level affiliated with a church or operated by a religious order
- Mission societies sponsored by or affiliated with one or more churches or church denominations, if more than half of the societies' activities are conducted in or directed at persons in foreign countries
- Exclusively religious activities of any religious order
- State institutions whose income is excluded from gross income under §115
- Section 501(c)(1) organizations that are instrumentalities of the United States and organized under an act of Congress[16]
- Governmental units and their affiliates granted exemption under §501(a)[17]
- Religious and apostolic organizations described in §501(d) that file Form 1065
- A limited liability company (LLC) or limited liability partnership (LLP) that elects to be treated as a disregarded entity the transactions of which are reported as the parent's information[18]

(c) Why File Even If Not Required To?

Annual filings of Form 990EZ are advisable for organizations whose annual gross receipts are below the $25,000 mark to ensure that the organization remains on the IRS mailing list to receive the forms for annual filing and other announcements issued by the IRS every year or so. Particularly for a volunteer organization that changes treasurers each year it is useful to file to change the address as officers change. The amount of the gross receipts is input in Item K on Form 990EZ without completing any other information. Prudence also dictates that any organization seeking donations should ensure that its name is listed in IRS Publication 78, the master list of qualifying charitable organizations. Omission from the list may cause two problems: disallowance of charitable contribution deduction to donors and unwillingness of private foundations or other donors to grant funds to the organization.

The extended 27-month deadline for submitting applications for recognition of exemption[19] creates a possible dual filing dilemma. A new nonprofit organization should file a Form 990 for the first fiscal year closing even if it has not yet filed Form 1023 or 1024 for recognition of its exempt status. Item F at the top left of page 1 of Form 990 is checked to indicate "exemption application is pending." When the new nonprofit has not yet filed an application for exemption so that it cannot say the application is pending, the IRS may reject the return.

Until exempt status is entered into the master data bank, the IRS expects the yet-to-be-determined exempt status organization to file Form 1120 or 1041. Even if the application for federal identification number lists the organization as a nonprofit, it is considered a taxpaying entity due to file income tax returns until the application for exemption is filed. When revenues in excess of expenses exist, tax is due to be paid even if the tax is ultimately recovered on an amended return. If income tax returns are filed, gross income received in the form of voluntary donations should be treated as nontaxable income because such donations are gifts.[20]

Whether to submit a protective filing for an expectant exempt organization that is not required to file Form 990 can also be a tough call. Say the new organization is technically not required to file a 990 because its gross revenue in the first year or two is less than $25,000 or it is a church or church affiliate. The issue is whether voluntary filing of a protective 1120 to start the statute of limitations colors the IRS's consideration of its exemption and whether this remote possibility outweighs the value of protection from tax assessments and reduction of penalties. The submission of financial information on a 1023 has been found not to constitute the filing of a return,[21] so penalties for late filing may not be excusable. An added dimension faces a new organization that may possibly be denied exempt status. Filing of Form 990 by a not-yet-recognized organization, in the good faith belief that it qualifies as an exempt organization, starts the period of limitations for collection of income tax.[22] The time required to appeal an adverse determination can be years, so filing 990s may furnish valuable protection from tax assessments for an organization ultimately found not to be exempt. Such a filing may also provide a "reasonable cause" excuse to reduce or eliminate penalties for failure to file Forms 1120 or 1041 and pay the tax due.

The statute of limitations for assessment of the unrelated business income tax (UBIT) on Form 990-T starts to run when an organization submits a Form 990 that contains sufficient facts (shown in Part VII) from which the

UBIT can be determined.[23] Say, for example, an exempt organization lists an amount for affinity card revenues on its 990, Part VII, column D. The number is reported on line 103, labeled as royalty income, and identified in column C with the exclusion code 15 for "royalty income excluded by §512(b)(2)." Assume that, after years of fighting in court, the IRS prevails (actually it lost the battle) in treating part or all of the royalty payment as unrelated income.[24] If the revenue is clearly disclosed and identified, tax can be collected for only three years prior to the decision. Note that substantial underpayment penalties might be assessed for the open years.[25]

If recognition of exemption is received after the organization has been in existence for more than a year, treatment as a taxable entity may also occur on a state level. In Texas, for example, a new nonprofit corporation must either furnish evidence of the federal exemption or seek exemption within approximately 15 months of its creation, or pay a franchise tax. Otherwise, the charter is revoked. If tax is paid and the IRS subsequently issues recognition of exemption retroactive to the date of incorporation, the tax will be refunded.

(d) Filing Deadline

The due date for Forms 990 gives tax practitioners and exempt organizations a reprieve. The forms are due to be filed within 4½ months after the end of the organization's fiscal year, rather than the 2½ allowed for Form 1120 (for-profit corporations) and the 3½ months for Form 1041 (trusts). An extension of time can be requested if the organization has not completed its year-end accounting soon enough to timely file. The new extension Form 8868 has been issued for 2000 returns and is shown in Appendix 1A. For Forms 990-T and 990-PF, an extension of time to file does not extend the time to pay the tax.

The penalty for late filing is $20 a day (up from $10) for organizations with gross receipts under $1 million a year, not to exceed the greater of $10,000 or 5 percent of the annual gross receipts for the year of late filing.[26] The penalty can also be imposed if the form is incomplete as filed. The penalty for a large organization (more than $1 million of annual gross receipts) is $100 a day up to a maximum penalty of $50,000.

(e) Group Returns and Annual Affidavit

The parent organization in "general supervision or control" of a group of subsidiary exempt organizations covered by a group exemption letter may assume the burden of filing a consolidated Form 990 for its subordinate organizations or require each subordinate file its own return.[27] The parent files its own separate 990. The parent and the subordinates must each file separate 990-Ts. To be included in a group Form 990, there must be two or more consenting subordinate member organizations with the following attributes:

- Affiliated with the central organization at the time its annual accounting period ends
- Subject to the central organization's general supervision or control
- Exempt from tax under a group exemption letter that is still in effect
- Use the same accounting period as the central organization

When the parent or controlling member of the group takes responsibility for filing a consolidated Form 990, each affiliate member covered by the group exemption must annually give written authority for its inclusion in the group return. A declaration, made under penalty of perjury, that the financial information to be combined into the group Form 990 is true and complete is included. An attachment showing the name, address, and employer identification number of included local organizations is attached to the group return. An affiliate choosing not to be included in the group return files a separate return and checks block H(c) on page 1 of Form 990. Each year, 90 days before the end of the fiscal year, the parent organization separately reports a current list of subsidiary organizations to the Ogden, Utah, Service Center.[28]

1.3 PUBLIC INSPECTION OF FORMS 990 AND 1023 OR 1024

An actual copy of Forms 990, 990-PF, or 990-EZ for the three most recent years and Form 1023 or 1024 must be given by tax-exempt organizations to anyone requesting one.[29] If the request is made in person at the organization's office, the copy must be provided immediately. In response to a written request, the copy must be mailed within 30 days. Between 1987 and 1997, the returns had to be made available for inspection in the organization's offices. The Regulations provide the following rules:

- An organization may charge $1 for the first page and 15 cents for each subsequent page.
- Payments must be accepted in cash, money orders, personal checks, or credit cards.
- Written requests can be transmitted by mail, electronic mail, facsimile, or private delivery service, or in person and must contain the address to which the copies can be mailed.

- Alternative methods an organization can use to make the forms widely available through electronic media instead of furnishing copies.

If the organization that charges a fee for copying receives a request containing no payment, it must, within seven days of receipt of the request, notify the requester of its prepayment policy and the amount due. If the copy charge exceeds $20 and prepayment is not required, the organization must obtain the requesters consent to the charge. An organization can satisfy its public inspection requirement by making its returns available on the Internet either through its own site or a database of other exempt organizations on another site. The forms will be considered widely available only if it is posted in the same format used by the IRS to post forms and publication on the IRS Web site. The site must contain instructions to enable the user to download and print the forms without charge.

If the exempt organization is the subject of a harassment campaign, the regulations contain procedures for applying to the key district office for relief. As an example, the regulation indicates the receipt of 200 requests following a national news report about the organization is not considered harassment. Receipt of 100 requests from known supporters of another organization opposed to the policies and positions the organization advocates are said to be disruptive to the organization's operations and to thereby constitute harassment.

An organization having more than one administrative office must have a copy available at each office where three or more full-time employees work. Service-providing facilities are not counted for this purpose if management functions are not performed there. A branch organization which does not file its own Form 990 because it is included in a group return must make the group return available.

A request to see a copy of the return can also be sent to the District Director of the Internal Revenue Service in the area in which the organization is located, or to the National Office of the IRS. Form 4506-A can also be used to request a copy of any return, and a photocopying fee will be imposed.

Up to a $10,000 penalty can be imposed against the person(s) responsible for a failure to disclose the returns. The penalty is $20 for each day the failure continues. An additional $10 per day, up to a maximum of $5,000, can also be imposed if the organization's manager(s) refuse to furnish the required information after a written request by the IRS. If more than one person is responsible, they are jointly and severally liable for the penalties.[30]

(a) Disclosures Not Required

The names and addresses of the organization's contributors are not subject to public inspection and can be omitted from the copy made available to the public, except for private foundations and political organizations. All other parts of the form, including officer and key employee compensation and Schedule A for public charities (except for major donor list attached for Part VII-A) must be disclosed. Forms 990-T and 1120-POL are considered nonpublic returns and need not be made available. Certain political organizations are now required to file Forms 990 that must be available for public inspection.

(b) Private Foundations

Prior to 2000, the annual return of a private foundation, Form 990-PF, was made available under a system dating from 1969 that differed from the other Form 990 rules in several respects. The foundation managers made the form open for inspection by any citizen at the principal office during regular business hours, on request made within 180 days after the date of publication of notice of its availability.[31] Effective March 13, 2000, private foundations are subject to the rules outlined above for Form 990 filers, with one important difference. Private foundations must disclose the names of their contributors and amounts donated. Effective for returns filed after March 13, 2000, a newspaper notice of availability is no longer required, though the state of New York continues the requirement in that state.

1.4 ACCOUNTING ISSUES

Good accounting is the key to successful preparation of federal information returns for a nonprofit organization.[32] The trick is to allocate and attribute revenues and expenses to the proper lines and columns on Forms 990. Both for those organizations that want to properly reflect activity costs and those that want to maximize deductions to offset unrelated business income,[33] proper identification of allocable expenses is an important goal. The functional expense display found on page 2 of Form 990 is the same as the reporting prescribed by generally accepted accounting standards. Three types of expenses are reported: program, administrative, and fund-raising. The Better Business Bureau, National Center for Nonprofit Boards, regulatory agencies, and funders generally recommend that the sum of an organization's administrative and fund-raising costs equal no more than 25 percent of total expenditures. Thus the desired proportion for spending on programs and mission-related activities is 75 percent. The total for each type of expense is shown on page 1, lines 13, 14, and 15, and in detail on page 2, Part II, making it easy for viewers to calculate the ratios.

Documentation and cost accounting records must be designed to capture revenues and costs by function, including joint cost allocations. When expenses are attributable to more than one function, organizations must develop techniques to have verifiable bases upon which expenses may be related to program or supporting service functions. The functional classification of expenses permits an organization to tell the reader of the financial statements not only the nature of its expenses, such as salary, supplies, and occupancy, but also the purpose for which they were made. At a minimum, all 990 filing organizations need to maintain the following:

- A staff salary allocation system is essential for recording the time employees spend on tasks each day. The possibilities are endless. Each staff member should maintain an individual computer database or fill out a time sheet. The reports should be completed often enough to ensure accuracy, preferably weekly. In some cases, as when personnel perform repetitive tasks, preparing one week's report for each month or one month each year might be sufficient. Percentages of time spent on various functions can then be tabulated and used for accounting allocations.
- Office/program space utilization charts to assign occupancy costs can be prepared. All physical building space rented or owned must be allocated according to its usage. Floor plans must be tabulated to arrive at square footage of the space allocable to each activity center. In some cases, the allocation is made by using staff/time ratios, or the converse. For dual-use space, records must reflect the number of hours or days the space is used for each purpose.
- Direct program or activity costs should be captured whenever possible. The advantages include reduction of unrelated business income, proof of qualifying distributions for a private foundation, and insurance against an IRS challenge for low program expenditures. A minimal amount of additional time should be required by administrative staff to accumulate costs by programs. A departmental accounting system is imperative. Some long-distance telephone companies will assist in developing a coding system that quantifies the phone charges by department. As another example, the organization can establish separate accounts with vendors for different departments.
- Joint project allocations must be made on a reasonable and fair basis recognizing the cause-and-effect relationship between the cost incurred and where it is allocated. Four possible methods of allocating include: activity-based allocations (identifying departmental costs);

equal sharing of costs (e.g., if three projects, divide by three); cost allocated relative to stand-alone cost (e.g., what it would cost if that department had to hire and buy independently); and cost allocated in proportion to cost savings.[34]

- Supporting, administrative, or other management costs should be allocated to departments to which the work is directly related. The organization's size and the scope of administrative staff involvement in actual programs determine the feasibility of such cost attributions. Staff salaries are most often allocable. Say, for example, that the executive director is also the editor of the organization's journal. If a record of time spent is maintained, his or her salary and associated costs could be attributed partly to the publication. When allocating expenses to unrelated business income, an exploitation of exempt functions rule may apply to limit such an allocation.[35]
- A computer-based fund accounting system, in which department codes are automatically recorded as moneys are expended, is preferable. The cost of the software is easily recouped in staff time saved, improved planning, and possibly tax savings due to a reduction in income and excise taxes.

(a) Tax Accounting Methods

Plainly and simply, the instructions for Forms 990 say that an organization should generally use the same accounting method on the return to figure revenue and expenses as it regularly uses to keep its books and records.[36] So long as the method clearly reflects income, either the cash or accrual method may be used. For its simplicity, many organizations use the cash method in their early years, meaning only the actual cash received and expended is reported as the financial activity for the year. What is called the *accrual method* reports transactions when a binding obligation to pay or receive occurs. As discussed below, a promise to make a donation is counted under the accrual method when a unconditional pledge is received. Similarly, an expense is recorded when the obligation to pay for the goods and services occurs, not when paid. There are a number of reasons, however, that a new nonprofit might instead select the accrual method.

Once an organization adopts either the cash or accrual method for 990 reporting purposes, it must file Form 3115 to change the method under procedures outlined in Chapter 6. A change from the cash to accrual method of accounting may need to be made, for example, by an organization that has, in its initial years or for whatever reason, not used the accrual method and chooses to begin to do so. Customarily, this situation arises when the organization engages a CPA to issue audited reports of its financial condition.

An organization that changes its method of reporting contributions and grants to comply with a change required by the FASB standards, however, is not required to file Form 3115.[37] The prior year effect of such a change is reported on line 20 of Part I of Form 990 and Part III of Form 990-PF, rather than on the beginning balance sheet. The many exempt organizations that adopted the new standards in 1996 and 1997 made significant changes in their financial reporting systems without permission.

The cash method of accounting must be used by public charities for purposes of calculating public support percentages under §170(b)(1)(A)(vi) and §509(a)(2) on Schedule A.[38] Private foundations must also tally the §4942 minimum distribution requirements on a cash basis.[39]

(b) Professional Accounting Standards

The FASB issues the rules followed by CPAs in presenting financial information. The standards are referred to as generally accepted accounting principles (GAAP). Though an organization is not required to follow GAAP, the accountant's report must take exception in the covering opinion, or say, if the information not presented according to GAAP. It is said that a "clean" accountant's opinion can be issued only for financials prepared according to GAAP. Thus, many nonprofit organizations apply these rules in maintaining and reporting financial information. The FASB continually studies and improves financial reporting by nonprofit organizations, and readers should be alert for changes. The rules are found in the periodically updated AICPA Audit and Accounting Guide for Not-For-Profit Organizations.[40] A brief introduction to the accounting concepts follows.

Financial Accounting Standards Board Statement (SFAS) No. 116, Accounting for Contributions Received and Contributions Made, affects the manner in which contributions are to be reported on GAAP financial statements. This Statement of Financial Accounting Standard (SFAS) defines a contribution as "an unconditional transfer of cash or other assets to an entity, or as a settlement or cancellation of its liabilities in a voluntary non-reciprocal transfer by another entity acting as other than an owner." The FASB further provides that the following inflows of assets are not included in the definition of contributions:

- Transfers that are exchange transactions, in which both parties receive goods or services of commensurate value

- Transfers in which the organization is acting as an agent, trustee, or intermediary for the donor (i.e., the organization has little or no discretion concerning the use of the assets transferred)
- Tax exemptions, tax incentives, and tax abatements

Contributions received in the form of charitable pledges are included in revenue when the pledge is unconditionally made or promised, rather than when paid in cash or other assets. A condition is a future and uncertain event. Thus, a pledge to match funding the organization raises from others is conditional and not reported until the matching gifts have been received. For the value of a pledge to be reported, there must be "sufficient evidence in the form of verifiable documentation that a promise was made and received." Restricted and unrestricted gifts of all kinds and in whatever form—cash, securities, other property, or in-kind—are subject to reporting as current revenue under this rule. Factors indicating a bookable pledge are compared in the following list to those indicating the gift is conditional and therefore not recordable (noted in parenthesis):

- Written evidence exists (no written promise made).
- Documents contain language such as *promise, agree, will,* or *binding* (no *hope, intend, may,* or *expect*).
- Pledge payments are scheduled for specific dates in the future (no specific payment dates indicated in documents).
- Donor's economic position indicates ability to pay pledged amount (collectibility of pledge is questionable).
- Donor has history of timely payment of pledged amounts (donor has no history).
- Donee has taken specific steps—signed contract to build the new building or sought matching pledges—in reliance on pledge (no action taken or obligation entered into as result of pledge).
- Pledge was made in response to solicitation of formal pledges (promise is unsolicited or funding request sought no pledge).
- Public recognition or announcement of pledge made (no announcement).

Pledges of donations to be received beyond the current year are discounted by applying an appropriate rate of interest (return the organization is currently earning on its investments or cash reserves). The increase (called *accretion*) in the value of the pledge each year is reported as a donation in that year. An allowance for uncollectable pledges must be provided to cover the inevitable uncollectable pledge (and reflected as a reduction of the revenue, not as an expense).

Contributed services provided by volunteers are recognized as income for financial purposes (but not for tax purposes) if one of two conditions exists when the services are received:

- The services create or enhance nonfinancial assets (volunteers construct a building or set for a theater performance).
- Services are of a type that require specialized skills, are provided by individuals possessing those skills, and would typically have to be purchased if not provided by donations. SFAS No. 116 lists by example professions, such as doctors, lawyers, teachers, and carpenters.

Donated facilities produce recognizable income equal to the fair rental value of the facilities but not more than the organization would otherwise pay for its needed facilities. The present value of a binding multiyear lease is reported as income in the year the agreement is arranged. Again note that the value of such a donation is not reported as revenue on Form 990 or counted as support in calculating public charity status. In-kind donations of land, building, equipment, supplies, food, and other tangible property are recorded for both financial and tax reporting purposes. A testamentary bequest is recorded as income when the amount of the bequest can be accurately determined. A specific bequest of a sum certain amount or particular property is recorded when there is no uncertainty about its being subject to death taxes or other obligations of the decedent. The discounted present value of the organization's share of assets in a split-interest agreement is reported as a gift of current income in the year its ownership is made certain under the intention-to-give concepts defining unconditional gifts.

Increases or decreases in an organization's investment in an affiliated entity are reported on Part I, line 7 (990) as other investment income, or possibly on line 11 as other revenue, depending on the reason why the organization is holding the property. For tax purposes, affiliated but legally independent exempt organizations must each file their own Forms 990, except for members of an affiliated association holding a group exemption.

Contributions or grants paid out by the organization are recognized as an expense in the year the promise to pay is made, regardless of whether the cash or other asset is actually disbursed. Matching, conditional, or otherwise contingent promises to pay are booked at the time the uncertainty is removed because the condition is met.

SFAS No. 117, Financial Statements for Not-for-Profit Organizations, redesigned financial statement presentation and made obsolete the different systems previously prescribed for hospitals, colleges, health and welfare, and all other not-for-profit organizations. Donations received are identified as subject to one of three types of restrictions:

- *Permanently restricted net assets,* such as moneys to be used to pay scholarships only, an endowment fund from which only the dividends and interest may be used, and long-lived assets, such as buildings or collections.
- *Temporarily restricted net assets* funds given to accomplish a particular program service or to buy certain assets over a period of time.
- *Unrestricted net assets* will identify all other resources of the not-for-profit organization freely available for use in accomplishing the organization's purposes and subject only to the control of the organization's board or officers.

A *Statement of Activity* for all organizational funds and programs replaces the statement of financial position and results of operations, also called statement of revenues and expenses. The statement is designed to help donors, creditors, and others assess an organization's service efforts functionally. In other words, the total cost of major program services is reported along with separate amounts for supporting services (management, fund-raising, and membership development expenses). Additionally, health and welfare organizations report total expenses in their natural categories—personnel, occupancy, interest, grants to others, and so on. For hospitals and all other nonprofits, this report is encouraged but not required. Current earnings on all funds, including those permanently restricted, are to be reported on the statement of activity. Revenues subject to restrictions, such as capital gains on endowment funds, are separately identified but still reported as current earnings.

SFAS No. 124, Accounting for Certain Investments Held by Not-for-Profit Organizations, addresses the way in which nonprofit organizations account for equity securities, the value of which is readily determinable, and investments in debt securities. Investments in land, a partnership, a subsidiary corporation, or other investments are not addressed in this SFAS. Marketable equity and debt securities are reported at their fair market value. Such investments are initially reported at their acquisition cost (including brokerage and other transaction fees) if purchased and at fair value if they are received as donations or through an agency transaction. Changes in fair value of such investments are reflected in the statement of activity (income statement) as unrealized gain or loss and increase or decrease unrestricted net assets unless their use is temporarily or permanently restricted by donors to a specified purpose or future period. Such unrealized gains and losses are not recognized for tax purposes, but instead are reflected in Part I, line 20 (990), or Part III, line 3 or 5 (990-PF) as an item reconciling book to tax income. Consequently, the tax gain or loss reported upon sale or other disposition of such investments is different from that reflected for financial purposes. Similarly, the FASB permits investment revenues to be reported net of related expenses, such as custodial fees and investment advisory fees; such expenses are reported in Part II of Form 990.

SFAS No. 136, Transfers of Assets to a Not-for-Profit Organization or Charitable Trust That Raises or Holds Contributions for Others, sets forth the rules for "agency transactions." A nonprofit is an agent when it accepts a donation with the obligation to pay the money to another entity. Such a payment is recorded as a liability, rather than revenue, by the agent. If the agent, or collecting organization, possesses a "variance power," or some discretion and control over the regranting of the gift, it recognizes the payment as revenue. Also, if it receives the money on behalf of a financially interrelated organization over which it has the ability to influence the operating and financial decisions, and in which it has an ongoing economic interest, it reports revenue. This rule was effective for years beginning after December 15, 1999.

Statement of Position 94-3, Reporting of Related Entities by Not-for-Profit Organizations, was proposed in February 1999 to be issued as an SFAS entitled *Consolidated Financial Statements: Purposes and Policy*. Combined financial reports must be issued for organizations with interlocking control and economic interests. Federal tax returns must, however, be filed independently for each separate organization. Form 990 cannot be prepared from or readily compared to such financial statements.

Statement of Position 98-2, Accounting for Costs of Activities of Not-for-Profit Organizations and State and Local Governmental Entities That Include Fund Raising, provides standards for reporting money spent for materials and activities that combine fund-raising activities with educational or other elements. Direct mail, telethons, special events, and a variety of methods are used by nonprofits to concurrently raise money and advance the mission. An athletic contest for handicapped persons or a cancer-warning signs brochure may embody requests for funding alongside the program content. Three rather complicated tests—purpose, audience, and content—are applied to determine whether any of the joint costs of such activities can be allocated to program or management, rather than all being treated as fund-raising costs. As described in the introduction to this section, allocation of expenses to the three functions displayed on page 2 of Form 990 (program, management, and fund-raising) requires cost accounting systems that capture people's time, space, and expenses devoted to each function. To make a joint cost allocation, the content of written materials and audience solicited are examined to find the primary motivation for an activity. The FASB suggests a test that asks, "Does the program component of the joint activity call for specific action by the recipient that will help accomplish the organization's mission?"

Appendix 1A

Form **8868** (December 2000)
Department of the Treasury
Internal Revenue Service

Application for Extension of Time To File an Exempt Organization Return

▶ File a separate application for each return.

OMB No. 1545-1709

- If you are filing for an **Automatic 3-Month Extension, complete only Part I** and check this box . . . . ▶ ☐
- If you are filing for an **Additional (not automatic) 3-Month Extension, complete only Part II** (on page 2 of this form).

Note: ***Do not complete Part II unless you have already been granted an automatic 3-month extension on a previously filed Form 8868.***

Part I **Automatic 3-Month Extension of Time**—Only submit original (no copies needed)

Note: *Form 990-T corporations requesting an automatic 6-month extension—check this box and complete Part I only* . . . ▶ ☐

All other corporations (including Form 990-C filers) must use Form 7004 to request an extension of time to file income tax returns. Partnerships, REMICs and trusts must use Form 8736 to request an extension of time to file Form 1065, 1066, or 1041.

Type or print File by the due date for filing your return. See instructions.	Name of Exempt Organization	**Employer identification number**
	Number, street, and room or suite no. If a P.O. box, see instructions.	
	City, town or post office, state, and ZIP code. For a foreign address, see instructions.	

Check type of return to be filed (file a separate application for each return):

☐ Form 990	☐ Form 990-T (corporation)	☐ Form 4720
☐ Form 990-BL	☐ Form 990-T (sec. 401(a) or 408(a) trust)	☐ Form 5227
☐ Form 990-EZ	☐ Form 990-T (trust other than above)	☐ Form 6069
☐ Form 990-PF	☐ Form 1041-A	☐ Form 8870

- If the organization does **not** have an office or place of business in the United States, check this box . . . . ▶ ☐
- If this is for a **Group Return,** enter the organization s four digit Group Exemption Number (GEN) ____________ . If this is for the **whole** group, check this box ▶ ☐ . If it is for part of the group, check this box ▶ ☐ and attach a list with the names and EINs of all members the extension will cover.

1 I request an automatic 3-month (6-month, for **990-T corporation**) extension of time until .... , 20...., to file the exempt organization return for the organization named above. The extension is for the organization s return for:

▶ ☐ calendar year 20 ... or

▶ ☐ tax year beginning .... , 20..., and ending .... , 20....

2 If this tax year is for less than 12 months, check reason: ☐ Initial return ☐ Final return ☐ Change in accounting period

3a If this application is for Form 990-BL, 990-PF, 990-T, 4720, or 6069, enter the tentative tax, less any nonrefundable credits. See instructions . . . . $

b If this application is for Form 990-PF or 990-T, enter any refundable credits and estimated tax payments made. Include any prior year overpayment allowed as a credit . . . . $

c **Balance Due.** Subtract line 3b from line 3a. Include your payment with this form, or, if required, deposit with FTD coupon or, if required, by using EFTPS (Electronic Federal Tax Payment System). See instructions . . . . $

Signature and Verification

Under penalties of perjury, I declare that I have examined this form, including accompanying schedules and statements, and to the best of my knowledge and belief, it is true, correct, and complete, and that I am authorized to prepare this form.

Signature ▶ Title ▶ Date ▶

For Paperwork Reduction Act Notice, see Instruction Cat. No. 27916D Form **8868** (12-2000)

Form 8868 (12-2000) Page **2**

• If you are filing for an **Additional (not automatic) 3-Month Extension, complete only Part II** and check this box ▶ ☐

Note: ***Only complete Part II if you have already been granted an automatic 3-month extension on a previously filed Form 8868.***

• If you are filing for an **Automatic 3-Month Extension, complete only Part I** (on page 1).

Part II Additional (not automatic) 3-Month Extension of Time—Must File Original and One Copy.

Type or print

File by the extended due date for filing the return. See instructions.

Name of Exempt Organization	**Employer identification number**
Number, street, and room or suite no. If a P.O. box, see instructions.	For IRS use only
City, town or post office, state, and ZIP code. For a foreign address, see instructions.	

Check type of return to be filed (File a separate application for each return):

☐ Form 990 ☐ Form 990-EZ ☐ Form 990-T (sec. 401(a) or 408(a) trust) ☐ Form 1041-A ☐ Form 5227 ☐ Form 8870
☐ Form 990-BL ☐ Form 990-PF ☐ Form 990-T (trust other than above) ☐ Form 4720 ☐ Form 6069

STOP: Do not complete Part II if you were not already granted an automatic 3-month extension on a previously filed Form 8868.

• If the organization does **not** have an office or place of business in the United States, check this box ▶ ☐

• If this is for a **Group Return,** enter the organization s four digit Group Exemption Number (GEN) ________ . If this is for the **whole** group, check this box ▶ ☐ . If it is for **part** of the group, check this box ▶ ☐ and attach a list with the names and EINs of all members the extension is for.

4 I request an additional 3-month extension of time until ________ , 20___.

5 For calendar year ______ , or other tax year beginning ________ , 20___ and ending ________ , 20___ .

6 If this tax year is for less than 12 months, check reason: ☐ Initial return ☐ Final return ☐ Change in accounting period

7 State in detail why you need the extension ________

8a If this application is for Form 990-BL, 990-PF, 990-T, 4720, or 6069, enter the tentative tax, less any nonrefundable credits. See instructions . . . $

b If this application is for Form 990-PF, 990-T, 4720, or 6069, enter any refundable credits and estimated tax payments made. Include any prior year overpayment allowed as a credit and any amount paid previously with Form 8868 . . . $

c **Balance Due.** Subtract line 8b from line 8a. Include your payment with this form, or, if required, deposit with FTD coupon or, if required, by using EFTPS (Electronic Federal Tax Payment System). See instructions . . . $

Signature and Verification

Under penalties of perjury, I declare that I have examined this form, including accompanying schedules and statements, and to the best of my knowledge and belief, it is true, correct, and complete, and that I am authorized to prepare this form.

Signature ▶ Title ▶ Date ▶

Notice to Applicant—To Be Completed by the IRS

☐ We **have** approved this application. Please attach this form to the organization s return.

☐ We **have not** approved this application. However, we have granted a 10-day grace period from the later of the date shown below or the due date of the organization s return (including any prior extensions). This grace period is considered to be a valid extension of time for elections otherwise required to be made on a timely return. Please attach this form to the organization s return.

☐ We **have not** approved this application. After considering the reasons stated in item 7, we cannot grant your request for an extension of time to file. We are not granting a 10-day grace period.

☐ We **cannot consider** this application because it was filed after the due date of the return for which an extension was requested.

☐ Other ________

________ By: ________ ________

Director Date

Alternate Mailing Address — Enter the address if you want the copy of this application for an additional 3-month extension returned to an address different than the one entered above.

Type or print

Name
Number and street (include suite, room, or apt. no.) Or a P.O. box number
City or town, province or state, and country (including postal or ZIP code)

Form **8868** (12-2000)

CHAPTER TWO

Successful Preparation of Forms 990 and 990-EZ

The IRS instructions for the various Forms 990 total more than 80 pages and are quite helpful and thorough. They should be read alongside this handbook, which does not repeat but instead elaborates on the IRS directions. A sample Form 990 filled out for a fictitious organization—Campaign to Clean Up America—can be found in Appendix 2B. Note in the sample that all nonapplicable questions are answered with "N/A." It is also useful to enter "none" in the blank for any part's total where no amounts are entered. It is especially important to answer the questions on board and staff compensation. This chapter offers practical guidance for completing Form 990 and is keyed to the parts of that form.

The suggestions for completing Form 990 are also intended to be used to complete Form 990-EZ. To assist the reader, a blank copy of 990-EZ referenced to the appropriate sections of this chapter that contain instructions for the parallel parts of Form 990 can be found in Appendix 2A.

2.1 FORM 990-EZ—SHORT FORM

The abbreviated version of Form 990 found in Appendix 2A is filed by tax-exempt organizations whose gross receipts are normally more than $25,000 but less than $100,000. An organization's gross receipts include all cash receipts that represent revenues during a year, except for those amounts received as an agent on behalf of another organization. In an agency transaction, the recipient organization has no right to keep the money but only serves as a custodian. Borrowed money, interfund transfers, and expense reimbursements are also not treated as gross receipts for this purpose. The IRS instructions suggest that the annual federal filing requirement can be determined by adding together specified lines of Part I of Form 990-EZ. For the unusual 990-EZ filing organization that uses the accrual rather than cash method of accounting, amounts would be calculated using the cash method. To calculate gross receipts, as a general rule, the following lines of Form 990-EZ are added:

- Line 1: Contributions, gifts, and grants
- Line 2: Program service revenue
- Line 3: Membership dues and assessments
- Line 4: Investment income
- Line 5a: Gross amount from sale of assets other than inventory
- Line 6a: Special event proceeds (not including contribution portion)
- Line 7a: Gross sales of inventory, less returns and allowances
- Line 8: Other revenue

The total can be checked by adding back all the costs deducted on page 1 on lines 5b, 6b, and 7b to the total revenue on line 9. Form 990 filers can follow the same pattern using the slightly different designations found on the 11 lines of that form and adding back the expenses deducted to arrive at net income on lines 6, 8, 9, and 10.

Although no filing is required by organizations whose annual gross receipts are under $25,000, the author strongly suggests filing anyway for reasons outlined in Chapter 1§2(c). Those nonprofits that are not required to file can simply complete the information requested in items A through K at the top of the Form 990-EZ and have an officer sign the bottom of the second page. The organization keeps its address current, and most importantly, the organization remains in the IRS master list of qualifying organizations.

To qualify to file Form 990-EZ, the nonprofit's total assets shown on line 25, column B for the current year must be less than $250,000, and it may not be a private foundation. Form 990-PF must be filed even if the foundation has no revenue. Organizations qualified for exemption under IRC §501(c)(3) must also file Schedule A.

The filing requirement is not based solely on the current year's gross revenue but on the amount the organization "normally" receives. Normally receiving less than $25,000 of gross receipts occurs in the following circumstances and relieves the organization from filing Form 990-EZ:

- *New organization.* An organization up to one year old that receives, or has donors pledging to give, $37,500 or less during its first year.
- *One- to three-year-old organization.* Between one and three years of age, an organization may average $30,000 or less in gross receipts during its first two years and not have to file.
- *Three- or more-year-old organizations.* All other organizations that receive an average of $25,000 or less in the immediately preceding three tax years, including the year for which the return would be filed, are excused from filing.

Form 990-EZ was designed by the IRS to simplify reporting requirements for modest organizations and to reduce their auditing burden. Essentially, Form 990-EZ is a condensed version of the six-page Form 990. The information reported is basically the same, but it is combined and abbreviated with fewer compliance questions. Fortunately, the most complicated and difficult to prepare part of the 990—Part VII, Analysis of Income-Producing Activities (which pinpoints unrelated business income)—is absent.

2.2 FORM 990, PART I—INCOME AND EXPENSE

Although the title of Part I, Revenue, Expenses, and Changes in Net Assets or Fund Balances, is similar to that found in the accountants' financial statement, Part II, Statement of Functional Expenses (called "Statement of Activity" under generally accepted accounting principles [GAAP]), its arrangement, and in some cases the amounts, are very different. Also, the tremendous difference in the operations and purposes of different types of exempt organizations adds complexity to completing the form. As described more fully in Chapter 1, revenues and expenses for purposes of this part are reported in keeping with the system used by the organization to maintain its accounting records and report to its constituents. However, some tax concepts and labels require the following explanations.

Contributions are called support in Part I. Line 1 support means a gratuitous transfer and is essentially a type of revenue received only by a nonprofit organization, also referred to as a *donation.* Support represents money given to the organization for which the donor receives nothing in return. Payments for which the payer expects something specific in return (school tuition, patient fees, publication sales, etc.), called *exchange transactions*, are not line 1 support and instead are reported on other lines. Fund-raising event proceeds are fragmented on line 9 to extract the contributed portion that is included on line 1 from the exchange portion attributable to raffles, dinners, auctions, and the like, that are reported on line 9. Exchange revenues, however, may be treated as support for Schedule A purposes in determining qualification as a §509(a)(2) public charity. A labor union or a business league reports its member dues on line 3 instead of reporting them as support on line 1. A §501(c)(3) organization reports its member dues payments either on line 1 or line 3, dependent on whether the dues are a charitable contribution, rather than a purchase of services.[1]

Sales of tangible or intangible objects can be troublesome because they can be reported on line 2, 8, 9, or 10. Hospitals and colleges using special accounting procedures are allowed to report in accordance with their prescribed categories. Unrelated business income (UBI) is reported alongside related income without specific identification. Some speculate that lines 10 and 11 are troublesome because they are often the appropriate slot for UBI, although the instructions anticipate that both exempt function and unrelated sales will be included on line 10. It is noteworthy that the statute of limitations, or time during which the IRS can assess tax on UBI, closes three years beyond the date Form 990 is filed. Even if Form 990-T is not filed, the submission of sufficient information to allow the IRS to review the status of each category of revenue invokes the statutory period.[2]

The primary goal in classifying an exempt organization's revenues depends on the exemption category. For a charitable exempt organization, donations that enable it to satisfy the public support tests may be of utmost importance. A labor union is more concerned about distinguishing between member purchases of goods and services that might be treated as taxable business income from those that are dues in support of the leagues activities that benefit the group as a whole. All income, including unrelated business income, is reported on page 1. The following section discusses types of income that often cause classification questions.

(a) Line 1: Contributions, Gifts, Grants, and Other Similar Amounts Received

Many types of nonprofits qualifying for tax exemption under §501(c) receive voluntary contributions and grants that are reportable on line 1. Beginning in the year 2000, detailed listing of those contributors donating over $5,000 must be detailed on new Schedule B illustrated in Appendix 2C. As previously requested as an attachment, the name, address, and zip code of each donor of more than $5,000 and the amount of their cumulative gifts for the year is reported on the form. New are boxes to identify the donation as being from an individual, as a payroll deduction, or a noncash gift. For noncash gifts, Part II of Schedule B asks that the property be described in detail, its fair market value be entered plus the date the property was received by the nonprofit. The accounting profession defines those payments that are treated as donations in Statement of Financial Accounting Standard (SFAS) No. 116 discussed in Chapter 1§3(b). Contributions pledged to be unconditionally paid in the future, thereby treated as current-year revenue, are also reported by an accrual-basis exempt organization, except for Schedule A, which is prepared on a cash basis.

(i) *Individual Contributions.* Volunteer payments motivated by the desire to help finance the nonprofit organization's exempt activities, or what can be thought of as one-way street receipts (nothing is received in return) are line 1 revenues. Monies reported on this line include those paid with the intention of making a gift with no expectation of return or consideration other than intangible recognition, such as inclusion of a name on a sponsor list or on a church pew. For a §501(c)(3) organization, amounts that qualify for the §170 charitable deduction appear on this line. Amounts given in return for privileges or goods[3] and investment returns are reported on the other revenue lines.

(ii) *Business Donations.* Grants from corporations or other businesses are reported as direct public support when they represent a gift. Although it seems logical to call it an indirect gift, money raised by a business in a cause-related marketing campaign is reported here. The IRS instructions refer to such fundraising programs as *commercial co-ventures.* Typically, a business uses the charity's name in a sales promotion and promises to contribute a stated dollar amount for each item sold or upon the occurrence of some action on the public's part. Business sponsorships treated as acknowledgments[4] are reported here; those treated as advertising are reported on line 11.

(iii) *Grants from Other Organizations.* Grants received from other charitable organizations for support in operating the organization's programs, building its facilities, conducting its research, and the like are reported on line 1a, along with individual and corporate donations. Restricted grants to be used for a specific purpose, such as acquisition of a work of art to be owned and held by the grantee, are also reported on this line. Grants to perform services of benefit to the grantor are reported instead on line 2, as explained below.

(iv) *Indirect Public Support.* Line 1b includes amounts received through solicitation campaigns of federated fund-raising agencies, such as the United Way or a community trust. Support received from a parent or subordinate organization, supporting organization, or other group that raises funds on behalf of the organization is also to be reported here. Money collected by a professional society whose members voluntarily add designated donations to their dues payments and transferred to its charitable arm go here.

(v) *Noncash Donations.* Gifts of marketable securities, real estate, and other noncash property such as food, clothing, or medical supplies are included on line 1a at their fair market value on the date of gift.[5] For such gifts exceeding $500, the donor must attach Form 8283 to his or her individual return to claim a deduction. When a charity acknowledges a gift of property valued at $5,000 or more on a donor's Form 8283 and sells the property within two years from the date of the gift (rather than using it for its exempt purposes), Form 8282 must be filed by the charity to report the sale. This form is designed for two purposes: (1) to inform the IRS when property is sold for less than the value claimed as a charitable donation and (2) to enforce a rule that the full market value of tangible personal property is only deductible if the recipient charity uses the property in their exempt activities. The deductible amount of a gift to a charity auction is the donor's tax basis, or the current value, whichever is less.

(vi) *In-Kind Contributions.* Donations of time, services, or the use of property are not reported as support on page 1 or in Schedule A; although gifts of tangible goods that are sometimes described as in-kind are reported. This rule parallels the fact that no charitable deduction can be claimed for such donations. Donated services and facilities may be recorded for financial reporting purposes in accordance with GAAP discussed in Chapter 1§4(b). If they are so recorded, they can be reported for 990-T purposes as discussed in Chapter 5.

(vii) *Contributor Names.* An attachment of contributors who gave the organization money or other property worth $5,000 or more during the year is to be attached for federal filing purposes but may omitted for public disclosure purposes.[6] Organizations classified as §509(a)(1) public charities with donations of more than $250,000 on line 1(d) are allowed a higher threshold equal to 2 percent of line 1d. Gifts of less than $1,000 are not included in tallying a donor's total gifts. The donor's name, address, and amount given must be reported. For gifts of property other than cash, the date received and a description of the property must be reported on an attachment to this part. The employer's name, rather than individual employees, is reported for gifts accumulated through a paycheck reduction system.

(viii) *Special Fund-Raising Events/Token Benefits.* Such fund-raising efforts produce both contributions and exchange revenues. The donation portion of a payment received in connection with a fund-raiser is reported on line 1. Essentially, the total payment less the value of dinner, merchandise, or other benefits provided to the donor is reported as a contribution. When the token items are given to donors, their value can be ignored and the entire payment reported as a donation on line 1.[7] Special rules also apply to certain benefits provided to members discussed below.

(ix) *Government grants* reportable on line 1c are those awards that represent support for the recipient organization to carry on programs and activities that further its organizational objectives.[8] Such grants are said to give a direct benefit primarily to the general public rather than an economic or physical benefit to the payor of the grant. Instead, some grants are payments in exchange for services and not treated as contributions. When a sale of goods, performance of service, or admission to or use of a facility must be delivered or provided specifically to the grantor, program service revenue reported on line 2 is received; what GAAP calls an *exchange transaction* occurs. For example, Medicare funding a health care provider receives for treatment of patients is reported on line 2. The terms of the grant agreement indicating gross receipts from a service contract, as contrasted to (terms identifying a contribution), might include the following:

- Specific delivery of services is required within specific time frame (time for performance at discretion of grantee).
- Penalties beyond the amount of the grant can be imposed for failure to perform (only penalty is return of grant for not conducting specific program or other restriction).
- Goods or services furnished or delivered only to grantor (program benefits, or services provided to, recipients other than grantor).

A government grant that is treated as program service revenue for financial purposes may, for tax purposes, be treated as a contribution if the conditions described in the first sentence of this paragraph exist.

Membership dues may represent a charitable donation or fee for services depending on "commensurate rights and privileges" provided to members. A pure donation exists when the benefit is only the personal satisfaction of being of service to others and furthering the charitable cause in which the members have a common interest. Otherwise, an exchange transaction occurs and service revenue is realized. Due to the difficulty of valuing certain member privileges, the IRS in August 1995 significantly eased the disclosure requirements by extending the token item *de minimus* rules to apply to member benefits. Benefits provided to members can be disregarded if they are given as a part of a basic annual membership of $75 or less. The IRS reasoned that it was "often difficult to value membership benefits, especially rights or privileges, that are not limited as to use, such as free or discounted admission or parking, and gift shop discounts" and decided to allow "limited relief."[9]

Pass-through grants are not recognized as revenue to the organization acting as an agent for another organization. Such grants must be distinguished from indirect public support; contributions received from a fund-raising agency, such as a united giving campaign; or an affiliated or supporting organization. Pass-through contributions are those that are not the property of the reporting organization, but instead represent a liability to the ultimate donee. Because of the public disclosure requirements (and in some cases, public support test calculations), this distinction has far-reaching impact. See discussion of FASB No. 136 in Chapter 1 §4(b).

(b) Line 2: Program Service Revenue

Program service revenues are those received by a nonprofit in return for carrying out the mission for which it was granted tax exemption, also referred to as *exempt function revenues*. Examples are many, including student tuition, hospital patient fees, testing fees, golf course green fees, trade show admission, ticket sales for cultural events, interest on student or credit union loans, low-cost housing rent, and convention registrations. Royalties received from publication of a school's educational materials goes here, but royalty from a donated mineral interest is reported on line 7. Payments a VEBA[10] receives for voluntary member health, life, and other welfare benefits are reported as program revenue as well as rents and interest from investments the nonprofit makes to accomplish an exempt purpose.

Grants that represent payments for services rendered on behalf of the donor are reported here. A grant received by a scientific laboratory testing automobile emissions for a state under the standards described above for government grants would be service revenue. Sales of inventory, such as books, posters, reproductions, or other items sold in a bookstore; crafts produced by the handicapped; or tennis balls sold in the country club shop, even though they are related to exempt function activities, are not reported here but on line 10. Hospitals and colleges whose accounting systems do not allow them to readily extract the cost of goods sold attributable solely to inventory are permitted to report inventory sales on line 2. Line 2 revenues are counted as public support for those (c)(3) organizations qualifying as public charities under §509(a)(2) but not under §509(a)(1).[11]

Fees for services generated in an exempt activity but taxed as unrelated business income (UBI), such as advertising revenues from a exempt publication, are reported on this line. A social club reports all revenues from use of club facilities here, although the portion received from nonmembers will also be reported on Form 990-T. Part VII contains a detailed listing and explanation of program service revenues and must be prepared before this line is completed. The very important instructions in §2.8 should be carefully studied to be sure this type of income is correctly reported.

(c) Line 3: Membership Dues and Assessments

For all exempt organizations with members, a question must first be asked to decide where to report dues: What do members receive in return for their dues payments? The value attributable to services received by members is reported as membership dues and assessments. For most exempt organizations, the total amount of member dues used as general support by the organization is considered to equal value received and is reported on line 3. Separate charges for specific activities, such as an educational seminar conducted or publications sold by a business league, for example, are reported on line 2.

For a charitable exempt organization, the excess amount of dues over fair market value of benefits and privileges required to be valued is separately reported as a donation on line 1, as explained in §2.2(a). If the rights and privileges of membership are incidental to making the organization function, and if the benefit of membership is the personal satisfaction of being of service to others and furthering the exempt purposes, then the membership is a gift.[12] One example of the distinction between dues and donations is that Civil Air Patrol (CAP) members are considered to make contributions when their dues entitle them to receive training to perform services for the CAP for the benefit of the public and not for the member.[13] The IRS has ruled that an educational newsletter is incidental to the exempt purposes and is thus not an individual benefit unless it is a "commercial-quality" publication.[14] Particularly for a §509(a)(1) organization, this distinction is important for Schedule A purposes. For them, membership dues treated as a donation are counted as public support; dues treated as exempt function revenue are not.

(d) Line 4: Interest on Savings and Temporary Cash Investments

This line is mostly self-explanatory if you note the word *investment*. Clearly, interest earned the nonprofit's accumulated funds is reported on this line. Interest earned on program-related loans that serve an exempt purpose, such as money lent to build a low-income housing project or as student loans, are reported on line 2. IRS instructions say that dividends earned on money market accounts are actually interest. A money market account held in an investment portfolio to invest cash from sales of shares and dividends can also be reportable as a dividend on line 5.

Interest on a note receivable that is not an investment or program related, such as an employee loan, is reported on line 11. Interest on a note receivable from the sale of an exempt function asset would also be reported as other income on line 11. A labor union loaning funds to a faltering company to protect the jobs of its worker members, however, would report the interest on line 2 as program related.

(e) Line 5: Dividends and Interest from Securities

Income payment from investments in stocks, bonds, and security loans are reported on this line. Mutual fund capital gain dividends, however, are reportable on line 8. Dividends from a subsidiary operated as a program-related investment would be reported on line 2; dividends from a for-profit subsidiary would be reported here.

(f) Line 6: Gross Rents

Rents from real estate and personal property not used for exempt purposes are reported on line 6. Rents produced through exempt programs, such as low-income housing, are included on line 2. Rental of office space to unaffiliated exempt organizations are reportable as rents here. Such rents are reported only on line 2 as exempt function income, if the rental rate is well below the fair rental value of the property, and if the rental itself serves the lessor exempt organization's mission.

Expenses directly connected with obtaining and maintaining the property producing the rental income are deducted on line 6b but need not be itemized. Repairs, interest on mortgages, depreciation, and other direct costs are placed here and are not included on page 2. Those costs associated with program-related rental properties are reported on page 2.

(g) Line 7: Other Investment Income

Income produced by assets reported in Part IV, line 56, as "Investments—other" is reported on line 7. Mineral royalties and distributions from a sub S corporation or a partnership are good examples of income reported on this line. Such income is expected to be explained, and the information can be tied to the balance sheet, where an explanation is also requested. However, the instructions specifically provide that the unrealized gains or losses on investments carried at market value are to be reported, not on this line but on line 20 as an "other change in fund balance."

(h) Line 8: Capital Gains and Losses

Gains or losses from sales of all types of capital assets (does not include goods held in inventory for regular sale), including those held for investment, those held for exempt purposes, and those that produce UBI, are reported on line 8. A detailed attachment similar to that included in a normal income tax return is prepared, including the date acquired and date sold, gross sales price and selling expenses, cost basis, and any depreciation. Multiple sales of publicly traded securities can be aggregated and reported as one number for 990 (but not for 999-PF) reporting. Capital gains distributed from partnerships, trusts, and S corporations are reported here as well. Unrealized gains reported for financial statement purposes should be reported on line 20.

(i) Line 9: Fund-Raising Events

A popular fund-raising tool for nonprofits is an event at which food, drink, and entertainment are provided to participants. The ticket price for such an event embodies both a donation and a purchase of the goods and services—called a *quid pro quo*. When an organization provides *quid pro quo* benefits in connection with a solicitation of a payment of more than $75, the value of the benefits must be disclosed on the invitation or receipt for payment.[15] Penalties are imposed for failure to disclose. Services or goods received are to be valued at their fair market value, which is often difficult to determine. The cost of the event is not necessarily determinative of its value. Technically, a payment of less than $75 must also be reduced by benefits (unless *de minimus*)[16] for tax deductibility purposes; the helpful nonprofit makes a valuation disclosure in connection with all solicitations.

This line fragments event proceeds into two parts:

1. That amount equal to the value of the goods or services provided in connection with payments for tickets or admission is reported on this line.

2. The excess, if any, of the payment over the value of services or goods received is reported as a donation on line 1 and noted in parentheses on line 9a.

Proceeds of an auction, car wash, cookie sale, dinner, or other event are included here. When the cost of the goods provided in connection with fund-raising efforts—a T-shirt, coffee cup, or poster, for example—is less than a *de minimus* amount, the item or benefit is treated as having no value. The total payment made to the organization is then treated as a gift and reported on line 1, with no amount reported on line 9. Also, the expenses associated with purchase of the *de minimus* items are reported on page 2 as fund-raising expense, and not on line 9.

Fund-raising campaign contributions for which donors receive nothing in return for their gifts are totally reported on line 1. The instructions direct §501(c)(3) organizations to keep both their solicitations and the receipts they furnish to participants in events, as well as proof of the method used to determine the noncontribution portion of the proceeds. An attachment displaying details of the three largest events sponsored during the year is requested. The cost of direct benefits (the food, drink, prizes, etc.) provided during the event are deducted on line 9b to arrive at the net income. The portion of the administrative and fund-raising department expenses attributable to management of and solicitation for the event is not reported on this line but on the applicable line of Part II.

(j) Line 10: Gross Sales Minus Returns and Allowances

Sales of inventory property made or purchased for resale, not including sales of capital assets, are reported here. An educational center's books, a retirement home's or a hospital's pharmaceuticals, a thrift shop's used clothing, or other objects purchased for resale constitute inventory items. Prior to 1994, hospitals and colleges could report sales of inventory on line 3, but are now instructed to report them on line 10. Cost of goods sold includes direct and indirect labor, materials and supplies consumed, freight, and a portion of overhead expenses. A detailed attachment is requested. Marketing and distribution expenses are reported in Part II.

(k) Line 11: Other Revenues

Interest earned on loans not made as investment or program purposes, such as an employee advance or officer loan, are cited by the IRS instructions as reportable on this line. Royalties paid for use of the exempt organization's name, logo, and mailing list are also reported here. Amounts reported on this line should be clearly described in Part VII.

(l) Lines 13 through 15: Expense Totals

Organizations that are §501(c)(3) and (4) and §4947(a)(1) charitable trusts must complete these lines. All other Form 990 filers are not required to complete these lines because they do not complete columns B through D on Part II. Totals from Part II on page 2, when expenses are divided into functional categories, are reported here. The organization should note that the ratio between these lines is an evaluation tool used by some observers. For example, assume:

Line 13	Program services	$600,000	67%
Line 14	Management and general	$200,000	22%
Line 15	Fund-raising	$100,000	11%
Line 17	Total expenses	$900,000	100%

Some advisors in the nonprofit community have opinions about the proper level of program spending as compared to management and general and fund-raising expenses. The Better Business Bureau has traditionally thought that program services of an exempt organization should equal 75 percent or more of the total expense. Spending 67 percent as shown above may be questionable in their view. Grant-making foundations and other donors to tax-exempt organizations like to see as much of their money as possible spent on programs and also carefully evaluate this expense ratio.

(m) Line 16: Payments to Affiliates

Required payments, such as dues to a national, state, or other closely related organization under a predetermined formula for sharing support or dues, are deducted here. A list of the name and address of each affiliate receiving fund is attached. Expenses paid on behalf of affiliates not connected to the functioning of the reporting entity may also be reported here. Payments voluntarily made in support of an affiliate would be reported on line 22, as would allocations paid over by federated fund-raising organizations to the agencies for whom it seeks funding. The IRS instructions for this line are extensive and can be studied for further guidance.

(n) Lines 18–21: Fund Balances

The information reported for Form 990 purposes is reconciled to the organization's financial records on these lines. The balance sheet in Part IV is reported according to the organization's financial statements, and the lines of this part reflect the differences so that line 73 of Part IV agrees with the last line of page 1, or line 21. The most common difference between tax and book income is an unrealized increase or decrease in the carrying value of investments recommended by SFAS No. 124, but not reported as tax revenue. The value of volunteer labor in building a new facility would be capitalized for financial purposes but not shown as tax revenue reported on line 1 of Part I.

Differences in reporting treatment can stem from a change in accounting method or from an adjustment of a prior year's mistake in reporting. Though as a rule permission is required to change accounting methods, nonprofits are afforded leniency.[17] An organization that changes its method of reporting contributions and grants to comply with a change required by the Financial Accounting Standards Board (FASB) standards is not required to seek permission. The prior-year effect of such a change is reported on line 20 rather than on the beginning balance sheet. For a charity whose public status is based on its revenue, Schedule A, however, should be adjusted to reflect the increase or decrease in contributions.

The exempt organization must consider whether a change or mistake is significant enough to require amendment of the previously filed Form 990. When the return is posted on the Internet on the Guidestar.org site, an amendment might be filed to provide a more accurate financial picture. If not, the difference is simply reported on line 20 along with an explanation. The IRS could conceivably question a correction if it reflects an overall accounting method change for which permission was not secured in advance and the amount is material. If the change affects amounts that might be taxed as unrelated income, an amended return may be proper.[18] In the author's experience, the IRS has not questioned amounts reported on line 20.

2.3 PART II—STATEMENT OF FUNCTIONAL EXPENSES

In this part, all 990 filers report operating expenses in column A by object classification, such as salaries, occupancy, and so on. The total organizational expenses are reported according to the accounting method used for the nonprofit's financial reporting. Preparers might find it useful to review the introductory materials about cost allocations and accounting theory in Chapter 1 before completion of this part. An organization might also consider designing its chart of accounts and cost centers to parallel the display of expense accounts in this part. The listing is common to that suggested by many national organizations; its use facilitates comparison of a nonprofit's financial reports to other nonprofits using the standard display. Organizing the account system to also quantify the cost of programs described in Part III is appropriate.

While it might seem wrong, expenses associated with unrelated business activities are reported alongside expenses of conducting program services and managing the organization's properties. The form's design combines all organizational expenses in this part just like the combined revenue reporting in Part I. Expenses deductible in calculating taxable income on Form 990-T may appear on any of the lines in columns B and C, but not D, according to the instructions. Grants reported on line 22 may qualify as a charitable deduction in calculating the UBI tax. Chapter 5 discusses unrelated income and associated deductions and defines direct and indirect costs–an accounting concept that applies in preparing this part.

The challenge in this part for (c)(3) and (c)(4) organizations is dividing the expenses into functional categories of program service, management and general (M&G), and fund-raising. The colum totals allow the IRS and others to evaluate the proportion of costs devoted to exempt activities—optimally, a high proportion. Conversely, fund-raising costs should be low; some states limit them to 20 percent to 25 percent of total expenses. The administrative (M&G) expense level depends on the nature of the organization. Some say the combined management and fund-raising costs should be less than 75 percent of the total. Completing columns B, C, and D to break down an organization's total expenses according to its departments for program services, M&G expenses, and fund-raising is optional for:

- Voluntary employee benefit associations and other exempt organizations substituting Department of Labor forms
- All exempt organizations except §501(c)(3) and §501(c)(4) organizations
- Organizations whose receipts are normally under $25,000 annually

Program services are those activities performed to accomplish the purposes for which the organization is exempt (its exempt function). Direct expenses specifically incurred in association with a project are included, along with an allocable part of indirect costs, such as salaries of employees directly involved in the project, occupancy cost for space utilized, and the cost of printing the reports. Colleges and hospitals whose internal accounting systems allocate indirect costs into cost centers have options for reporting such costs and should read the IRS instructions carefully.

Management and general expenses include overhead and administration—those expenses that are not allocable to programs or fund-raising. The executive director or controller and her or his staff and expenses, personnel and accounting departments, auditors, and lawyers are reported in column C. The administrative staff of a modest organization might perform all three functions so that their compensation and associated costs are allocated. The cost of organizational meetings, such as the annual membership meeting; monthly board, staff, and committee meetings; and other meetings unrelated to a specific program or fund-raising are reported in column C. The investment or cash management function, budgeting, auditing, personnel, and staff cafeteria operations typify the costs reported here. Organizational and officer and director liability coverage is a management expense.

Fund-raising includes expenses incurred in soliciting donations, memberships, and grants voluntarily given to the exempt organization, including:

- Annual giving campaign costs of printing, publicity, mailing, staffing, and the like
- Professional fees to plan and execute the campaign or to draw documents for planned giving
- Development or grant-writing department
- Costs of collecting fund campaign pledges
- Portion of event costs not reported on line 8b
- Advertisements soliciting support

Fund-raising expenses do not include:

- Unrelated business expenses (these go in column B or C, or possibly only on page 1 if directly related to rents or inventory items)
- Fund-raising event, rental, and direct inventory expenses deducted directly from the gross receipts on page 1 (lines 6b, 8b, 9b, or 10b)
- Costs associated with collecting exempt income, such as student tuition or seminar registration fees (report these in column B)

(a) Line 22: Grants and Allocations

Grants to other exempt organizations and to certain individuals are reported on line 22 in keeping with the amounts expensed per books. Pledges of grants accrued according to GAAP rules are reported as current-year grants by accrual-basis organizations. Cash-basis organizations would not report unbooked pledges, similarly to private foundations, which are only allowed to report grants actually paid as qualifying distributions. An attachment listing the following detailed information must reflect:

- The names of the individual and organizational recipients of grants, their addresses, and amount received are reported. An important exception allows colleges, universities, and schools subject to the Family Educational Rights and Privacy Act to omit the names of individual scholarship and financial aid recipients and report only the amount of each type of aid and the number of recipients.
- Grants should be grouped by class or type of grant, such as scholarships, fellowships, educational research, or building construction.
- The relationship, if any, between the grantor and its directors or trustees and an individual grantee is reported. This information allows the IRS to identify private inurement, or those payments that benefit those who control the organization rather than the class of beneficiaries for which exemption was granted.

Voluntary payments to affiliated organizations are reported on this line, rather than on line 16, where required payments to affiliates are reported. Scholarship, fellowship, and research grants to individuals are reported on line 22, even though it may seem surprising, given the title of line 23. Only the grant award amounts are reported; the cost of administering the grant program, such as selection of recipients and monitoring compliance, are included on lines 25 through 43. If the grant is made in property rather than cash, more details are required. A description of the property, its book value, how the fair market value was determined, and the date of the gift are to be listed. Any difference between the value and book value of the property granted is reported on line 20 in Part I.

(b) Line 23: Specific Assistance to Individuals

Medical care, food, clothing, and cash given to indigents or other members of a charitable class are reported on line 23. An attachment providing a summary by type of assistance is requested. The individual names are not reported. A (c)(3) organization must be alert to defining its charitable class and avoiding challenges that it benefits particular individuals or families—a condition that prevents tax exemption. A grant to another organization that operates a homeless shelter to buy food and clothes is reported on line 22, but a direct purchase of food and clothing to give out to homeless individuals is reported on this line.

(c) Line 24: Benefits Paid to or for Members

Payment of member benefits is usually antithetical to the purposes of an organization classified as exempt under §501(c)(3) or (c)(4). As charities and social welfare organizations, they must operate to benefit the public rather than particular individuals. This line is suited to labor unions, fraternal benefit societies, voluntary employee beneficiary associations, unemployment benefit trusts, and other nonprofit associations formed to benefit their members in a nonprofit mode. They set aside and spend monies for member benefits as a part of their underlying exempt function. An attachment reflecting the amount and type of benefits paid for sickness, death, unemployment, and the like is attached and the total reported on this line. Similar payments and the insurance premiums associated with such protection paid on behalf of a nonprofit's employees are reported on lines 27 and 28.

(d) Line 25: Compensation of Officers, Directors, Etc.

Total officer compensation reported on this line should be coordinated with amounts reported in columns C, D, and E of Part V. Salaries, fees, commissions, and other types of compensation, including pension plan contributions, deferred compensation accruals (even if unfunded), health insurance, and other employee benefits (taxable and nontaxable) are included as further described in the suggestions for Part V. Amounts earned by directors in their capacity as directors and/or as staff or management are reported. The compensation of an officer treated as an independent contractor is also reported on this line. Also amounts paid on behalf of leased employees who are officers and key employees are reported here. Some recommend that the amounts reports on lines 26 and 27 combined should agree with the total of Forms 941 filed to report compensation to employees during the year, an impossibility for a non-calendar year organization. The suggestion is that those lines should reconcile to amounts reported as payroll. The author considers it more important that these amounts be reconciled to Part V where amounts reported on Forms 1099 or not reported at all because the persons are leased must be included as compensation. Accurate reporting of these amounts can be critical to satisfy the rebuttable presumption of reasonableness in an intermediate sanction dispute.[19]

(e) Lines 26, 27, 28, and 29: Salaries, Wages, Pension Contributions, Employee Benefits, and Payroll Taxes

Total compensation payments to all salaried individuals, other than officers reported on line 25, are reported on line 26. Other reporting requirements are signaled to the IRS by the numbers on these lines. In addition to payroll taxes mentioned above, unemployment taxes may be due, and Form 5500 may be due for pension plans. Nonprofits classified as §501(c)(3) organizations are exempt from all federal, as well as some state, unemployment taxes. To properly report personnel costs by function, the organization's employees customarily must maintain time reports or other evidence of the portion of their efforts devoted to programs, management, and fund-raising, as discussed in Chapter 1§3.

(f) Lines 30, 31, and 32: Professional Fund-Raising, Accounting, and Legal Fees

These lines report compensation paid to independent advisors for fund-raising, accounting, auditing, financial consulting, and legal services. Note that the combination of lines 25 through 32 represent the direct amounts paid by the organization to individuals for services rendered. If this total number is high in relation to the overall expenses of the organization shown on line 44, an alarm may be sounded in someone's mind. The IRS, an inspecting member of the general public (see Chapter 1§3), a news reporter, or a potential contributor may ask questions. Organizations and their return preparers must remember that Form 990 is now available to all on the Internet at Guidestar.org. Some states require charitable registration, and amounts reported on line 32 may signal to them the need for additional compliance.

(g) Lines 33 through 43: Supplies, Telephone, Postage, Occupancy, Etc.

These lines are largely explained by their titles, although some comments are in order.

(i) *Travel.* An organization reporting travel should use a system of documentation designed to prove the travel's exempt purpose. Expense vouchers reflecting the nature of the expenditures and indicating any personal elements are appropriate. Staff members using an organization's vehicles must maintain a log of their mileage to prove what use is devoted to organization affairs, as well as any personal use. The personal portion, if any, is part of compensation and reportable on line 25, 26, or 28 (and for W-2 purposes). Vehicle expense is reported either as a part of travel or shipping.

(ii) *Interest.* Amounts paid for interest on rental property are not reported here but on line 6b of Part I, and, for property occupied by the organization for its own operations, on line 36. Otherwise, interest expense is reported on line 41. The total interest reported on the three lines mentioned should be coordinated with the answer to indebtedness in Part IV, Balance Sheets.

(iii) *Depreciation.* An attachment showing how depreciation is computed must be prepared and should include the current expense, accumulated depreciate reserves, asset costs, and useful lives. Neither a detailed asset listing, annual additions and deletions, nor the date acquired is required by the IRS instructions. Assets can simply be combined in broad categories according to their useful lives. It is useful to prepare one attachment that reflects depreciation included on line 6b of Part I and line 42 of Part II, and details requested as an attachment for the balance sheet of Part IV at lines 55 and 57. The attachment for the Campaign to Clean Up America in Appendix 2B reflects this presentation. Only if the organization applies MACRS (Modified Accelerated Cost Recovery System) to compute depreciation should Form 4562 is attached. Unless an asset is producing unrelated business income, adoption of the somewhat artificial tax depreciation methods is unnecessary.

(iv) *Joint Costs.* An organization that has costs associated with a combined educational campaign and fund-raising solicitation included in program costs is asked to explain how it allocates costs. To allocate costs that are of benefit to more than one function of the organization's operations, the IRS suggests, "Use an appropriate basis for each kind of cost." Some expenses, such as salaries, are allocated based on time expended. Occupancy can be based on space assigned or people using it (and may be partly based on their time allocation). The accounting profession provides some guidance for allocating materials that serve both an educational and informational purpose.[20]

Other Expenses. Due to the fact that the returns are open to public inspection and reproduced on the Internet, it is advisable to try to condense accounts. It is preferable to avoid attachments for other expenses in order to be concise, and to combine expenses so that all of the amounts can appear on this page.

2.4 PART III—STATEMENT OF PROGRAM SERVICE ACCOMPLISHMENTS

Due to the fact that a copy of Form 990 must be furnished to anybody who is willing to pay for it[21] and returns are entering the electronic age, the prudent organization should carefully prepare this part. It can be considered an opportunity to "toot the organization's horn" and to convince funders to support the organization. At least it should tell the story the organization wants conveyed in electronic media. This part should be prepared with extreme care, with a view to influencing the words that Guidestar.org chooses to describe the organization in its database summary reporting the organization's mission and activities.

Part III first asks the filing organization to describe its primary exempt purpose in about five to eight words (depends on font size used). Again, the author strongly recommends careful choice of words. Do not prepare an attachment; use 5 to 8 words. Why cause Guidestar.org or some other information service to abbreviate a lengthy attachment? Next, this part asks that the organization explain its mission achievements in a "clear and concise manner." To explain the exempt organization's accomplishments, up to four major programs are described along with numerical data concerning how many members are served, classes taught, meals served, patients healed, sites restored, books published, products certified, or similar data evidencing benefit to the organization's exempt constituents. IRS instructions suggest the organization "discuss achievements that are not measurable." Again, it is advisable to avoid attachments; tax return preparers should ask the organization to write this part in their own words, limiting them to the space provided, if possible.

A private elementary school with 400 students can easily answer this question. A 400-bed hospital would report the number of patients served and quantify the amount of charity care, if any. Reasonable estimates can be furnished if the exact number of recipients is not known. If numerical results are not pertinent or available, the project objectives for the return period and the long-range plans can be described. An exempt organization conducting research on heart disease and testing a controlled group of 100 women over a five-year period would say so. Similarly, an organization commissioning a study of an area's history would say it expects the project to take 10 years and possibly describe its research modality to evidence the work's educational nature. Brochures, publication lists, and rate sheets can also be attached to convey a picture of the organization's activities. The instructions suggest that donated services might be disclosed in this part.

Section 501(c)(3) and (4) organizations and wholly charitable trusts (optional for other categories of Form 990 filers) must also report the cost of program activities, including the amount of grants and allocations paid to other individuals and organizations as reported on lines 22 and 23 of Part II. In other words, the organization must take the expenses reported in column B of Part II and further identify them by particular projects, reporting the total for its major programs. Functional accounting records maintained by program are clearly a must for completing this part. For all other types of nonprofits, submission of total expenses by program service category is not required.

2.5 PART IV—BALANCE SHEET AND RECONCILIATION

An exempt organization's beginning and ending assets, liabilities, and fund balances or net assets are reported in Part IV, using the same method it uses for maintaining its normal accounting books and records. Beginning in 1995, this part of Form 990 reflects changes to the Net Asset section to accommodate the financial reporting changes. For organizations not following SFAS No. 117, lines 70 through 73 combine the former titles and add traditional fund balance titles—endowment and plant fund—as shown on the form in Appendix 2B. Fair market value of the assets may be reported if the organization's normal accounting method adjusts its carrying value to the current value. The amounts are often reported at original cost, or "book value." If detailed attachments are requested, only the year-end numbers must be furnished. The instructions for this part are quite good and need not be repeated here.

(a) Loans

Certain lines in this part alert the IRS to problem issues, and in those cases detailed attachments are requested. For most loans receivable by or payable by the organization, 10 detailed items of information are required: borrower's name and title, original amount, balance due, date of note, maturity date, repayment terms, interest rate, security provided by borrower, purpose of the loan, and description and fair market value of consideration furnished by the lender. Loans to and from officers, directors, trustees, and key employees are presented as a separate total on line 50. Significant amounts on this line, particularly if high in relation to the overall asset amounts, might indicate impermissible private benefit to insiders and should be very carefully disclosed. A $10,000 loan for purchase of a residence to a new vice president may not cause additional scrutiny, but a $100,000 loan to refinance his credit cards might.

(b) Coordinated Attachments

Schedules for depreciable assets should be prepared to coordinate with the information attached for Parts I and II. Likewise, receivable and payable information can be tied to interest expense.

(c) Incomplete Information

In its instructions, the IRS cautions the preparer that penalties are imposed for failure to complete any part of the return. The IRS thoughtfully reminds the organization that the reports are open to public inspection and recommends that an effort be made to correctly complete the report. Labor unions filing Form LM-2 or LM-3 with the U.S. Department of Labor and certain employee benefit plans may substitute those forms for this part.

Parts IV-A and IV-B, Reconciliation of Revenues and Expenses per Audited Financial Statements with Expenses per Return, were added in 1995 to clarify items for which there are reporting differences for tax and financial purpose similar to Schedule M on Form 1120. These parts are completed by an organization receiving an audited financial statement. They are optional for a group return. A common reconciling item is revenue from donated services or the use of facilities and the corresponding expense for professional services, rent, or similar item. This part reminds organizations that such revenues are not deductible contributions for tax purposes.[22] Unrealized gains or losses on investments recognized for financial reporting purposes are not shown as revenue in Part I but instead as a change in fund balance on line 20.

2.6 PART V—LIST OF OFFICERS, DIRECTORS, AND TRUSTEES

Part V calls for the names, addresses, titles, and average time devoted to the positions for all members of the exempt organization's governing body and key employees, or "those persons having responsibilities or powers similar to those of officers, directors, or trustees," regardless of whether they are compensated. All such persons are to be listed, even if there are 50 board members. If an attachment is prepared, consider entering totals across the bottom of the form or noting "none" in each column where applicable.

Total compensation paid to persons serving on the governing board for all services rendered is to be reported, whether they are employees or independent contractors. For persons serving in more than one position—for example, as both a director and officer or staff member—the compensation for each respective position should be separately presented. The total gross wages or fees reported as paid to an individual should also be corroborated with Forms 941, W-2, and/or 1099 that are separately filed with the IRS to report the individual compensation and tax withholding. The IRS emphasized this subject during large case examinations during the late 1990s. This part contains five columns of information to be listed about each official, regardless of whether they are compensated.

To describe the requirements of tax-exempt status, IRC §501 uses the word *inures* to limit the activities of §501(c)(3), (4), (6), (7), (9), (10), (13), and (19) organizations. These subsections all require that, "no part of the net earnings inure to the benefit of any private shareholder or individual." With this part, the IRS seeks information to allow them and other authorities to identify organizations that pay compensations amounts that are excessive and therefore could provide inurement. Since 1995, the tax code has contained intermediate sanctions to impose penalties if excess benefits are paid by 501(c)(3) or (4) organizations. An organization reporting total compensation in excess of $80,000 to an officer, the threshold for application of the sanctions, must contemporaneously document its process for determining reasonable amounts to pay.[23]

(a) Column A: Name and Address

The name and address of each person who served at any time during the year as an officer, director, trustee, or key employee is entered. The address at which they want to be contacted by the IRS if necessary is shown; the organization's address can be used. Key employees include the chief management and administrative officials of an organization (such as an executive director or chancellor) but does not include the heads of separate departments or smaller units within the organization. Both a chief financial officer and the officer in charge of administration or program operations are key employees if they have the authority to control the organization's activities, its finances, or both. It is extremely important to coordinate the inclusion of persons on this part with the intermediate sanction rules.

(b) Column B: Title and Average Hours per Week Devoted to Position

Each person's title and the average hours per week devoted to the position is reported. Often, such officials serve as volunteers and may not keep a record of time they spend in carrying out the position. If the persons are uncompensated, it is sufficient to give an estimate such as "4 to 6 hours," "as needed," or "part-time." For compensated persons (particularly highly paid ones), records substantiating actual time spent are critical.

(c) Column C: Compensation

Salary, fees, bonuses, and severance benefits paid, including current-year payments of deferred compensation reported in column D in a year past, are reportable here. Note that this number is not necessarily equal to the amount reported on one's W-2 or Form 1099. Certain taxable benefits and allowances are reported in column E. Cash and noncash payments are counted. For purposes of reporting compensation paid by related organizations to determine if someone receives a combined amount of more than $100,000, stock bonuses or options granted by a taxable subsidiary would be also includible, even if not currently taxable. Payments to a management service company for work performed by an officer or key employee is included as if it had been paid to the individual directly. Ideally, the amounts entered in this part should agree in total with the amount on Part II, line 25.

(d) Column D: Contributions to Employee Benefit Plans and Deferred Compensation

All forms of deferred compensation—whether funded or unfunded, whether pursuant to a qualified or unqualified plan, whether accrued or earned for the current year—are reportable in this column. Qualified pension plans include defined contribution, defined benefit, and money purchase plans under §401(a), employee plans under §403(b), and IRA/SEP plans under §408. In a duplicative manner, the current-year amount set aside is reported in this column as it accrues, whereas the actual payment made in a later year is reported in column C. Medical, dental, disability, and life insurance premiums paid by the organization are included. Tuition, child care, sick leave, and family leave allowances would be counted. All amounts payable under a cafeteria plan, for example, would be included. Estimated cost is to be used if exact amounts per person are not available.

(e) Column E: Expense Account and Other Allowances

Both taxable and nontaxable fringe benefits are reportable. Examples include amounts for which the recipient did not account to the organization or allowances that were more than the person spent serving the organization. A flat automobile, travel, book, or similar allowance would be included (also reportable on Form W-2). The IRS instructions say that payments made under indemnification arrangements and the value of the personal use of housing, automobiles, or other assets owned or leased by the organization (or provided for the organization's use free of charge) should be reported here. The IRS devoted an entire chapter to this subject in its exempt organization specialists' annual training manual for 1996.[24] The chapter reminds the specialists that Internal Revenue Code §§132, 162, and 274 apply to define compensation and fringe benefits. The training materials recommend following the regulations to distinguish between reportable fringes and nonreportable *de minimus* fringe benefits to tally up total compensation. Reportable benefits include season tickets to the theater or ballgames, commuting use of the organization's car, club memberships, below-market loans, group term insurance on spouses or children, weekend use of an apartment or hunting lodge, and spousal travel absent a bona fide business purpose. The following question appears at the end of this part:

> Did any officer, director, trustee, or key employee receive aggregate compensation of more than $100,000 from your organization and all related organizations, of which more than $10,000 was provided by the related organizations? ☐ Yes ☐ No

This question allows the IRS to gather statistics and choose candidates for examination due to excessive compensation. Compensation for this purpose includes all of the items reportable in Part V combined for all related entities. When compensation above the $100,000/$10,000 floor is paid, a supporting schedule adding together the total compensation to any one individual must be attached.

Essentially, Part V intends to reveal compensation paid to personnel of an affiliated group on a consolidated basis. There is some question whether the related organization compensation must be revealed for an officer who receives no compensation from the reporting organization. The question literally asks the organization to combine the compensation of its officers with any compensation they receive from other related entities. Certainly, that is the intention. Another aspect of this issue is the potential for reallocation of compensation among the members of the controlled group.[25]

A *related organization* for this purpose is any entity, tax exempt or not, that is either controlled or owned by or controls or owns the exempt organization. Control and ownership begin at a 50 percent level, with the Form 990 instructions very specifically providing:

- *Owns* means possessing 50 percent or more of the voting membership rights, voting stock, profits interest, or beneficial interest.
- *Control* exists where (1) 50 percent or more of the exempt organization's officers, directors, trustees, or key employees are also officers, directors, trustees, or key employees of the second organization being tested for control; (2) The exempt organization appoints 50 percent or more of the officers, directors, trustees, or key employees of the second organization; or (3) 50 percent or more of the exempt organization's officers, directors, trustees, or key employees are appointed by the second organization.
- Supporting groups operated to benefit another member of the commonly controlled group are treated as controlled or owned, regardless of whether a 50 percent control level exists. *Supporting* for this purpose includes §509(a)(3) organizations as well as other organizations that "operate in connection with the exempt organization where one of the purposes of the supporting organization is to benefit or further the purposes of your organization." The IRS instructions suggest that a hospital auxiliary that raises funds for the hospital or coordinates volunteer programs would be treated as a supporting organization.

Shares issued to unrelated but closely associated individuals or organizations may be scrutinized. The structure may be challenged if its purpose was to keep the ownership under 50 percent for purposes of this reporting requirement. Clearly, a broad net is to be cast with the intention of reflecting all compensation paid to individuals by related organizations.

2.7 PARTS VI AND IX—OTHER INFORMATION

Part VI requests information with which the IRS can evaluate an organization's ongoing qualification for tax exemption. The IRS instructions for this part are quite extensive and the questions survey a wide range of issues. Some of the questions are germane to a particular class of §501(c) organization. Part IX is completed in response to a positive answer to Question 88 in Part VI. Certain answers can cause serious problems for the organization, as outlined in the following discussion.

Line 76 alerts the IRS to review organizational changes by asking if the organization "engaged in any activities not previously reported to the IRS." The question is sometimes hard to answer when the organization's activity has evolved or expanded, but has not necessarily changed in its focus or overall purpose. When there is any doubt, it is prudent to answer "yes" and attach an explanation. The issue raised by this question is whether the organization wants written IRS approval for its evolving or new activity. Simply answering this question "yes" and attaching a detailed description of a change does not result in an IRS response in most cases. The exempt organization must decide whether to instead report the changes to the Ohio District Director with a request for determination of their impact on exempt status. The choice is discussed in Chapter 6.

Line 77 serves a function similar to line 76 by asking if "changes were made in the organizing or governing documents, but not reported to the IRS." Conformed copies (either signed or accompanied by a sworn statement of an authorized official that they are true and correct copies of the original) should be attached if the answer is "yes." Again, it is not customary to get an IRS response to any information submitted. Chapter 6 should be studied to decide if the Cincinnati, Ohio, office should instead be informed directly.

Line 78 tells the IRS that the organization has unrelated business income in excess of $1,000 and that Form 990-T is due to be filed. This answer should be coordinated with Part VII where reportable UBI is input in column B. Woe to the organization that checks this question "yes" and fails to do so!

Line 79 reveals whether a liquidation, termination, or substantial contraction has occurred. Mergers, bankruptcy, and other reasons for terminating the organization's existence are reported. Articles of dissolution, preferably approved by local authorities, should be attached when the organization ceases to exist. A donation of a substantial portion of the assets to another organization constitutes a substantial contraction. If the transfer(s) is made in accordance with the nonprofit's charter, no adverse issues should arise. A (c)(3) organization, for example, must distribute its assets only for one of the eight named (c)(3) purposes. An attachment describing the recipient and indicating suitability is requested. The instructions provide specific information to be attached if the answer is "yes"; direct the preparer to read the regulations for special rules and exceptions.[26]

Line 80 asks "Is the organization related . . . to any other exempt or nonexempt organization?" If so, the entity is to be named. Such relationships are permitted and do not necessarily expose the organization to loss of its exemption. Line 88 and Part IX of Form 990 also request information about taxable subsidiaries and Part VII of Schedule A asks about transactions with non–charitable exempt organizations.[27]

Line 81 asks for the amount of political expenditures. "None" must be the answer for (c)(2) and (c)(3) organizations. Political activity for this purpose is that aimed at influencing the election of persons who make local, state, or national laws, not to be confused with lobbying, which is influencing the elected persons once they are in office. An excise tax is imposed on any (c)(3) involved in elections,[28] and its exemption may be revoked. Such activity is not absolutely prohibited for many types of exempt organizations.

Line 81a asks if Form 1120-POL was filed. New filing requirements for political organizations are discussed in §2.9.

Line 82 allows an organization to voluntarily report any donated services or facilities it receives during the year and to indicate their value. Such donations are not included on page 1 or Schedule A because they are not deductible to the donor and are difficult to value. Because returns are open to public inspection, it is desirable for the organization to reveal such support here. If in-kind donations are reported for financial purposes, the number is also shown in Part IV-A and B and can be noted in Part III.

Line 83a asks whether the organization has complied with the public inspection rules discussed in Chapter 1§3. Failure to comply leads to imposition of penalties.

Line 83b asks, "Did the organization comply with the disclosure requirements relating to quid pro quo contributions?" A fully deductible contribution is one for which nothing is received in return *(quid pro quo)* for the gift. As more fully described in §2.2, the value of benefits provided to a donor in connection with soliciting the gift must be reported to the donor on fund-raising materials and receipts. The old refrain used by charities for many years—"deductible to the extent allowed by law"—is not acceptable. A penalty is imposed for failure to disclose so the answer should either be "yes" or "N/A."

Line 84a asks, "Did the organization solicit any contributions or gifts that were not tax deductible?" Line 84b asks if so, were required disclosures made? This question applies to non–(c)(3) organizations with over $100,000 annual gross receipts that must expressly disclose on solicitations that payments are not deductible as donations under §170.[29] Organizations eligible to receive deductible gifts answer this question "N/A."

Line 85 asks eight questions pertaining to the requirement that §501(c)(4), (5), and (6) organizations disclose the portion of their member dues attributable to nondeductible lobbying. These questions seek to ascertain whether civic associations, unions, and business leagues that conduct lobbying meet the notification and proxy tax requirements.

Line 86 requests the statistics needed to calculate a social club's ongoing qualification, based on the proportionate amount of nonmember receipts and investment income.[30]

Line 87 similarly tests compliance for benevolent life insurance associations, including mutual ditch or irrigation companies, mutual or cooperative telephone companies, and like organizations that must receive 85 percent or more of their income from members.

Line 88 is related to Line 80, discussed previously.

Line 89a asks that the amount of penalty tax for excessive lobbying or political campaign intervention imposed on the (c)(3) organization itself be reported. Information reported on Schedule A, Part VI-A or B is designed to allow the IRS to decide whether this answer should be "yes."

Line 89b asks whether a (c)(3) or (c)(4) organization engaged in any excess benefit transactions during the year or became aware it had done so in a past year. A "yes" answer indicates Form 4720 should be filed to report intermediate sanctions penalties.

Line 89c reports the amount of penalty taxes imposed on the organization's managers and other insiders.

Line 89d asks for the amount of penalty taxes reimbursed by the organization to persons mentioned in line 90c.

Line 90a asks for a list of the states in which Form 990 is filed.

Line 90b requests the number of employees during the March 12 pay period reported on Form 941 or 943, not 942. It is presumed that this information will be matched up with the information from the actual payroll returns filed by the organization, but no report of such action has yet been released. For fiscal-year filers with years ending after March 31, the information bears no relation to the 990 year.

Line 91 asks for the name and telephone number of the person who is in care of the books. This person will receive the call if the IRS wishes to examine the organization's records, or if some member of the interested public wants to ask a question. The phone number for the organization is also input on the first page. Folks disagree on whether the numbers should be the same or different.

2.8 PART VII—ANALYSIS OF INCOME-PRODUCING ACTIVITY

Part VII was added to Form 990 in 1989 and contains a host of pitfalls and traps for the unwary. At the behest of Congress, the IRS designed this part as an audit trail to find unrelated business income. Selection of the appropriate inclusion (column a) or exclusion (column b) code to identify income is difficult in some cases and can have adverse consequences. Some choices are not absolute, and discretion can be important. For example, a column (c) exclusion code 40 highlights activities conducted for nonexempt purposes and operated at a loss—possibly indicating use of exempt organization funds for private purposes that result in inurement.[31] Such losses are also not available to offset against profit-motivated UBI.[32]

A review of the unrelated business income provisions can be found in Chapter 5.[33] An understanding of the terms *regularly carried on*, *member convenience*, *related* and *unrelated*, and *fragmented* is absolutely necessary for correct completion of this page. The form forces the organization to report items of revenue appearing on page 1, lines 2 through 11 (except for contributions) in one of three categories—unrelated and taxable, unrelated but not taxable, and received from performing exempt functions.

(a) What the Columns Include

(i) *Columns (a) and (b): Unrelated Business Income.* Income from unrelated business activities is reported in column (b). Any amounts included here must be reported on Form 990-T and are subject to income tax if a profit is generated from the activity. Column (a) codes are used in Form 990-T (Appendix 5A) to identify the type of business conducted—mining, construction, manufacturing, services, and so on. The UBI codes shown in Appendix 2D, which are very similar to those used in Forms 1120 and 1065 for corporate and partnership income tax returns, were redesigned for 1998.

(ii) *Columns (c) and (d): Revenues Excluded or Modified from Tax.* Income from investments, fund-raising events, and business activities statutorily excluded from tax are included in these columns. The reason for exclusion of the income from tax is claimed by inserting one of 40 code numbers (explained below by line numbers and shown in Appendix 2E) in column (c). If more than one exclusion code applies, the lowest applicable code number is used according to the instructions. Certain codes, such as bingo (9), membership lists (13), and royalties (15), which are the subjects of IRS versus taxpayer battles, may be troublesome, as the IRS uses this page to choose the exempt organizations it will examine, such as social clubs during 1997–98.

(iii) *Column (e): Related or Exempt Function Income.* Income generated through charges for services rendered or items sold in connection with the organization's underlying exempt (program) activities are entered in column (e). Student tuition and fees, hospital charges, admissions, publication sales, handicraft or other by-product sales, seminar registrations, and all other revenues received in return for providing exempt functions[34] are included. This column is a safe harbor because it contains income not potentially subject to the UBI tax: that income generated by "substantially related" activities (those with a causal relationship, contributing importantly to the organization's programs). An explanation of the related aspect of each number in this column must be entered in Part VIII below.

Some exempt function income is also described by specific exclusion codes. Rentals from low-income housing fits into code 16 and therefore could also properly be placed in columns (c) and (d). It is preferable to place such an item in column (e) because the taint of UBI character is removed. Interest income earned under a student loan program or by a credit union and royalties from scientific research patents are other examples of potential dual classifications.

(b) Line-by-Line Description

First, note that for certain lines gross income before any deductions is reported, and for others (lines 97, 98, 100, and 101) net income is reported.

(i) *Line 93: Program Service Revenue.* Revenues produced from activities forming the basis for exemption, described under column (e), are considered program service revenues. As a general rule, all revenues on this line would be reportable in column (e). One important exception is fees for social club services charged to nonmembers, which must be reported in column (b) and labeled with UBI code 713900. A short description of the type of income—student tuition, admission fees, and so on—is entered under line 93 (a through f). Program service revenue in the form of interest, dividend, rent, or royalty is entered on this line. Sales of goods or "inventory items," such as student books, blood bank sales, or museum gift shop items are not entered here but on line 102, except for hospitals and colleges. According to the instructions to page 1, they may include inventory sales items as program services revenue when it is consistent with their overall reporting system under GAAP. Governmental grants for services rendered, not entered as contributions on line 1(c) of page 1, are entered on line 93(g). Contractual services, such as research, student testing, medical and food services, child welfare program fees, and similar services performed on a fee basis for governmental agencies are to be included here.

(ii) *Line 94: Membership Dues and Assessments.* Dues and other charges for services rendered to members are included on this line. When a member pays dues primarily to support the organization's activities, rather than to derive benefits of more than nominal monetary benefit, that dues payment represents a contribution. To the extent that a (c)(3) organization's membership dues are treated as a contribution because they have no monetary value, they are not included here. Member items that are not required to be assigned value include non–commercial quality publications, discounts on admission or store purchases, free admission, educational classes, and other certain other items members can use frequently throughout the year.

A business league, labor union, social club, veterans group, or similar organization would report its members' dues, not including any portion allocable to inventory items sold or program services, such as decals or group insurance. Varying levels of membership with different amounts of dues, such as associate or junior members, raise a question. As long as the privileges given to a different class of member do not provide special benefit to any individuals, all types of dues can be aggregated.[35] Dues would be most commonly placed in column (e). To the extent that member services (such as group insurance or job placement services) are considered UBI, they would be included in column (b) and labeled with a UBI code (524292-524298 for insurance and 561300 for placement services).

(iii) *Line 95: Interest on Savings and Temporary Cash Investment.* Payments from savings and loan, bank, and credit union cash deposits are entered on this line. Typically, this income is entered in column (d) and identified with code 14. Interest income on student, low-income housing, and other program-related loans are reported on line 93. Interest on a loan to an officer or employee would be reported as other revenue, line 103, in column (d), unless the loan is in the nature of compensation (e.g., a temporary loan to buy a new home), in which case it could be reported in column (e).

(iv) *Line 96: Dividends and Interest from Securities.* Dividends earned on common or preferred stock, money market accounts, mutual fund shares, U.S. or local government and corporate bonds, and any other securities are usually reported on line 96 in column (d) and are also labeled with code 14. Dividends received from an 80 percent–owned for-profit subsidiary would also be reported in column (d). However, interest, rent, or other payments deductible to the subsidiary go in column (b). Capital gains distributed by a mutual fund are reported on line 100.

Securities purchased with borrowed funds, either through a margin account or other debt (called *acquisition indebtedness*), produce UBI. Income from such indebted securities is reported in column (b); in the case of partial indebtedness, only the portion calculated in the ratio of the cost to the debt would be reported in column (b) (UBI code 900000), with the balance reported in column (d).

(v) *Line 97: Net Rental Income (Loss) from Real Estate.* The net income, calculated after deduction of expenses such as depreciation, interest on debt, and other direct costs of maintaining real property, is reported on line 97 (code 16). This line does not come directly from page 1. On page 6, real estate and personal property rentals are separated. Also, this is the first line on page 6 where the net income, instead of gross, is entered in column (b), (d), or (e). Real estate rentals can be classified under one of 10 exclusion codes, and careful study of §§512 through 514 may be necessary to ensure correct property classification under particular facts and circumstances. The majority of real property rentals are received on non–indebted property held for investment, the income from which is reported in column (d) and identified with code 16. Lease rentals dependent upon the tenants' profits are classed as UBI and must be reported in column (b). Rents on program-related real estate properties are placed in column (e) on line 93.

Codes 30 through 38 apply specifically to debt-financed income reportable in column (d) but excludable from UBI classification due to a statutory exception. The portion of income attributable to acquisition indebtedness that is not excluded (see Chapter 5) is reported in column (b), line 97a (513110 series code).

Rents paid by a 50 percent or more owned subsidiary are reported in column (b) as taxable UBI. If services are rendered to benefit the individual occupant, such as in a hotel, boarding house, parking lot, or storage facility, the rental is also classed as UBI (531110 series code). Services customarily provided for all tenants, such as utilities, security, cleaning of public entrances, elevators, and other common areas do not constitute services rendered to individual tenants.

(vi) *Line 98: Net Rental Income (Loss) from Personal Property.* Rentals from personal property earned for purely investment purposes create UBI (whether indebted or not) and are reported in column (b) and identified with the appropriate business code, such as 532420. Such rentals could be program related, in which case they are reported on line 93 in column (e) with no code.

If more than 50 percent of a combined real and personal property lease revenue is attributable to personal property, the rental is reported on line 98, column (b), and is subject to UBI. A manufacturing or printing plant, a scientific research facility, and an exhibition hall with booths are examples of the types of rentals that might fall into this category. A Form 990-T code again applies and this income, net of directly allocable expenses, is entered in column (b).

(vii) *Line 99: Other Investment Income.* Royalty income from mineral or intellectual property interests are entered on this line. In most cases, such income is entered in column (d) and identified with exclusion code 15. Royalties from educational publications or research patents might be classed as program service revenue on line 93 and entered in column (e) instead. (See line 103 for certain royalties.) Changes in unrealized gain or loss on an investment portfolio is not considered as current income on page 1 or page 6, but is entered as a surplus adjustment on line 20 of page 1.

(viii) *Line 100: Gain (Loss) from Sales of Assets Other Than Inventory.* Capital gains and losses reported on line 8 of page 1 from the disposition of all organization assets, other than inventory, are reported on this line (code 18). Gains and losses from the sale of investment portfolio assets, real estate, office equipment, program-related assets, partnership interest, and all sorts of property are included. Most gains or losses are reportable in column (d), except for debt-financed property that must be shown in column (b). Exempt organizations with sophisticated UBI activity may realize gain from sale of assets used in that business which would also be reportable in column (b). Gain (loss) from the sale of program-related assets is reported in column (e).

Gain or loss on purchase, sale, or lapse of security options can be reported on this line (code 19). It has been suggested that revenue attributable to lapsed options, as distinguished from options sold or "covered" before maturity, should be reportable on line 99. However, the IRS instructions are silent and, for convenience, all option activity can be combined.

(ix) *Line 101: Net Income from Special Fund-Raising Events.* Fund-raising event net income, excluding any portion allocated to donations (not reported in this part), is technically UBI. The typical charitable event is excepted from UBI under the irregular (code 01) or volunteer (code 02) exception, and the net profit is reported in column (d). When the primary purpose of the event is educational or otherwise exempt, such as a cultural festival, it is conceivable that the profits could be reported as related income in column (e). Any other fund-raising profits must be reported as UBI in column (b) (711110).

(x) *Line 102: Gross Profit (Loss) from Sales of Inventory.* Gross revenues from the sale of inventory, less returns and allowances and cost of goods sold (line 10c on page 1), is entered here. Inventory includes objects purchased or made for resale, rather than held as an investment. In contrast to the instruction for rents and interest produced from program-related investments, exempt function inventory sales are to be reported on this line, rather than on line 93.

(xi) *Line 103: Other Revenue.* Revenues not suitable for inclusion on lines 93 through 102 are entered here. Two particular types of revenue that fit on this line are the subject of constant battles between the IRS and exempt organizations. Advertising revenues not classified as program related can be entered in either column (b) or (d). Ads produce unrelated income (column (b), code 541800) unless the irregular or the volunteer exception applies. Likewise, royalties from use of the organization's name, logo, or mailing list could be entered in either column. If the organization disagrees with the IRS's current position that such income is unrelated, such revenue would be entered in column (d) with modification code 15. See code 13 for the narrow exception available to (c)(3)s and certain veterans organizations for exchanges or rentals of lists between similar types of organizations.

Some have speculated that use of code 15 is an invitation to be examined, because the IRS will scrutinize organizations claiming modification of royalties, despite the fact that some royalties are clearly passive income.

Recoveries of prior-year expenditures, interest on loans not made for investment or program purposes (e.g., to employees or managers), and any other items of revenue not properly reported elsewhere would also be entered on line 103.

(c) Rationale for Column (e) Amounts

Part VIII, Relationship of Activities to the Accomplishment of Exempt Purposes, asks the organization to explain how each activity for which income is reported in column (e) fosters the accomplishment of its exempt purposes (other than by providing funds for such purposes). Dues payments reported on line 3 of Part I providing funds to support the organization's exempt activities are included here. Not much room is provided and it is hard to know how much information to submit. There are two types of answers to this question, depending on the nature of the income. For clearly and unquestionably related types of revenue, such as student tuition, hospital room fees, symphony performance admission tickets, and member dues, the answer can simply be such a description. For revenues received in activities that might arguably produce UBI, such as charges for computer services, sale of standard forms, advertising, or logo sales, a more convincing description of exempt purpose is recommended.

The IRS sample contained in the instructions suggests sentences like: "Fee from county for finding foster homes for two children—this furthers our exempt purpose of ensuring quality care for foster children," and "Members are social services workers who receive information and advice on problem cases from our staff as part of our counseling, adoption, and foster care programs." The explanation here need not repeat the same information, but can refer back to Part III, Statement of Program Service Accomplishments, where very similar information is furnished.

(d) The Codes

Each numerical entry on page 6 is individually explained either with a code or literal description. The type of revenue in column (b) is identified by column (a) codes (Appendix 2D) that mimic those used for the unrelated business income tax return, Form 990-T. These codes describe the type of business and are easy to assign because they are so literal—dance studio or physical fitness facility, for example. Each major category has a miscellaneous number. There is little harm in choosing the wrong code, because the organization is already admitting that the income is UBI.

Column (d) is described by exclusion codes (Appendix 2E), and the correct choice of these is very important. These codes explain that, although the organization is admitting it has unrelated business income, it claims that the UBI is not taxable for one of 40 different reasons. A review of Chapter 5 may be useful in making the choices.

2.9 REPORTING BY POLITICAL ORGANIZATIONS

Effective July 1, 2000, a political organization that intends to be tax-exempt must notify the IRS no later than 24 hours from its creation and provide specific information evidencing its qualification for exemption.[36] The recognition will be effective only prospectively from the date of notification. Preexisting political organizations were given until July 31, 2000, to file; the filings must be made both electronically and physically. Except for charitable organizations, all other categories of nonprofit organizations qualify without making notification.[37] Failure to file notification in a timely fashion results in the political organization's being treated as a normal taxpayer subject to income tax on all of its income. The exempt function expenses, or disbursements for political campaign activity, would not be deductible,[38] and income is taxed at the highest current corporate rate (currently 35 percent). So a committee that fails to make notice will not only have to pay tax on net investment income, but also on its campaign contributions.

Effective for years beginning after June 30, 2000, all political organizations that are required to file Form 1120-POL must now file Form 990 or 990-EZ and, for those described below, new Forms 8871 and 8872.

(a) Public Disclosure Reports—Forms 8871 and 8872

After a flurry of demands for disclosure of campaign contributors, Congress imposed enhanced reporting rules on certain §527 organizations. The rules are designed to require reporting for those so-called "soft money" organizations not previously required to report donor and expenditure information to either the IRS or the Federal Election Commission (FEC). Such political action committees (PACs) receive unlimited donations used to support political parties rather than individual candidates. The rules also apply to congressional leadership PACs that are not required to make FEC reports.

It is important to note that Form 1120-POL must still be filed to report tax on a PAC's investment income. Additionally, Form 990 or 990-EZ is now also due to be filed. The following political organizations are *not* subject to these new requirements[39]:

- An entity required to report to the Federal Election Commission[40] (not including local and state reporters) as a political committee (the so-called "hard money" organizations)
- Organizations that reasonably anticipate that their annual gross receipts will always be less than $25,000 each year (not an average)
- Otherwise tax-exempt organizations described in 501(c) that are subject to 527(f)(1) when they make an "exempt function" expenditure[41]

Effective immediately upon its passage,[42] all other political groups must file both electronically[43] and on paper the following with the IRS (reproduced in Appendixes 2F and 2G):

- Form 8871, Political Organization, Notice of Section 527 Status
- Form 8872, Report of Contributors and Expenditures filed both annually and periodically (during an election year at least quarterly)

Form 8871 must contain the following:

- The name and both the physical mailing and electronic address of the organization
- The purpose of the organization
- The names and addresses of its officers, highly compensated employees, contact person, custodian of the records, and members of the board of directors
- The name and address of, and relationship to, any related entities

The IRS must make information submitted by political organizations available at its officers and on the Internet no later than five business days after it receives the notice. The political organization itself must make Form 8871 available for public inspection under the same rules application to Form 990 and 1023 availability.[44]

The term *highly compensated employees*, for this purpose, means the five employees (other than officers or directors) who are expected to have the highest annual compensation in excess of $50,000. Cash and noncash payments, whether paid currently or deferred, are included. For an organization existing when the rules were imposed, the 12-month period began on July 1, 2000.

The term *related entity* is defined to include one of two types:

- The related entity and the organization have significant common purposes and substantial common members *or* substantial common direction or control, whether direct or indirect.
- The related entity or the organization owns, directly or indirectly through one or more entities, at least 50 percent capital or profits interest in the other.

Form 8872 is to be filed annually each year and also periodically during a year. The political organization can choose to file monthly or quarterly/semiannually. The monthly filer must submit the form by the 20th day after the close of each month, except the December report can be included in the annual report due January 31. During an election year, the monthly filer must report no later than 12 days before and 30 days after the general election. Quarterly/semiannual filers submit a report for the first half of the year by July 31 and for the second half by January 31. Why organizations were given the choice of a more frequent, monthly filing option is not stated. Certainly, the monthly reports would be shorter and inspire regular attention to record keeping.

During election years, reports must be filed quarterly, plus a preelection report is filed 12 days before the election and post–general election report 30 days after the election. An election is defined for this purpose to include a general, special, primary, or runoff election for a federal office; a convention or caucus of a political party with authority to nominate a candidate for federal office; a primary election to select delegates to a national nominating convention; or a primary election to express a preference for the nomination of an individual for election to the office of president. Local and state elections are not included for filing requirement purposes.

For donors giving $200 or more and for vendors paid $500 or more during the calendar year, the name, address, and, if an individual, the occupation and employer of any person must be reported. Independent expenditures made without the authorization, suggestion, or request of a candidate need not be reported. Form 8872 is filed with the Ogden Service Center. The penalty for failure to file is a tax equal to the amount not disclosed multiplied by the highest corporate tax rate. Form 8872 must be made available for public inspection.[45] Also, organizations that are tax exempt under §501(c)(4), (5), and (6) are now required to disclose all assistance they provide to §527 organizations. Those that spend $10,000 or more on political expenditures must also disclose the names of contributors of $1,000 or more.

Appendix 2A

Form **990-EZ**

Department of the Treasury
Internal Revenue Service

Short Form

Return of Organization Exempt From Income Tax

Under section 501(c) of the Internal Revenue Code (except black lung benefit trust or private foundation), section 527, or section 4947(a)(1) nonexempt charitable trust

For organizations with gross receipts less than $100,000 and total assets less than $250,000 at the end of the year.

The organization may have to use a copy of this return to satisfy state reporting requirements.

OMB No. 1545-1150

2000

Open to Public Inspection

A For the 2000 calendar year, OR tax year beginning and ending

B Check if: ☐ Change of address ☐ Change of name ☐ Initial return ☐ Final return ☐ Amended return

C Name of organization
Consult the chapter references below for instructions to this form

Number and street (or P.O. box, if mail is not delivered to address)

City, town, or country State ZIP code

D Employer identification number

E Telephone number

F Check if ☐ if application pending

H Enter 4-digit group exemption number (GEN)

G Accounting method: ☐ Cash ☐ Accrual ☐ Other (specify)

I Organization type (check only one)- ☐ 501(c) ( ) (insert no.) ☐ 527 or ☐ 4947(a)(1)

Section 501(c)(3) organizations and 4947(a)(1) nonexempt charitable trusts must attach a completed Schedule A (Form 990 or 990-EZ).

J Check ☐ if the organization's gross receipts are normally not more than $25,000. The organization need not file a return with the IRS; but if the organization received a Form 990 Package in the mail, it should file a return without financial data. Some states require a complete return.

K Add lines 5b, 6b, and 7b, to line 9 to determine gross receipts; if $100,000 or more, file Form 990 instead of Form 990-EZ $

L Check this box if the organization is not required to attach Schedule B (Form 990 or 990-EZ) ☐

Part I Revenue, Expenses, and Changes in Net Assets or Fund Balances

Section	Line	Description	Sub-line	Sub-amount	Line	Amount
Revenue	1	Contributions, gifts, grants, and similar amounts received			1	2.2 a
	2	Program service revenue including government fees and contracts			2	2.2 b
	3	Membership dues and assessments			3	2.2 c
	4	Investment income			4	2.2 d,e,g
	5a	Gross amount from sale of assets other than inventory	5a	2.2 h		
	b	Less: cost or other basis and sales expenses	5b			
	c	Gain or (loss) from sale of assets other than inventory (line 5a less line 5b) (attach schedule)			5c	
	6	Special events and activities (attach schedule):				
	a	Gross revenue (not including $ ____ of contributions reported on line 1)	6a	2.2 i		
	b	Less: direct expenses other than fundraising expenses	6b			
	c	Net income or (loss) from special events and activities (line 6a less line 6b)			6c	
	7a	Gross sales of inventory, less returns and allowances	7a	2.2 j		
	b	Less: cost of goods sold	7b			
	c	Gross profit or (loss) from sales of inventory (line 7a less line 7b)			7c	
	8	Other revenue (describe ____)			8	2.2 f,k
	9	Total revenue (add lines 1, 2, 3, 4, 5c, 6c, 7c, and 8)			9	
Expenses	10	Grants and similar amounts paid (attach schedule)			10	2.3 a
	11	Benefits paid to or for members			11	2.3 c
	12	Salaries, other compensation, and employee benefits			12	2.3 d&e
	13	Professional fees and other payments to independent contractors			13	2.3 f
	14	Occupancy, rent, utilities, and maintenance			14	2.3 g
	15	Printing, publications, postage, and shipping			15	2.3 g
	16	Other expenses (describe ____)			16	2.3 g
	17	Total expenses (add lines 10 through 16)			17	
Net Assets	18	Excess or (deficit) for the year (line 9 less line 17)			18	
	19	Net assets or fund balances at beginning of year (from line 27, column (A)) (must agree with end-of-year figure reported on prior year's return)			19	2.2 n
	20	Other changes in net assets or fund balances (attach explanation)			20	
	21	Net assets or fund balances at end of year (combine lines 18 through 20)			21	

Part II Balance Sheets If Total assets on line 25, column (B) are $250,000 or more, file Form 990 instead of Form 990-EZ.

Line	(See Specific Instructions on page 37.)	(A) Beginning of year	Line	(B) End of year
22	Cash, savings, and investments		22	
23	Land and buildings **See Chapter 2.5**		23	
24	Other assets (describe ____)		24	
25	Total assets		25	
26	Total liabilities (describe ____)		26	
27	Net assets or fund balances (line 27 of column (B) must agree with line 21)		27	

For Paperwork Reduction Act Notice, see page 1 of the separate instructions. (HTA) Form 990-EZ (2000)

Form 990-EZ (2000) Consult the chapter references below for instructions Page 2

Part III Statement of Program Service Accomplishments (See Specific Instructions on page 38.)

Expenses (Required for 501(c)(3) and (4) organizations and 4947(a)(1) trusts; optional for others.)

What is the organization's primary exempt purpose?

Describe what was achieved in carrying out the organization's exempt purposes. In a clear and concise manner, describe the services provided, the number of persons benefited, or other relevant information for each program title.

28 See Chapter 2.4
(Grants $ | 28a

29
(Grants $ | 29a

30
(Grants $ | 30a

31 Other program services (attach schedule) . . . . (Grants $ | 31a

32 Total program service expenses (add lines 28a through 31a) . . . . | 32

Part IV List of Officers, Directors, Trustees, and Key Employees (List each one even if not compensated. See Specific Instructions on page 38.)

(A) Name and address	(B) Title and average hours per week devoted to position	(C) Compensation (If not paid, enter -0-.)	(D) Contributions to employee benefit plans & deferred compensation	(E) Expense account and other allowances
See Chapter 2.6				

Part V Other Information (See Specific Instructions on page 38 and General Instruction V on page 14.) See Chapter 2.7 — Yes or No

33 Did the organization engage in any activity not previously reported to the Internal Revenue Service? If "Yes," attach a detailed description of each activity . . . . Yes or No

34 Were any changes made to the organizing or governing documents but not reported to the IRS? If "Yes," attach a conformed copy of the changes . Yes or No

35 If the organization had income from business activities, such as those reported on lines 2, 6, and 7 (among others), but NOT reported on Form 990-T, attach a statement explaining your reason for not reporting the income on Form 990-T.

a Did the organization have unrelated business gross income of $1,000 or more or 6033(e) notice, reporting, and proxy tax requirements? . . . . Yes or No

b If "Yes," has it filed a tax return on Form 990-T for this year? . . . . Yes or No

36 Was there a liquidation, dissolution, termination, or substantial contraction during the year? (If "Yes," attach a statement) . . . Yes or No

37a Enter amount of political expenditures, direct or indirect, as described in the instructions | 37a

b Did the organization file Form 1120-POL for this year? . . . . Yes or No

38a Did the organization borrow from, or make any loans to, any officer, director, trustee, or key employee OR were any such loans made in a prior year and still unpaid at the start of the period covered by this return? . . . . Yes or No

b If "Yes," attach the schedule specified in the line 38 instructions and enter the amount involved . . | 38b

39 501(c)(7) organizations. - Enter: a Initiation fees and capital contributions included on line 9 | 39a

b Gross receipts, included on line 9, for public use of club facilities . . . . | 39b

40a 501(c)(3) organizations. - Enter: Amount of tax imposed on the organization during the year under: section 4911 ______ ;section 4912 ______ ;section 4955 ______

b 501(c)(3) and (4) organizations. Did the organization engage in any section 4958 excess benefit transaction during the year or did it become aware of an excess benefit transaction from a prior year? If "Yes," attach an explanation. . . . . Yes or No

c Amount of tax imposed on organization managers or disqualified persons during the year under 4912, 4955, and 4958 . . . .

d Enter: Amount of tax on line 40c, above, reimbursed by the organization . . . .

41 List the states with which a copy of this return is filed.

42 The books are in care of ______ Telephone no. ______
Located at ______ ZIP + 4 ______

43 Section 4947(a)(1) nonexempt charitable trusts filing Form 990-EZ in lieu of Form 1041- Check here ☐
and enter the amount of tax-exempt interest received or accrued during the tax year . . . . | 43

Please Sign Here

Under penalties of perjury, I declare that I have examined this return, including accompanying schedules and statements, and to the best of my knowledge and belief, it is true, correct, and complete. Declaration of preparer (other than officer) is based on all information of which preparer has any knowledge. (IMPORTANT: See General Instruction W, page 14.)

Signature of officer | Date | Type or print name and title. | Title

Paid Preparer Use Only			
Preparer's signature	Date	Check if self-employed X	Preparer's SSN or PTIN 400-00-0000
Firm's name (or yours if self-employed) and address, and ZIP code	A Qualified CPA Firm 1001 Main Street Hometown, Texas 77777	EIN 45-5555555 Phon (444) 422-2222	

Form 990-EZ (2000)

Appendix 2B

Form **990** | **Return of Organization Exempt From Income Tax** | OMB No.1545-0047 **2000**

Under section 501(c) of the Internal Revenue Code (except black lung benefit trust or private foundation), section 527, or section 4947(a)(1) nonexempt charitable trust

Department of the Treasury
Internal Revenue Service

The organization may have to use a copy of this return to satisfy state reporting requirements.

Open to Public Inspection

A For the 2000 calendar year, OR tax year period beginning July 1st , 2000, and ending June 30th 2001

B Check if: ☐ Change of address ☐ Change of name ☐ Initial return ☐ Final return ☐ Amended return

C Name of organization: **Hometown Chapter, Campaign to Clean Up America**

Number and street (or P. O. box if mail is not delivered to street address): **1111 Any Street**

City or town: **Hometown** State or Country: **Texas** ZIP code: **77777**

D Employer identification number: **44-4444444**

E Telephone number: **(444) 444-4444**

F Check ☐ if application is pending

Note: H and I are not applicable to section 527 orgs.

H(a) Is this a group return for affiliates? ☐ Yes [X] No

H(b) If "Yes," enter number of affiliates

H(c) Are all affiliates included? ☐ Yes ☐ No (If "No," attach a list. See inst.)

H(d) Is this a separate return filed by an organization covered by a group ruling? [X] Yes ☐ No

I Enter 4-digit group exemption number (GEN) 1010

L Check this box if the organization is not required to attach Schedule B (Form 990 or 990-EZ) ☐

G Organization type (check only one) [X] 501(c) (3)(insert no.) ☐ 527 or ☐ 4947(a)(1)

Section 501(c)(3) organizations and 4947(a)(1) nonexempt charitable trusts MUST attach a completed Schedule A (Form 990 or 900-EZ).

J Accounting method: ☐ Cash [X] Accrual ☐ Other (specify)

K Check here ☐ if the organization's gross receipts are normally not more than $25,000. The organization need not file a return with the IRS; but if the organization received a Form 990 Package in the mail, it should file a return without financial data. Some states require a complete return.

Part I Revenue, Expenses, and Changes in Net Assets or Fund Balances (See Specific Instructions on page 16.)

Revenue	1	Contributions, gifts, grants, and similar amounts received:				
	a	Direct public support	1a	877,200		
	b	Indirect public support	1b			
	c	Government contributions (grants)	1c	80,000		
	d	Total (add lines 1a through 1c) (cash $ 757,200 noncash $ 200,000)			1d	957,200
	2	Program service revenue including government fees and contracts (from Part VII, line 93)			2	49,700
	3	Membership dues and assessments			3	
	4	Interest on savings and temporary cash investments			4	400
	5	Dividends and interest from securities			5	4,000
	6a	Gross rents	6a	4,500		
	b	Less: rental expenses	6b	1,600		
	c	Net rental income or (loss) (subtract line 6b from line 6a)			6c	2,900
	7	Other investment income (describe)			7	
	8a	Gross amount from sales of assets other than inventory	8a	(A) Securities 1,400; (B) Other		
	b	Less: cost or other basis and sales expenses	8b	(A) 200		
	c	Gain or (loss) (attach schedule)	8c	(A) 1,200		
	d	Net gain or (loss) (combine line 8c, columns (A) and (B))			8d	1,200
	9	Special events and activities (attach schedule)				
	a	Gross revenue (not including $ 20,000 of contributions reported on line 1a)	9a	55,000		
	b	Less: direct expenses other than fundraising expenses	9b	47,000		
	c	Net income or (loss) from special events (subtract line 9b from line 9a)			9c	8,000
	10a	Gross sales of inventory, less returns and allowances	10a	40,000		
	b	Less: cost of goods sold	10b	10,000		
	c	Gross profit or (loss) from sales of inventory (attach schedule) (subtract line 10b from line 10a)			10c	30,000
	11	Other revenue (from Part VII, line 103)			11	
	12	Total revenue (add lines 1d, 2, 3, 4, 5, 6c, 7, 8d, 9c, 10c, and 11)			12	1,053,400
Expenses	13	Program services (from line 44, column (B))			13	484,200
	14	Management and general (from line 44, column (C))			14	133,300
	15	Fundraising (from line 44, column (D))			15	83,500
	16	Payments to affiliates (attach schedule)			16	10,000
	17	Total expenses (add lines 16 and 44, column (A))			17	711,000
Net Assets	18	Excess or (deficit) for the year (subtract line 17 from line 12)			18	342,400
	19	Net assets or fund balances at beginning of year (from line 73, column (A))			19	43,800
	20	Other changes in net assets or fund balances (attach explanation)			20	5,200
	21	Net assets or fund balances at end of year (combine lines 18, 19, and 20)			21	391,400

For Paperwork Reduction Act Notice, see page 1 of the separate instructions. (HTA) Form 990 (2000)

Form 990 (2000) Hometown Chapter, Campaign to Clean Up America 44-4444444 Page 2

Part II Statement of Functional Expenses All organizations must complete column (A). Columns (B), (C), and (D) are required for section 501(c)(3) and (4) organizations and section 4947(a)(1) nonexempt charitable trusts but optional for others. (See Specific Instructions on page 20.)

Do not include amounts reported on line 6b, 8b, 9b, 10b, or 16 of Part I.		(A) Total	(B) Program services	(C) Management and general	(D) Fundraising
22 Grants and allocations (attach schedule) (cash $ 2,500 noncash $)	22	2,500	2,500		
23 Specific assistance to individuals (attach schedule)	23				
24 Benefits paid to or for members (attach schedule)	24				
25 Compensation of officers, directors, etc.	25	50,000	30,000	15,000	5,000
26 Other salaries and wages	26	270,000	205,000	50,000	15,000
27 Pension plan contributions	27				
28 Other employee benefits	28	25,000	18,000	5,000	2,000
29 Payroll taxes	29	25,000	17,000	5,000	3,000
30 Professional fundraising fees	30	20,000			20,000
31 Accounting fees	31	10,000		10,000	
32 Legal fees	32	10,000		10,000	
33 Supplies	33	8,000	6,300	1,200	500
34 Telephone	34	18,000	12,000	4,000	2,000
35 Postage and shipping	35	7,000	5,700	800	500
36 Occupancy	36	60,000	43,000	14,000	3,000
37 Equipment rental and maintenance	37	10,000	10,000		
38 Printing and publications	38	52,000	42,000	2,000	8,000
39 Travel	39	25,000	16,000	3,000	6,000
40 Conferences, conventions, and meetings	40	7,000	6,000	1,000	
41 Interest	41	3,000		3,000	
42 Depreciation, depletion, etc. (attach schedule)	42	25,500	24,200	800	500
43 Other expenses (itemize) a	43a				
b Advertising	43b	47,000	26,000	3,000	18,000
c Dues/library	43c	5,500	2,500	3,000	
d Outside consultants	43d	18,000	16,000	2,000	
e Miscellaneous	43e	2,500	2,000	500	
f	43f				
44 Total functional expenses (add lines 22 through 43). Organizations completing columns (B) - (D), carry these totals to lines 13 - 15	44	701,000	484,200	133,300	83,500

Reporting of Joint Costs. Did you report in column (B) (Program services) any joint costs from a combined educational campaign and fundraising solicitation? [X] Yes [ ] No

If "Yes," enter (i) the aggregate amount of these joint costs $ 31,500 ; (ii) the amount allocated to Program services $ 20,500

(iii) the amount allocated to Management and general $ ______ ; and (iv) the amount allocated to Fundraising $ 11,000

Part III Statement of Program Service Accomplishments (See Specific Instructions on page 23.)

What is the organization's primary exempt purpose? Charitable - to promote civic betterment

All organizations must describe their exempt purpose achievements in a clear and concise manner. State the number of clients served, publications issued, etc. Discuss achievements that are not measurable. (Section 501(c)(3) and (4) organizations and 4947(a)(1) nonexempt charitable trusts must also enter the amount of grants and allocations to others.)

	Program Service Expenses (Required for 501(c)(3) and (4) orgs., and 4947(a)(1) trusts; but optional for others.)
a VOLUNTEER TEAMS: To prevent litter and organize pick-up teams, the campaign holds community meetings to recruit volunteers. Teams are provided equipment, including rakes, shovels, gloves, and trash bags with which to clean up their communities. Over 300 persons volunteered this year. Samples of toxic garbage are collected for testing by the Environmental Protection Agency. (Grants and allocations $ 2,500)	249,400
b PUBLIC EDUCATION: Literature describing Campaign's mission to rid America of litter and clean up our cities, towns, and countrysides is prepared and distributed. Mailings, newspaper and magazine advertisements, and pamphlets are used. Over 500,000 packages were mailed and over 10,000 pamphlets sold. (Grants and allocations $)	146,600
c SEMINARS: The Campaign sponsors educational meetings to bring together government officials, businesses, and citizens to discuss new methods of trash collections, recycling, and litter reduction. Over 2,000 persons participated in programs this year. (Grants and allocations $)	78,200
d LEGISLATIVE ACTIVITY: The Campaign promotes the passage of legislation to reduce litter, including a bottle ordinance to require use of returnable bottles. (Grants and allocations $)	10,000
e Other program services (attach schedule) (Grants and allocations $)	
f Total of Program Service Expenses (should equal line 44, column (B), Program services)	484,200

Form 990 (2000)

Form 990 (2000) Hometown Chapter, Campaign to Clean Up America 44-4444444 Page 3

Part IV Balance Sheets (See Specific Instructions on page 23.)

Note: Where required, attached schedules and amounts within the description column should be for end-of-year amounts only.			(A) Beginning of year		(B) End of year
Assets					
45 Cash - non-interest-bearing				45	
46 Savings and temporary cash investments			12,000	46	29,000
47a Accounts receivable	47a	2,000			
b Less: allowance for doubtful accounts	47b			47c	2,000
48a Pledges receivable	48a				
b Less: allowance for doubtful accounts	48b			48c	
49 Grants receivable				49	12,000
50 Receivables from officers, directors, trustees, and key employees (attach schedule)				50	
51a Other notes and loans receivable (attach schedule)	51a				
b Less: allowance for doubtful accounts	51b			51c	
52 Inventories for sale or use				52	
53 Prepaid expenses and deferred charges				53	
54 Investments - securities (attach schedule) ☐ Cost	☒ FMV		19,000	54	255,400
55a Investments - land, buildings, and equipment: basis	55a				
b Less: accumulated depreciation (attach schedule)	55b			55c	
56 Investments - other (attach schedule)				56	
57a Land, buildings, and equipment: basis	57a	187,000			
b Less: accumulated depreciation (attach schedule)	57b	27,000	18,000	57c	160,000
58 Other assets (describe)				58	
59 Total assets (add lines 45 through 58) (must equal line 74)			49,000	59	458,400
Liabilities					
60 Accounts payable and accrued expenses			5,200	60	14,000
61 Grants payable				61	
62 Deferred revenue				62	18,000
63 Loans from officers, directors, trustees, and key employees (attach schedule)				63	
64a Tax-exempt bond liabilities (attach schedule)				64a	
b Mortgages and other notes payable (attach schedule)				64b	35,000
65 Other liabilities (describe)				65	
66 Total liabilities (add lines 60 through 65)			5,200	66	67,000
Net Assets or Fund Balances					
Organizations that follow SFAS 117, check here ☒ and complete lines 67 through 69 and lines 73 and 74.					
67 Unrestricted			25,800	67	191,200
68 Temporarily restricted				68	70,000
69 Permanently restricted			18,000	69	130,200
Organizations that do not follow SFAS 117, check here ☐ and complete lines 70 through 74.					
70 Capital stock, trust principal, or current funds				70	
71 Paid-in or capital surplus, or land, bldg., and equipment fund				71	
72 Retained earnings, endowment, accumulated income, or other funds				72	
73 Total net assets or fund balances (add lines 67 through 69 OR lines 70 through 72; column (A) must equal line 19 and column (B) must equal line 21)			43,800	73	391,400
74 Total liabilities and net assets/fund balances (add lines 66 and 73)			49,000	74	458,400

Form 990 is available for public inspection and, for some people, serves as the primary or sole source of information about a particular organization. How the public perceives an organization in such cases may be determined by the information presented on its return. Therefore, please make sure the return is complete and accurate and fully describes, in Part III, the organization's programs and accomplishments.

Form 990 (2000) Hometown Chapter, Campaign to Clean Up America 44-4444444 Page 4

Part IV-A Reconciliation of Revenue per Audited Financial Statements with Revenue per Return (See Specific Instructions, page 25.)

a	Total revenue, gains, and other support per audited financial statements		a	1,087,700
b	Amounts included on line a but not on line 12, Form 990:			
(1)	Net unrealized gains on investments	5,200		
(2)	Donated services and use of facilities	27,500		
(3)	Recoveries of prior year grants			
(4)	Other (specify): Rental expense	1,600		
	Add amounts on lines (1) thru (4)		b	34,300
c	Line a minus line b		c	1,053,400
d	Amounts included on line 12, Form 990 but not on line a:			
(1)	Investment expenses not included on line 6b, Form 990			
(2)	Other (specify):			
	Add amounts on lines (1) and (2)		d	
e	Total revenue per line 12, Form 990 (line c plus line d)		e	1,053,400

Part IV-B Reconciliation of Expenses per Audited Financial Statements with Expenses per Return

a	Total expense and losses per audited financial statements		a	740,100
b	Amounts included on line a but not on line 17, Form 990:			
(1)	Donated services and use of facilities	27,500		
(2)	Prior year adjustments reported on line 20, Form 990			
(3)	Losses reported on line 20, Form 990			
(4)	Other (specify): Rental expense	1,600		
	Add amounts on lines (1) thru (4)		b	29,100
c	Line a minus line b		c	711,000
d	Amounts included on line 17, Form 990 but not on line a:			
(1)	Investment expenses not included on line 6b, Form 990			
(2)	Other (specify):			
	Add amounts on lines (1) and (2)		d	
e	Total expenses per line 17, Form 990 (line c plus line d)		e	711,000

Part V List of Officers, Directors, Trustees, and Key Employees (List each one even if not compensated; see Specific Instructions on page 25.)

(A) Name and address	(B) Title and average hours per week devoted to position	(C) Compensation (if not paid, enter -0-)	(D) Contributions to employee benefit plans & deferred compensation	(E) Expense account and other allowances
John J. Environmentalist	President 4 hours per week	None	None	None
Jane D. Environmentalist	Secretary/Treasurer 3 hours per week	None	None	None
James F. Friend	Vice-President 2 hours per week	None	None	None
Samantha Engineer	Director 1 hour per week	None	None	None
Andrew Organized	Executive Director +40 hours per week	50,000	5,000	None
All officers and directors listed may be contacted at: 1111 Any Street, Hometown, Texas 77777				

75 Did any officer, director, trustee, or key employee receive aggregate compensation of more than $100,000 from your organization and all related organizations, of which more than $10,000 was provided by the related organizations? ☐ Yes ☒ No
If "Yes," attach schedule - see Specific Instructions on page 26.

Form 990 (2000)

Hometown Chapter, Campaign to Clean Up America 44-4444444 Page 5

Part VI Other Information (See Specific Instructions on pages 26.)

				N/A	Yes or No
76	Did the organization engage in any activity not previously reported to the Internal Revenue Service? If "Yes," attach a detailed description of each activity.			76	No
77	Were any changes made in the organizing or governing documents, but not reported to the IRS? If "Yes," attach a conformed copy of the changes.			77	No
78a	Did the organization have unrelated business gross income of $1,000 or more during the year covered by this return?			78a	Yes
b	If "Yes," has it filed a tax return on Form 990-T for this year?			78b	Yes
79	Was there a liquidation, dissolution, termination, or substantial contraction during the year? If "Yes," attach a statement			79	No
80a	Is the organization related (other than by association with a statewide or nationwide organization) through common membership, governing bodies, trustees, officers, etc., to any other exempt or nonexempt organization?			80a	No
b	If "Yes," enter the name of the organization ________ and check whether it is ☐ exempt OR ☐ nonexempt.				
81a	Enter the amount of political expenditures, direct or indirect, as described in the instructions for line 81	81a	None		
b	Did the organization file Form 1120-POL for this year?			81b	N/A
82a	Did the organization receive donated services or the use of materials, equipment, or facilities at no charge or at substantially less than fair rental value?			82a	Yes
b	If "Yes," you may indicate the value of these items here. Do not include this amount as revenue in Part I or as an expense in Part II. (See instructions for reporting in Part III.)	82b	27,500		
83a	Did the organization comply with the public inspection requirements for returns and exemption applications?			83a	Yes
b	Did the organization comply with the disclosure requirements relating to quid pro quo contributions?			83b	Yes
84a	Did the organization solicit any contributions or gifts that were not tax deductible?			84a	No
b	If "Yes," did the organization include with every solicitation an express statement that such contributions or gifts were not tax deductible?			84b	N/A
85	501(c)(4), (5), or (6) organizations. (a) Were substantially all dues nondeductible by members?			85a	N/A
b	Did the organization make only in-house lobbying expenditures of $2,000 or less? If "Yes" to either 85a or 85b, do not complete 85c through 85h below unless the organization received a waiver for proxy tax owed for the prior year.			85b	N/A
c	Dues, assessments, and similar amounts from members	85c	N/A		
d	Section 162(e) lobbying and political expenditures	85d	N/A		
e	Aggregate nondeductible amount of section 6033(e)(1)(A) dues notices	85e	N/A		
f	Taxable amount of lobbying and political expenditures (line 85d less 85e)	85f	N/A		
g	Does the organization elect to pay the section 6033(e) tax on the amount in 85f?			85g	N/A
h	If section 6033(e)(1)(A) dues notices were sent, does the organization agree to add the amount in 85f to its reasonable estimate of dues allocable to nondeductible lobbying and political expenditures for the following tax year?			85h	N/A
86	501(c)(7) orgs. - Enter: (a) Initiation fees and capital contributions included on line 12	86a	N/A		
b	Gross receipts, included on line 12, for public use of club facilities	86b	N/A		
87	501(c)(12) orgs. - Enter: a Gross income from members or shareholders	87a	N/A		
b	Gross income from other sources. (Do not net amounts due or paid to other sources against amounts due or received from them.)	87b	N/A		
88	At any time during the year, did the organization own a 50% or greater interest in a taxable corporation or partnership, or an entity disregarded as separate from the organization under Regulations sections 301.7701-2 and 301.7701-3? If "Yes," complete Part IX			88	No
89a	501(c)(3) organizations - Enter: Amount of tax paid during the year under: section 4911 None ; section 4912 None ; section 4955 None				
b	501(c)(3) and 501(c)(4) orgs. Did the organization engage in any section 4958 excess benefit transaction during the year or did it become aware of an excess benefit transaction from a prior year? If "Yes," attach a statement explaining each transaction			89	No
c	Enter: Amount of tax imposed on the organization managers or disqualified persons during the year under section 4912, 4955 and 4958.				None
d	Enter: Amount of tax in 89c, above, reimbursed by the organization				None

90a List the states with which a copy of this return is filed None

b Number of employees employed in the pay period that includes March 12, 2000 (See inst.) 90b 10

91 The books are in care of Joan Controller Telephone no. (444) 444-4444

Located at 1111 Any Street, Hometown, Texas ZIP code 77777

92 Section 4947(a)(1) nonexempt charitable trusts filing Form 990 in lieu of Form 1041-- Check here ☐
enter the amount of tax-exempt interest received or accrued during the tax year 92

Form 990 (2000)

Form 990 (2000) Hometown Chapter, Campaign to Clean Up America 44-4444444 Page 6

Part VII Analysis of Income-Producing Activities (See Specific Instructions on pages 30.)

Enter gross amounts unless otherwise indicated.	Unrelated business income (A) Business code	(B) Amount	Excluded by section 512, 513, or 514 (C) Exclusion code	(D) Amount	(E) Related or exempt function income
93 Program service revenue:					
a Volunteer team samples					12,000
b Public education					13,800
c Seminar fees					23,900
d					
e					
f Medicare/Medicaid payments					
g Fees and contracts from government agencies					
94 Membership dues and assessments					
95 Interest on savings and temporary cash investment			14	400	
96 Dividends and interest from securities			14	4,000	
97 Net rental income (loss) from real estate:					
a debt-financed property					
b not debt-financed property					
98 Net rental income or (loss) from personal property	900002	2,900			
99 Other investment income					
100 Gain or (loss) from sales of assets other than inventory			18	1,200	
101 Net income or (loss) from special events			1,2	8,000	
102 Gross profit or (loss) from sales of inventory					30,000
103 Other revenue					
b					
c					
d					
e					
104 Subtotal (add cols. (B), (D), and (E))		2,900		13,600	79,700
105 TOTAL (add line 104, columns (B), (D), and (E))					96,200

Note: (Line 105 plus line 1d, Part I, should equal the amount on line 12, Part I.)

Part VIII Relationship of Activities to the Accomplishment of Exempt Purposes (See Specific Instructions on page 31.)

Line No.	Explain how each activity for which income is reported in column (E) of Part VII contributed importantly to the accomplishment of the organization's exempt purposes (other than by providing funds for such purposes).
93a	Toxic garbage samples are collected for testing by the Environmental Protection Agency. See Part III, line a.
93b	Pamphlets on recycling and litter clean-up are sold for $5.00 each. See Part III, line b.
93c	One-day seminars presenting educational information were held in Texas, California and New York. See Part III, line c.
102	Garbage bags bearing the organization's slogan, "CLEAN UP AMERICA", are sold in 50-count boxes for $5.00 each.

Part IX Information Regarding Taxable Subsidiaries and Disregarded Entities (See Specific Instructions on page 31.)

(A) Name, address, and EIN of corporation, partnership, or disregarded entity	(B) Percentage of ownership interest	(C) Nature of activities	(D) Total income	(E) End-of-year assets

Part X Information Regarding Transfers Associated with Personal Benefit Contracts (See Specific Instructions on page 31.)

(a) Did the organization, during the year, receive any funds, directly or indirectly, to pay premiums on a personal benefit contract? ☐ Yes ☒ No

(b) Did the organization, during the year, pay premiums, directly or indirectly, on a personal benefit contract? ☐ Yes ☒ No

Note: If " Yes" to (b), file Form 8870 and Form 4720 (see instructions).

Please Sign Here

Under penalties of perjury, I declare that I have examined this return, including accompanying schedules and statements, and to the best of my knowledge and belief, it is true, correct, and complete. Declaration of preparer (other than officer) is based on all information of which preparer has any knowledge. (IMPORTANT: See General Instruction W, on page 14.)

[signature] 4/30/01 President

Signature of officer — Date — Type or print name — Title

Paid Preparer's Use Only

Preparer's signature	a. Good, C.P.A	Date 4/28/01	Check if self-employed ☒	Preparer's SSN or PTIN 400-00-0000
Firm's name (or yours if self-employed) and address, and ZIP code	A Qualified CPA Firm 1001 Main Street Hometown, Texas 77777-4222		EIN Phone	45-5555555 (444) 422-2222

Form 990 (2000)

Hometown Chapter, Campaign to Clean Up America **44-4444444**
2000 Form 990

Part I, Line 8 - Sale of assets other than inventory

200 shares Environmental Growth Inc.

Gross amount from sale	$ 1,400
Cost basis	200
Net gain	$ 1,200

Part I, Line 9 - Special Events

Earth Day 2000

Gross revenue	$ 75,000
Less contribution portion	(20,000)
	55,000
Less direct expenses	(47,000)
Net income	$ 8,000

Part I, Line 10 Sales of Inventory

Sale of garbage bags bearing slogan, "CLEAN UP AMERICA"	$ 40,000
Less: Cost of goods sold	(10,000)
Gross profit from sales of inventory	$ 30,000

Part I, Line 16 - Payments to Affiliates

National Campaign to Clean Up America Anytown, Missouri 20012	Annual affiliation fee	$ 10,000

Part I, Line 20 - Other changes in net assets or fund balances

Increase in value of securities reported under *SFAS No. 124*
(Accounting for Certain Investments Held by Not-for-Profit Organizations)

Attachment to Part I, Lines 8, 9, 10, 16 and 20

Hometown Chapter, Campaign to Clean Up America **44-4444444**
2000 Form 990

Part II, Line 22 - Grants and Allocations

Name & Address	Purpose of Grant	Amount
Mr. John Doe 1234 Main Street, Hometown TX 77777	Volunteer Service Award	$ 750
Ms. B. Smart 1010 Center Drive, Hometown TX 77777	Volunteer Service Award	1,250
Mr. Z. Books 25 Money Tree Lane, Hometown TX 77777	Volunteer Service Award	500
Total grants and allocations		$ 2,500

Grant recipients are unrelated to persons that have an interest in the organization.

Part II, Line 42 and Part IV, Line 57b - Equipment/Depreciation

	Cost	Accumulated Depreciation	Current Provision
Office furnishings (10 yr SL)	26,000	1,200	800
Computers (3 yr SL)	20,000	1,900	1,300
Vans (8 yr SL)	45,000	6,000	6,000
Lawn equipment/tools (5 yr)	96,000	17,900	17,900
	$ 187,000	$ 27,000	$ 26,000
Depreciation included in Part I, line 6			500
Depreciation included in Part II, line 42			$ 25,500

Part IV, Line 54 - Investments - securities

Short-term government obligations	$ 95,400
Publicly traded common stock	160,000
Total investments - securities	$ 255,400

Attachment to Part II Lines 22 and 42, Part IV Lines 54 and 57b

Hometown Chapter, Campaign to Clean Up America **44-4444444**
2000 Form 990

Part IV, Line 64b - Mortgages and Other Notes Payable

Lender	Campaign to Clean Up America
Original amount	$ 40,000
Balance due	$ 35,000
Date of note	8/1/2000
Maturity date	7/1/2002
Repayment terms	Principal and interest due annually
Interest rate	8.50%
Security/purpose	Purchase of vans and lawn equipment

Attachment to Part IV, Line 64b

Appendix 2C

Schedule B (Form 990 or 990-EZ) Department of the Treasury Internal Revenue Service	**Schedule of Contributors** Supplementary Information for line 1d of Form 990 or line 1 of Form 990-EZ (see instructions)	OMB No. 1545-0047 **2000**

Name of organization	Employer identification number
Hometown Chapter, Campaign to Clean Up America	**44-4444444**

Organization type (check one)-Section: [X] 501(c)(3) (enter number) [ ] 527 or [ ] 4947(a)(1) nonexempt charitable trust

A Section 501(c)(7), (8), or (10) organizations-
Check this box if the organization had no charitable contributors who contributed more than $1,000 during the year. (But see General rule below.) . . . . [ ]
Enter here the total gifts received during the year for a religious, charitable, etc., purpose $

Note: This form is generally not open to public inspection except for section 527 organizations.

(HTA) Schedule B (Form 990 or 990-EZ) (2000)

Schedule B (Form 990 or 990-EZ)(2000) Page 1 to 1 of Part I

Name of organization	Employer identification number
Hometown Chapter, Campaign to Clean Up America	**44-4444444**

Part I Contributors

(a) No.	(b) Name, address and zip code	(c) Aggregate contributions	(d) Type of contribution
1	John & Jane Environmentalist 333 First Street Hometown, Texas 77777	$ 200,000	Individual ☐ Payroll ☐ Noncash ☒ (Complete Part II if a noncash contribution.)
2	Friendly Corporation 101 Business Tower Hometown, Texas 77777	$ 200,000	Individual ☒ Payroll ☐ Noncash ☐ (Complete Part II if a noncash contribution.)
3	National Campaign to Clean Up America 2525 Capital Street Capital City, D.C. 01010	$ 150,000	Individual ☒ Payroll ☐ Noncash ☐ (Complete Part II if a noncash contribution.)
4	Environmentalist Fund 111 Any Street Hometown, Texas 77777	$ 160,000	Individual ☒ Payroll ☐ Noncash ☐ (Complete Part II if a noncash contribution.)
5	Waste Disposal Company 290 Allied Tower Chicago, IL 60555	$ 50,000	Individual ☒ Payroll ☐ Noncash ☐ (Complete Part II if a noncash contribution.)
6	Environmental Protection Agency 11110 Constitution Avenue Washington, D.C. 20000	$ 80,000	Individual ☒ Payroll ☐ Noncash ☐ (Complete Part II if a noncash contribution.)

Schedule B (Form 990 or 990-EZ) (2000)

Schedule B (Form 990 or 990-EZ)(2000) Page 1 to 1 of Part II

Name of organization	Employer identification number
Hometown Chapter, Campaign to Clean Up America	**44-4444444**

Part II Noncash Property

(a) No. from Part I	(b) Description of noncash property given	(c) FMV (or estimate) (see instructions)	(d) Date received
1	30,000 shares of Environmental Growth, Inc.	$ 200,000	8/2/2000

(a) No. from Part I	(b) Description of noncash property given	(c) FMV (or estimate) (see instructions)	(d) Date received
		$	/ /

(a) No. from Part I	(b) Description of noncash property given	(c) FMV (or estimate) (see instructions)	(d) Date received
		$	/ /

(a) No. from Part I	(b) Description of noncash property given	(c) FMV (or estimate) (see instructions)	(d) Date received
		$	/ /

(a) No. from Part I	(b) Description of noncash property given	(c) FMV (or estimate) (see instructions)	(d) Date received
		$	/ /

(a) No. from Part I	(b) Description of noncash property given	(c) FMV (or estimate) (see instructions)	(d) Date received
		$	/ /

Schedule B (Form 990 or 990-EZ) (2000)

Appendix 2D

Codes for Unrelated Business Activity

(If engaged in more than one unrelated business activity, select up to two codes for the principal activities. List first the largest in terms of unrelated income, then the next largest.)

AGRICULTURE, FORESTRY, HUNTING, AND FISHING

Code
110000 Agricultural, forestry, hunting, and fishing
111000 Crop production

MINING

Code
211110 Oil and gas extraction
212000 Mining (except oil and gas)

UTILITIES

Code
221000 Utilities

CONSTRUCTION

Code
230000 Construction
233000 Building, developing, and general contracting

MANUFACTURING

Code
311000 Food manufacturing
312100 Beverage manufacturing
312200 Tobacco manufacturing
313000 Textile mills
315000 Apparel manufacturing
316000 Leather and allied product manufacturing
321000 Wood product manufacturing, except furniture
322000 Paper manufacturing
323100 Printing and related support activities
323117 Book printing
323119 Other commercial printing
324110 Petroleum refineries
325000 Chemical manufacturing
325200 Resin, synthetic rubber, artificial and synthetic fiber and filament manufacturing
327000 Nonmetallic mineral product manufacturing
331000 Primary metal manufacturing
332000 Fabricated metal product manufacturing
333000 Machinery manufacturing
334000 Computer and electronic product manufacturing
335000 Electrical equipment, appliance, and component manufacturing
336000 Transportation equipment manufacturing
337000 Furniture and related product manufacturing
339000 Miscellaneous manufacturing
339110 Medical equipment and supplies manufacturing

WHOLESALE TRADE

Code
421000 Wholesale trade, durable goods
422000 Wholesale trade, nondurable goods

RETAIL TRADE

Code
441100 Automobile dealers
442000 Furniture and home furnishings stores
443120 Computer and software stores
444100 Building materials and supplies dealers
445100 Grocery stores
445110 Supermarkets and other grocery stores
445200 Specialty food stores
445291 Baked goods stores
446110 Pharmacies and drug stores
446130 Optical goods stores
447100 Gasoline stations
448000 Clothing and clothing accessories stores
451110 Sporting goods stores
451211 Book stores
451212 News dealers and newsstands
452000 General merchandise stores
453000 Miscellaneous store retailers
453100 Florists
453220 Gift, novelty, and souvenir stores
453310 Used merchandise stores
454110 Electronic shopping and mail-order houses

TRANSPORTATION AND WAREHOUSING

Code
481000 Air transportation
482110 Rail transportation
483000 Water transportation
484000 Truck transportation
485000 Transit and ground passenger transportation
485510 Charter bus Industry
487000 Scenic and sightseeing transportation
493000 Warehousing and storage

INFORMATION

Code
511110 Newspaper publishers
511120 Periodical publishers
511130 Book publishers
511190 Other publishers
512000 Motion picture and sound recording industries
513100 Radio and television broadcasting
513300 Telecommunications
514000 Information services and data processing services

FINANCE AND INSURANCE

Code
522110 Commercial banking
522120 Savings institutions
522130 Credit unions
522190 Other depository credit intermediation
522210 Credit card issuing
522290 Other non-depository credit intermediation
523100 Securities, commodity contracts, and other intermediation and brokerage
524113 Direct life insurance carriers
524114 Direct health and medical insurance carriers
524121 Property and casualty insurance carriers
524126 Direct property and casualty insurance carriers
524130 Reinsurance carriers
524292 Third party administration for insurance and pension funds
524298 All other insurance related activities
525100 Insurance and employee benefit funds
525920 Trusts, estates, and agency accounts
525990 Other financial vehicles

REAL ESTATE AND RENTAL AND LEASING

Code
531110 Lessors of residential buildings and dwellings
531120 Lessors of nonresidential buildings, except miniwarehouses
531190 Lessors of other real estate property
531210 Offices of real estate agents and brokers
531310 Real estate property managers
531390 Other activities related to real estate
532000 Rental and leasing services
532291 Home health equipment rental
532420 Office machinery and equipment rental and leasing
533110 Lessors of nonfinancial intangible assets (except copyrighted works)

PROFESSIONAL, SCIENTIFIC, AND TECHNICAL SERVICES

Code
541100 Legal services
541200 Accounting, tax preparation, bookkeeping, and payroll services
541300 Architectural, engineering, and related services
541380 Testing laboratories
541500 Computer systems design and related services
541511 Custom computer programming services
541610 Management consulting services
541700 Scientific research and development services
541800 Advertising and related services
541860 Direct mail advertising
541900 Other professional, scientific, and technical services

MANAGEMENT OF COMPANIES AND ENTERPRISES

Code
551111 Offices of bank holding companies
551112 Offices of other holding companies

ADMINISTRATIVE AND SUPPORT AND WASTE MANAGEMENT AND REMEDIATION SERVICES

Code
561000 Administrative and support services
561300 Employment services
561439 Other business service centers (including copy shops)
561450 Credit bureaus
561499 All other business support services
561500 Travel arrangement and reservation services
561520 Tour operators
561700 Services to buildings and dwellings
562000 Waste management and remediation services

EDUCATIONAL SERVICES

Code
611110 Elementary and secondary schools
611310 Colleges, universities, and professional schools
611510 Technical and trade schools
611600 Other schools and instruction

HEALTHCARE AND SOCIAL ASSISTANCE

Code
621000 Ambulatory health care services
621110 Offices of physicians
621210 Offices of dentists
621300 Offices of other health practitioners
621400 Outpatient care centers
621410 Family planning centers
621500 Medical and diagnostic laboratories
621610 Home health care services
621910 Ambulance services
621990 All other ambulatory health care services
621991 Blood and organ banks
622000 Hospitals
623000 Nursing and residential care facilities
623990 Other residential care facilities
624000 Social assistance
624100 Individual and family services
624200 Community food and housing, and emergency and other relief services
624310 Vocational rehabilitation services
624410 Child day care services

ARTS, ENTERTAINMENT, AND RECREATION

Code
711110 Theater companies and dinner theaters
711120 Dance companies
711130 Musical groups and artists
711190 Other performing arts companies
711210 Spectator sports (including sports clubs and racetracks)
711300 Promoters of performing arts, sports, and similar events
712100 Museums, historical sites, and similar institutions
713110 Amusement and theme parks
713200 Gambling industries
713900 Other amusement and recreation industries (including golf courses, skiing facilities, marinas, fitness centers, and bowling centers)

ACCOMMODATION AND FOOD SERVICES

Code
721000 Accomodation
721110 Hotels (except casino hotels) and motels
721210 RV (recreational vehicle) parks and recreational camps
721310 Rooming and boarding houses
722100 Full-service restaurants
722210 Limited-service eating places
722320 Caterers
722410 Drinking places (alcoholic beverages)

OTHER SERVICES

Code
811000 Repair and maintenance
812300 Drycleaning and laundry services
812900 Other personal services
812930 Parking lots and garages

OTHER

Code
900000 Unrelated debt-financed activities other than rental of real estate
900001 Investment activities by section 501(c)(7), (9), or (17) organizations
900002 Rental of personal property
900003 Passive income activities with controlled organizations
900004 Exploited exempt activities

Appendix 2E

Exclusion Codes

General Exceptions

01— Income from an activity that is not regularly carried on (section 512(a)(1))

02— Income from an activity in which labor is a material income-producing factor and substantially all (at least 85%) of the work is performed with unpaid labor (section 513(a)(1))

03— Section 501(c)(3) organization— Income from an activity carried on primarily for the convenience of the organization's members, students, patients, visitors, officers, or employees (hospital parking lot or museum cafeteria, for example) (section 513(a)(2))

04— Section 501(c)(4) local association of employees organized before May 27, 1969—Income from the sale of work-related clothes or equipment and items normally sold through vending machines; food dispensing facilities; or snack bars for the convenience of association members at their usual places of employment (section 513(a)(2))

05— Income from the sale of merchandise, substantially all of which (at least 85%) was donated to the organization (section 513(a)(3))

Specific Exceptions

06— Section 501(c)(3), (4), or (5) organization conducting an agricultural or educational fair or exposition— Qualified public entertainment activity income (section 513(d)(2))

07— Section 501(c)(3), (4), (5), or (6) organization—Qualified convention and trade show activity income (section 513(d)(3))

08— Income from hospital services described in section 513(e)

09— Income from noncommercial bingo games that do not violate state or local law (section 513(f))

10— Income from games of chance conducted by an organization in North Dakota (section 311 of the Deficit Reduction Act of 1984, as amended)

11— Section 501(c)(12) organization— Qualified pole rental income (section 513(g))

12— Income from the distribution of low-cost articles in connection with the solicitation of charitable contributions (section 513(h))

13— Income from the exchange or rental of membership or donor list with an organization eligible to receive charitable contributions by a section 501(c)(3) organization; by a war veterans' organization; or an auxiliary unit or society of, or trust or foundation for, a war veterans' post or organization (section 513(h))

Modifications and Exclusions

14— Dividends, interest, payments with respect to securities loans, annuities, income from notional principal contracts, other substantially similar income from ordinary and routine investments, and loan commitment fees, excluded by section 512(b)(1)

15— Royalty income excluded by section 512(b)(2)

16— Real property rental income that does not depend on the income or profits derived by the person leasing the property and is excluded by section 512 (b)(3)

17— Rent from personal property leased with real property and incidental (10% or less) in relation to the combined income from the real and personal property (section 512(b)(3))

18— Gain or loss from the sale of investments and other non-inventory property and from certain property acquired from financial institutions that are in conservatorship or receivership (sections 512(b)(5) and (16)(A))

19— Gain or loss from the lapse or termination of options to buy or sell securities or real property, and on options and from the forfeiture of good-faith deposits for the purchase, sale, or lease of investment real estate (section 512(b)(5))

20— Income from research for the United States; its agencies or instrumentalities; or any state or political subdivision (section 512(b)(7))

21— Income from research conducted by a college, university, or hospital (section 512(b)(8))

22— Income from research conducted by an organization whose primary activity is conducting fundamental research, the results of which are freely available to the general public (section 512(b)(9))

23— Income from services provided under license issued by a federal regulatory agency and conducted by a religious order or school operated by a religious order, but only if the trade or business has been carried on by the organization since before May 27, 1959 (section 512 (b)(15))

Foreign Organizations

24— Foreign organizations only—Income from a trade or business NOT conducted in the United States and NOT derived from United States sources (patrons) (section 512(a)(2))

Social Clubs and VEBAs

25— Section 501(c)(7), (9), or (17) organization—Non-exempt function income set aside for a charitable, etc., purpose specified in section 170(c)(4) (section 512(a)(3)(B)(i))

26— Section 501(c)(7), (9), or (17) organization—Proceeds from the sale of exempt function property that was or will be timely reinvested in similar property (section 512(a)(3)(D))

27— Section 501(c)(9) or (17) organization— Non-exempt function income set aside for the payment of life, sick, accident, or other benefits (section 512(a)(3)(B)(ii))

Veterans' Organizations

28— Section 501(c)(19) organization— Payments for life, sick, accident, or health insurance for members or their dependents that are set aside for the payment of such insurance benefits or for a charitable, etc., purpose specified in section 170(c)(4) (section 512(a)(4))

29— Section 501(c)(19) organization— Income from an insurance set-aside (see code 28 above) that is set aside for payment of insurance benefits or for a charitable, etc., purpose specified in section 170(c)(4) (Regs. 1.512(a)–4(b)(2))

Debt-Financed Income

30— Income exempt from debt-financed (section 514) provisions because at least 85% of the use of the property is for the organization's exempt purposes. (**Note:** *This code is only for income from the 15% or less non-exempt purpose use.*) (section 514(b)(1)(A))

31— Gross income from mortgaged property used in research activities described in section 512(b)(7), (8), or (9) (section 514(b)(1)(C))

32— Gross income from mortgaged property used in any activity described in section 513(a)(1), (2), or (3) (section 514(b)(1)(D))

33— Income from mortgaged property (neighborhood land) acquired for exempt purpose use within 10 years (section 514(b)(3))

34— Income from mortgaged property acquired by bequest or devise (applies to income received within 10 years from the date of acquisition) (section 514(c)(2)(B))

35— Income from mortgaged property acquired by gift where the mortgage was placed on the property more than 5 years previously and the property was held by the donor for more than 5 years (applies to income received within 10 years from the date of gift (section 514(c)(2)(B))

36— Income from property received in return for the obligation to pay an annuity described in section 514(c)(5)

37— Income from mortgaged property that provides housing to low and moderate income persons, to the extent the mortgage is insured by the Federal Housing Administration (section 514(c)(6)). (**Note:** *In many cases, this would be exempt function income reportable in column (e). It would not be so in the case of a section 501(c)(5) or (6) organization, for example, that acquired the housing as an investment or as a charitable activity.*)

38— Income from mortgaged real property owned by: a school described in section 170(b)(1)(A)(ii); a section 509(a)(3) affiliated support organization of such a school; a section 501(c)(25) organization; or by a partnership in which any of the above organizations owns an interest if the requirements of section 514(c)(9)(B)(vi) are met (section 514(c)(9))

Special Rules

39— Section 501(c)(5) organization—Farm income used to finance the operation and maintenance of a retirement home, hospital, or similar facility operated by the organization for its members on property adjacent to the farm land (section 1951(b)(8)(B) of Public Law 94-455)

40— Annual dues, not exceeding $112 (subject to inflation), paid to a section 501(c)(5) agricultural or horticultural organization (section 512(d))

Trade or Business

41— Gross income from an unrelated activity that is regularly carried on but, in light of continuous losses sustained over a number of tax periods, cannot be regarded as being conducted with the motive to make a profit (not a trade or business)

Appendix 2F

Form **8871** (July 2000)
Department of the Treasury
Internal Revenue Service

Political Organization Notice of Section 527 Status

OMB No. 1545-1693

Part I General Information

1 Name of organization — **Employer identification number**

2 Mailing address (P.O. Box or number, street, and room or suite number)

City or town, state, and ZIP code

3 E-mail address of organization

4a Name of custodian of records — **4b** Custodian's address

5a Name of contact person — **5b** Contact person's address

6 Business address of organization (if different from mailing address shown above). Number, street, and room or suite number

City or town, state, and ZIP code

Part II Purpose

7 Describe the purpose of the organization

Part III List of All Related Entities (see instructions)

8a Name of related entity	**8b** Relationship	**8c** Address

For Paperwork Reduction Act Notice, see page 4. Cat. No. 30405V Form **8871** (7-2000)

Form 8871 (7-2000) Page 2

Part IV List of All Officers, Directors, and Highly Compensated Employees (see instructions)

9a Name	**9b** Title	**9c** Address

Sign Here

Under penalties of perjury, I declare that the organization named in Part I is to be treated as an organization described in section 527 of the Internal Revenue Code, and that I have examined this notice, including accompanying schedules and statements, and to the best of my knowledge and belief, it is true, correct, and complete.

Signature of authorized official | Date

Form **8871** (7-2000)

Appendix 2G

Form **8872** (July 2000)
Department of the Treasury Internal Revenue Service

Political Organization Report of Contributions and Expenditures

See separate instructions.

OMB No. 1545-1696

A For the period beginning , 20 and ending , 20

B Check applicable boxes: ☐ Initial report ☐ Change of address ☐ Amended report ☐ Final report

1 Name of organization | **Employer identification number**

2 Mailing address (P.O. Box or number, street, and room or suite number)

City or town, state, and ZIP code

3 E-mail address of organization | **4** Date organization was formed

5a Name of custodian of records | **5b** Custodian's address

6a Name of contact person | **6b** Contact person's address

7 Business address of organization (if different from mailing address shown above). Number, street, and room or suite number

City or town, state, and ZIP code

8 Type of report (check only one box)

a ☐ First quarterly report (*due by April 15*)

b ☐ Second quarterly report (*due by July 15*)

c ☐ Third quarterly report (*due by October 15*)

d ☐ Year-end report (*due by January 31*)

e ☐ Mid-year report (*Non-election year only-due by July 31*)

f ☐ Monthly report for the month of: ____________
(*due by the 20th day following the month shown above, except the December report, which is due by January 31*)

g ☐ Pre-election report (*due by the 12th or 15th day before the election*)
(1) Type of election: ____________
(2) Date of election: ____________
(3) For the state of: ____________

h ☐ Post-general election report (*due by the 30th day after general election*)
(1) Date of election: ____________
(2) For the state of: ____________

9 Total amount of reported contributions (total from all attached **Schedules A**)	**9**	
10 Total amount of reported expenditures (total from all attached **Schedules B**)	**10**	

Sign Here

Under penalties of perjury, I declare that I have examined this report, including accompanying schedules and statements, and to the best of my knowledge and belief, it is true, correct, and complete.

Signature of authorized official | Date

For Paperwork Reduction Act Notice, see separate instructions. Cat. No. 30406G Form **8872** (7-2000)

Form 8872 (7-2000)

Schedule B **Itemized Expenditures**

Schedule B page ___ of ___

Name of organization	Employer identification number

Recipient's name, mailing address and ZIP code	Name of recipient's employer / Recipient's occupation	Amount of each expenditure reported for this period
Recipient's name, mailing address and ZIP code	Name of recipient's employer Recipient's occupation	Amount of each expenditure reported for this period $
Recipient's name, mailing address and ZIP code	Name of recipient's employer Recipient's occupation	Amount of each expenditure reported for this period $
Recipient's name, mailing address and ZIP code	Name of recipient's employer Recipient's occupation	Amount of each expenditure reported for this period $
Recipient's name, mailing address and ZIP code	Name of recipient's employer Recipient's occupation	Amount of each expenditure reported for this period $
Recipient's name, mailing address and ZIP code	Name of recipient's employer Recipient's occupation	Amount of each expenditure reported for this period $
Recipient's name, mailing address and ZIP code	Name of recipient's employer Recipient's occupation	Amount of each expenditure reported for this period $
Recipient's name, mailing address and ZIP code	Name of recipient's employer Recipient's occupation	Amount of each expenditure reported for this period $
Recipient's name, mailing address and ZIP code	Name of recipient's employer Recipient's occupation	Amount of each expenditure reported for this period $
Recipient's name, mailing address and ZIP code	Name of recipient's employer Recipient's occupation	Amount of each expenditure reported for this period $
Subtotal of expenditures reported on this page only. Enter here and also include this amount in the total on line 10 of Form 8872		$

Form **8872** (7-2000)

CHAPTER THREE

Form 990, Schedule A: For §501(c)(3) Organizations

Organizations that qualify as charities under Internal Revenue Code (IRC) §501(c)(3) and §501(a), (e), (f), (k), and (n), and nonexempt wholly charitable trusts furnish information to enable the IRS to review their ongoing qualification for tax-exempt and public charity (if applicable) status on Schedule A (reproduced in Appendix 3A). The author has suggested to the IRS for several years that this form be collapsed into one summary page that asks questions and prompts attachments for applicable information similar to Forms 1023 and 1024. Readers might join in asking the IRS to revise the form, as they find that for almost all Schedule A filers one or more of the pages is inapplicable. This chapter contains rather brief instructions regarding the seven different parts of Schedule A illustrated in Appendix 3A. The issues addressed in this form are complex, and an adequate explanation of the genesis of the questions is beyond this book. The IRS, however, provides rather complete instructions, and preparers will be well informed by studying them. The chapters in the author's tax book where additional information can be found are also referenced.

3.1 PARTS I AND II—COMPENSATION

Both of these parts look for private benefit paid to highly compensated personnel and consultants, other than those key employees, officers, and directors reported on Form 990, Part V. Technically, private benefit (to those that control the organization) in the past was thought to be not as damaging to the organization's exempt status as private inurement (to those that do not control). However, the IRS considers excess compensation to persons not controlling an exempt organization to be almost as bad as such payments made to insiders.[1]

To describe the requirements of tax-exempt status, IRC §501 uses the word *inures* to limit the activities of §501(c)(3) organizations and requires that "no part of the net earnings inure to the benefit of any private shareholder or individual." Inurement occurs when an organization transfers financial resources to an individual solely by virtue of his or her relationship to the organization, and without regard to accomplishing exempt purpose. Whether private benefit is incidental to overall public benefit or interest hinges on the nature and quantum of the activity under consideration and the manner in which the public benefit will be derived.[2] Factors the IRS suggests its agents look for that might allow inurement to occur include close control by persons with whom the organization has financial transactions and management agreements.[3]

It is permissible, however, for a tax-exempt organization to pay compensation and have financial transactions with individuals, including those that serve on its governing body. Payments to individuals cannot be unreasonable or excessive in relation to the property or services provided to the organization. The tax code contains intermediate sanctions to impose if excess benefits are paid. The measure of excess is determined by using a "like, like, like, like" test: Is the compensation a *like* amount that would be paid to a *like* person doing a *like* job in a *like* circumstance? An organization is expected to obtain comparable salary statistics, independent opinions, appraisals, and other contemporaneous documentation to prove the amounts paid to its officials and other employees is reasonable. Persons independent of the person receiving the payments must approve the payments. A person that receives excess benefits faces not only a 25 percent penalty, but must also return the excessive payments.[4]

For both Part I and Part II, the level above which compensation must be reported has been $50,000 since 1994. All forms of compensation and benefits are reported under the same instructions provided for the same columns of Part V of Form 990 found in Chapter 2§6. Payments to employees are reported in Part I. Payments to independent contractors of all sorts (including corporations) who performed personal services of a professional nature for the organization are reported in Part II. Only the fee portion of contractor payments, not expense reimbursements, are reported.

3.2 PART III—STATEMENT ABOUT ACTIVITIES

Part III canvasses a host of sins. Positive responses to the questions in this part require submission of additional information, but a "yes" answer is not necessarily a bad answer. A "yes" in answer to questions 2(a) through 2(e) deserve special attention. These questions seek to determine whether the organization has operated to benefit its insiders. Transactions with the persons who control a public charity are not strictly prohibited but are subject to scrutiny to prove that the insiders do not unfairly benefit at the expense of the organization and its charitable constituents. Is too high a price paid for property sold to the executive director? Does the organization need to maintain a New York apartment for its treasurer's use in monitoring the investments? If such a transaction has occurred, the organization must explain in Part III how its exempt purposes were served. Whether the amount involved in the transaction was the fair value for the services or property received or given is extremely important to disclose. If independent appraisals or other evidence of the value was obtained, it's good to mention.

Question 1 asks whether the organization has spent any money on lobbying efforts, and a positive response prompts submission of details on either Part VI-A or VI-B of Schedule A. A description of lobbying activity is requested for those that complete Part VI-B. Only a limited amount of lobbying activity is permissible for public charities.

Question 2 asks whether any of five different types of financial transactions have taken place between the organization and its trustees, directors, officers, creators, key employees, or members of their families, or with any taxable organization with which any such person is affiliated as an officer, director, trustee, majority owner, or principal beneficiary. Reporting of transactions is required whether the organization is the buyer or seller, lessee or lessor, or lender or borrower. A "detailed statement explaining the transactions" is requested. Adequate information to document lack of private inurement in the transaction is imperative. A "yes" answer to question 2(b) that asks if money has been lent or borrowed can be answered by referring to the required balance sheet attachment for the receivable on line 50 of Part IV or for the payable on line 63 of Part IV, whichever is applicable. If compensation is paid to an insider, resulting in a positive answer to question 2(d), a reference can be made to the information in Part V. Positive answers to questions 2(a), (c), or (e) deserve very carefully prepared answers.

Question 3 asks whether the organization makes grants for scholarships, fellowships, student loans, and the like. If the answer to this question is "yes," information is submitted in answer to question 4(b).

Question 4(a) asks whether the organization has a §403(b) plan for its employees. It is a new question, added in 1998 as a result of the IRS's finding excess funding for such plans when it conducted audits of hospitals and universities in the mid-1990s.

Question 4(b) asks for a statement to explain how the organization determines that individuals or organizations receiving grants or loans from it in furtherance of its charitable purposes qualify to receive those payments. The instructions suggest the charitable class and how the aid helps them be described. Examples would include help for the aged and poor or training teachers and social workers in underdeveloped countries. As it regards scholarships, fellowships, and student loan payments, the answer should contain information that evidences the choice was made in an objective and nondiscriminatory fashion without favoritism to insiders or their relatives. Standards applied to choose recipients can be described; the actual application form might be attached. Periodic reports required by grantees that receive payments over a period of time should be described. In some circumstances, the program descriptions submitted in Part III of Form 990 might be referred to rather than repeating information.

3.3 PART IV—REASON FOR NON–PRIVATE FOUNDATION STATUS: §509(a)(1)

The "reason for non–private foundation status" rests on the organization's ability to qualify as a public charity and to fit into one of the 11 boxes (presented as items 5 through 14) on page 2 of Schedule A. These distinctly different categories of public charity are described in IRC §509(a)(1), (2), and (3), and are briefly discussed below.[5] The author apologizes for the extensive use of code citations in this subchapter but recommends that 990 preparers become conversant with them due to their extreme importance.

(a) 509(a)(1)

A wide variety of organizations qualify as public charities under this category. The (a)(1) category includes all §501(c)(3) tax-exempt organizations that are described in IRC §170(b)(1)(A)(i)–(vi), the tax code section that lists organizations eligible to receive deductible charitable contributions.[6] The definition is complicated and rather unwieldy because it includes six distinct types of exempt entities. Because of the code's design, the categories are labeled with numerical letters.

The first five categories include those organizations that perform what the IRS calls *inherently public activity*. The first three achieve public status because of the nature of their activities without regard to sources of funds with which they pay their bills—even if they are privately supported. The fourth and fifth are closely connected with governmental support and activities. Last, but certainly not least, because of the large number variety of charities included, the sixth category embodies those organizations balancing their budgets with donations from a sizeable group of supporters, such as the United Way or the American Red Cross. These organizations must meet a mathematically measured contribution base formula and are referred to as *donative public charities*. A consideration of the rules that pertain to both donative public charities and service provider entities[7] is important in understanding public charities.

(b) Churches

The first category of IRC §509(a)(1) includes a "church, convention, or association of churches." Churches are narrowly defined and not all religious organizations are regarded as churches.[8] Perhaps due to the need to separate church and state, neither the Internal Revenue Code nor the IRS regulations define a church. The fact that churches are not required to file Form 990 makes checking of this box a rarity.

(c) Schools

IRC §170(b)(1)(A)(ii), the second category, includes formal schools. A school is an "educational organization that normally maintains a regular faculty and curriculum and normally has a regularly enrolled body of pupils or students in attendance at the place where its educational activities are regularly carried on." The presentation of formal instruction must be the primary function of a school. The term *school* includes primary, secondary, preparatory, and high schools, and colleges and universities. Schools publicly supported by federal, state, and local governments qualify for this category, and in some cases also qualify as governmental units under (e), discussed below.

What the regulations call *noneducational* activities must be incidental. A recognized university can operate a museum or sponsor concerts and remain a school. A museum's art school, however, does not make the museum a school. All four elements must be present to achieve recognition as a school: regular faculty, students, curriculum, and facility. A home-tutoring entity providing private tutoring was held not to be an educational organization for this purpose. Likewise, a correspondence school was not approved under this section because it lacked a physical site where classes were conducted.

What constitutes a "regular curriculum" was loosely construed in one case, permitting an elementary school to qualify despite the fact that it had no "formal course program" and espoused an open learning concept. However, leisure learning classes, in the eyes of the IRS, do not present a sufficiently formal course of instruction to qualify as a school. Lectures and short courses on a variety of general subjects not leading to a degree or accreditation do not constitute a curriculum. Also, invited authorities and personalities recognized in the field are not considered to be members of a regular faculty. The duration of the courses was not considered a barrier to qualification for a particular outside survival school. Though classes lasted only 26 days and part of the facilities it used were wide open spaces, regular teachers, students, and a regular course study existed.[9]

(d) Hospitals and Medical Research Organizations

This class of public charity includes hospitals, the principal purpose or function of which is providing medical or hospital care, medical education, or medical research. An organization directly engaged in continuous, active medical research in conjunction with a hospital may also qualify if, during the year in which the contribution is made to the organization, the funds are committed to be spent within five years.

Medical care includes the treatment of any physical or mental disability or condition on an inpatient or outpatient basis. A rehabilitation institution, outpatient clinic, or community mental health or drug treatment center may qualify. Convalescent homes, homes for children or the aged, handicapped vocational training centers, and medical schools are not considered to be hospitals. An animal clinic was also found not to be a hospital. The issues involved in qualifying for exemption as a hospital are evolving, and close attention must be paid to the latest information.

Medical research is the conduct of investigations, experiments, and studies to discover, develop, or verify knowledge relating to the causes, diagnosis, treatment, prevention, or control of physical or mental diseases and impairments of man. "Appropriate equipment and qualified personnel necessary to carry out its principal function must be regularly used." The disciplines spanning the biological, social, and behavioral sciences, such as chemistry, psychiatry, biomedical engineering, virology, immunology, biophysics, and associated medical fields, can be studied. Such organizations must conduct research directly. Granting funds to other organizations, while possible, may not be a primary purpose. The rules governing medical research organizations' expenditure of funds and endowment levels are complicated, and the regulations must be studied to understand this type of public organization.[10]

(e) College and University Support Organizations

An entity operating to receive, hold, invest, and administer property and to make expenditures to or for the benefit of a college or university qualifying under §170(b)(1)(A)(ii) are public charities. Such entities must normally receive a substantial part of their support from governmental grants as well as contributions from the general public, rather than exempt function revenue.

(f) Governmental Units

The United States, District of Columbia, states, possessions of the United States, and their political subdivisions are classified as governmental units. They are listed as qualifying as a public charity although they are not actually tax exempt under IRC §501(c)(3). In essence, they are public charities because they are responsive to all citizens. The regulations contain no additional definition or explanation of the meaning of this term, but IRS rulings and procedures and the courts have provided some guidance.[11]

(g) Donative Public Charities

Public charities in this category are organizations that normally receive at least 33⅓ percent of their annual support in the form of donations from members of the general public (not including fees and charges for performing exempt functions). *Normally* is based on an aggregation of the four years preceding the year in question and the succeeding year: for example, the basis for qualification as a public charity for the tax years 2002 and 2001 is the revenue received during the four years 1997 through 2000. A five-year period is applied during an organization's initial advanced ruling period. This calculation is made in Part IV-A of Schedule A, lines 15 through 26. Fortunately, the IRS in 1997 added lines that reflect whether the organization meets the test.

(h) What Is Support?

The 33⅓ percent support formula for donative public charities does not include revenues the organization receives from performing its exempt activities—student tuition or patient fees, for example—as does the formula for service providers.[12] Donations of services for which a contribution deduction is not allowed[13] are also excluded. Donations from other donative public charities and governmental entities are fully included in the numerator and denominator for this test, but other types of donations are partly or fully excluded as explained next. Supporting organization grants and split-interest trust donations are subject to the 2 percent limit. An organization that is primarily dependent upon exempt function revenues (receives a minimum amount of donations) cannot qualify as a donative public charity.[14]

(i) Two Percent Gifts

There is a 2 percent ceiling for donations included as public support. Contributions from each donor, whether an individual, corporation, trust, private foundation, or other type of entity (after combining related parties) during each four-year period are counted only up to 2 percent of the charity's total support. For example, say an organization receives total support during the four-year test period of $1 million. In such a case, contributions from each donor up to $20,000 could be counted as public donations. If one person gave $20,000 each year for a total of $80,000 for 4 years, only $20,000 is counted. The $1 million organization must receive at least $333,333 in public donations of $20,000 or less from each donor. It could receive $666,666 from one source and $10,000 from 33 sources or $20,000 from 17 sources, for example.

A public donation = Up to and no more than 2% of total support
$20,000 = 2% of $1 million

(j) Not All Public Charity Grants Count

Voluntary grants and donations received by a donative public charity from other charities listed in §170(b)(1)(A) and governmental units, including foreign governments,[15] are not subject to the 2 percent limit and instead are fully counted as donations from the general public (unless the gift was passed through as a donor-designated grant).[16] Grants from a service-providing entity[17] and from a supporting organization are subject to the 2 percent inclusion limitation.[18]

(k) Facts and Circumstances Test

When the percentage of an organization's public donations falls below the precise 33⅓ percent test, it may be able to sustain public charity status by applying the *facts and circumstances test*. The history of the organization's fund-raising efforts and other factors are considered as an alternative method to the strict mathematical formula for qualifying for public support under §509(a)(1). This test is not available for charities qualifying as public under §509(a)(2). An organization may need to apply this test at different times during its life. It can seek such qualification when it originally files Form 1023. In that instance, the IRS will scrutinize the facts and issue its approval or disapproval. The test may also be applied later in its life if support falls below the 33⅓ percent level. At this point there are two choices: The information can be submitted as an attachment to Schedule A of the annual Form 990. The words "Facts and Circumstances Apply" should be noted next to box 26f that shows an amount less than 33⅓ percent. The problem with this choice is that the IRS does not customarily respond to such a filing. Though prior IRS approval is not required, an organization might choose to seek approval by submitting the information to the Cincinnati office responsible for determinations.[19] For the facts and circumstances test to apply, the following factors must be present:

- Public support must be at least 10 percent of the total support, and the higher the better.
- The organization must have an active "continuous and bona fide" fund-raising program designed to attract new and additional public and governmental support. Consideration will be given to the fact that, in its early years of existence, it limits the scope of its solicitations to

those persons deemed most likely to provide seed money in an amount sufficient to enable it to commence its charitable activities and to expand its solicitation program.

Other favorable factors must be present, such as:

- The composition of the board is representative of broad public interests (rather than those of major contributors).
- Some support comes from governmental and other sources representative of the general public (rather than a few major contributors).
- Facilities and programs are made available to the general public, such as a museum or symphonic society.
- Programs appeal to a broadly based public (and in fact the public participates).

(l) Unusual Grants

When inclusion of a substantial donation(s) causes an organization to fail the 33⅓ percent public support test, public charity status may still be sustained by excluding such gift(s). A qualifying *unusual grant* can be excluded from gross revenue in calculating total support for both (a)(1) and (a)(2) purposes. A grant is unusual if it is an unexpected and substantial gift attracted by the public nature of the organization *and* received from a disinterested party. A number of factors are taken into account; no single factor is determinative, and not all factors need be present. The positive factors are shown below, along with their opposites in parentheses:

1. The contribution is received from a party with no connection to the organization. (The gift is received from a person who is a substantial contributor, board member, or manager, or related to a board member or manager of the organization.)
2. The gift is in the form of cash, marketable securities, or property that furthers the organization's exempt purposes. (The property is illiquid, difficult to dispose of, and not pertinent to the organization's activities—useless, in other words.) A gift of a painting to a museum, or a gift of wetlands to a nature preservation society would be useful and appropriate property.
3. No material restrictions are placed on the gift. (Strings are attached.)

4. The organization attracts a significant amount of support to pay its operating expenses on a regular basis, and the gift adds to an endowment or pays for capital items. (The gift pays for operating expenses for several years and is not added to an endowment.)
5. The gift is a bequest. (The gift is an *inter vivos* transfer.)
6. An active fund-raising program exists and attracts significant public support. (Fund solicitation programs are unsuccessful.)
7. A representative and broadly based governing body controls the organization. (Related parties control the organization.)
8. Prior to the receipt of the unusual grant, the organization qualified as publicly supported. (The unusual grant exclusion was relied upon in the past to satisfy the test.)

If the grant is payable over a period of years, it can be excluded each year, but any income earned on the sums would be included. The IRS has provided a set of "safe harbor" reliance factors to identify unusual grants. If the first four factors listed above are present, unusual grant status can automatically be claimed and relied upon. As to item 4, the terms of the grant cannot provide for more than one year's operating expense.

3.4 PART IV—SERVICE-PROVIDING PUBLIC CHARITIES: §509(a)(2)

Like those organizations said to conduct "inherently public" activities—churches, schools, and hospitals—the second major category of public charity includes entities that also provide services to the public—museums, libraries, low-income housing projects, and the like. Unlike churches, schools, and hospitals that qualify without regard to their sources of support, §509(a)(2) service providers must meet public support tests. Also unlike donative public charities that disregard fee-for-service revenue in calculating public support, service providers count exempt function revenues as support when their qualification is calculated on line 27 of Part IV-A. Thus, this type of public charity usually includes organizations receiving a major portion of their support from fees and charges for activity participation such as day care centers, animal shelters, theaters, and educational publishers. A two-part support test must be met to qualify under this category:

1. Investment income cannot exceed one third of the total support (all revenue except capital gains). Gifts from supporting organizations

and split-interest trusts retain their character as investment income for purposes of calculating this limitation.

2. Over one third of the total support must be received from exempt function sources made up of a combination of the following:
   - Gifts, grants, contributions, and membership dues received from non-disqualified persons. Unusual grants can be excluded.
   - Admission to exempt function facilities or performances, such as theater or ballet performance tickets, museum or historic site admission fees, movie or video tickets, seminar or lecture fees, and athletic event charges.
   - Fees for performance of services, such as school tuition, day care fees, hospital room and laboratory charges, psychiatric counseling, testing, scientific laboratory fees, library fines, animal neutering charges, athletic facility fees, and so on.
   - Merchandise sales of goods related to the organization's activities, including books and educational literature, pharmaceuticals and medical devices, handicrafts, reproductions and copies of original works of art, by-products of a blood bank, and goods produced by handicapped workers.
   - Exempt function revenues received from one source are not counted if they exceed $5,000 or 1 percent of the organization's support, whichever is higher.

A qualifying service provider cannot receive over one third of its revenue from investment income. Dividends, interest, payments with respect to security loans, rents, royalties, and net unrelated business income (less the unrelated business income tax (UBIT)) are treated as investment income for this purpose. Program-related investments, such as low-income housing loans, do not produce investment income but rather exempt function gross receipts.

3.5 PART IV—SUPPORTING ORGANIZATIONS: §509(a)(3)

The third category of organizations that escape the stringent requirements placed on private foundations is a *supporting organization* (SO). If such organizations are sufficiently responsive to, controlled or supervised by, or in connection with one or more public charities, they are classified as public charities themselves, even if they are privately funded.

Basically, SOs dedicate all of their assets to one or more public charities that need not necessarily control them (except an SO cannot be controlled by disqualified persons). Beneficiary organization(s) must be specified, but can be changed under certain conditions. This flexibility makes SOs popular with benefactors that want neither to create a private foundation nor to make an outright gift to an established charity. The rules are not entirely logical, and the regulations are quite detailed and extensive.[20] The questions that must be answered on Form 1023, Schedule D, for organizations seeking this classification are also instructive. An SO must meet three unique organizational and operational tests as follows:

1. It must be organized, and at all times thereafter, operated exclusively for the benefit of, to perform the functions of, or to carry out the purposes of one or more specified public charities (*purpose*).
2. It must be operated, supervised, controlled by, or in connection with one or more public charities (*organizational test*).
3. It cannot be controlled, directly or indirectly, by one or more disqualified persons.

3.6 DIFFERENCES BETWEEN §509(a)(1) AND §509(a)(2)

Some organizations, including most churches, schools, and hospitals, can qualify for public status under both §509(a)(1) and (a)(2). The (a)(1) class is the preferred public charity category. For purposes of annual reporting, unrelated business, limits on deductions for donors, and most other tax purposes, the two categories are virtually the same, with one important exception: To receive a terminating distribution from a private foundation upon its dissolution, the charity must be an (a)(1) organization.

(a) Definition of Support

The items of gross income included in the requisite "support" is different for each category and does not equal total revenue under either class. "Support" forms the basis of public status for both categories, and the calculations are made on a four-year moving average basis using the cash method of accounting. For (a)(1) purposes, certain revenue is not counted as support and is not included in the numerator or the denominator:

- Exempt function revenue, or that amount earned through charges for the exercise or performance of exempt activities, such as admission tickets, patient fees, etc.

- Capital gains or losses
- Unusual grants
- Donations of in-kind services and facilities (although facility and service donations from governmental units are counted)

For (a)(2) purposes, total revenue less capital gains or losses, unusual grants, and in-kind service and facility donations equals total support.

(b) Major Gifts

Contributions received are counted as public support differently for each category. Under the (a)(1) category, a particular giver's donations (including grants from supporting organizations and §509(a)(2) organizations) are counted only up to an amount equal to 2 percent of the total "support" for the four-year period. Gifts from other public charities and governmental entities are not subject to this 2 percent floor.

For (a)(2) purposes, all gifts, grants, and contributions are counted as public support, except those received from disqualified persons. Such a person may be a substantial contributor, or one who gives over $5,000 if such amount is more than 2 percent of the organization's aggregate contributions for its life, a board member, trustee, or officer, a business controlled by a disqualified person, or a relative of such a person. For (a)(2) purposes, gifts from these insiders are not counted at all. Subject to the 2 percent ceiling, their gifts are counted for (a)(1) purposes.

(c) Membership Fees

For both categories, this may represent donations or charges for services rendered. In some cases, a combined gift and payment for services may be present. The facts in each circumstance must be examined to properly classify the revenue. A membership fee is a donation if it is paid by a person to support the goals and interests they have in common with organization rather than to purchase admission, merchandise, services, or the use of facilities.[21] The charitable deduction rules also provide that members provided *de minimus* benefits may treat the entire dues payment as a donation as discussed in Chapter 2§2(a) and (c). Particularly for (a)(1) purposes, this distinction is very important because dues treated as exempt function fees are not included in the public support calculations.

(d) Grants for Services

These grants, to be rendered for the granting organization such as a state government's funding for home health or prisoner care, are treated under both categories as exempt function income, not donations or grants. The accounting rules call such revenue *exchange function* when the recipient organization performs a service or provides a facility or product to serve the needs of the grantor. A grant is instead treated as a contribution when the payment is made to encourage the grantee organization to carry on certain programs or activities in furtherance of its own exempt purposes; no economic or physical benefit accrues to the grant maker.

Under both categories, this distinction is important to determine amounts qualifying as contributions. For (a)(2) status, the distinction has yet another dimension: Only the first $5,000 of fees, or 1 percent of the total revenue (whichever is higher), for such services received from a particular grantor or vendor is includible in public support. Government payments made on behalf of a third-party payor, such as Medicare or Medicaid patient receipts or blood bank charges collected by a hospital as agent for a blood bank, are treated as revenue from the individual patients.[22]

Pass-through grants received from another public charity are totally counted toward public support unless the gift represents an indirect grant expressly or implicitly earmarked by a donor to be paid to a subgrantee organization. In that case, the donor is the individual. *Donor-designated* grants, therefore, require careful scrutiny. The basic question is whether the intermediary organization received the gift as an agent or whether it can freely choose to regrant the funds. Donations received under a donor designation and donor-advised funds should qualify as public support to the initial recipient organization (and again to the ultimate recipient) because it retains ultimate authority to approve the regrants.

(e) In-Kind Gifts

These are counted differently for each category. For (a)(1) purposes, the regulation specifically says support does not include "contributions of services for which a deduction is not allowable." For (a)(2) purposes, the regulation says support includes the fair market or rental value of gifts, grants, or contributions of property or use of such property on the date of the gift. Back to (a)(1), the regulations and the IRS instructions to Form 990 are silent about gifts of property that are deductible. It is not stated whether the full fair market value of property for which the contribution deduction is limited to basis, such as a gift of clothing to the charity resale shop, is counted at full value or at basis. The organization, for accounting purposes, would count such gifts at their full value.

3.7 SOLVING TROUBLESOME PUBLIC STATUS PROBLEMS

To secure one of its major sources of funding, a public charity must carefully guard its status to be sure it can continue to receive grants from private foundations (PFs). One PF can give a grant to another PF only if it exercises expenditure responsibility, a paperwork requirement that many refuse to undertake. The test is based on revenues the charity *normally* receives. The normal period is the four years preceding the year in question and the succeeding year. The basis for qualification as a public charity for the tax years 2002 and 2001 is the revenue received during 1997 through 2000. This time lag provides opportunities for planning and seeking funding that might be needed to maintain the required greater than 33⅓ percent support ratio. For an organization with a support ratio below 50 percent, it is desirable to maintain ongoing projections of qualification. A few of problems that might arise and suggested solutions include:

- *Change of public charity category*. Sometimes, the sources of a public charity's revenue change, causing it to fail to qualify under one category or another. When the change indicated is reclassification from (a)(1) to (a)(2) or vice versa, the factors discussed in Chapter 6§6 can be considered. Simply reporting the financial information on Schedule A is sufficient to allow an organization to continue its public status; the issue is whether to seek a new determination letter to reflect the new category. Funders and other interested parties that compare Schedule A to the determination letter may want an explanation. IRS Publication 78 does not, however, list an organization's 509 category, but instead simply says the organization is a public charity.
- An organization could conceivably change annually, depending on the category into which it fits. The consequence is minimal, except §509(a)(2) organizations are not qualified recipients for a PF's terminating distribution, and grants received by a §509(a)(1) public charity from an (a)(2) public charity are subject to the 2 percent limit. Only loss of public status is truly harmful.
- *Loss of public status*. A more serious situation arises when the changes in support cause the organization to lose its public charity status. Important to note here is that the loss of status is not immediate; if the financial tally submitted with the organization's 2000 return reflects support for the years 1996 through 1999 was less than

the requisite one third, public status continues through the year 2000. If a material change in the organization's sources of support occurs that is not caused by an unusual grant, a five-year testing period may apply, and special rules apply for new organizations. Until a change of status is announced in the Internal Revenue Bulletin, contributors are entitled to rely upon the latest IRS letter. A donor who is responsible for or otherwise aware of the changes is not entitled to such reliance.[23]

- *Timing* can be extremely important for an organization that inadvertently loses its public status and becomes a private foundation. The organization can make an application to terminate PF status under a plan to raise an appropriate level of public donations during the following five years, referred to as a *60-month termination*. However, a notice of such a conversion plan must be filed for IRS approval prior to the period for which it is effective. An inattentive organization may not realize its need to file until after the end of the year in which the failure occurs.[24]
- *Change of operation*. An organization that has qualified as a public charity for reasons of its activity, such as a school or a hospital, loses it public status at the end of a year, if not technically on the day, it ceases to conduct the activity. Commonly, such an organization sells its assets, invests the proceeds, and converts to a grant-making private foundation. Because of the excise tax on investment income, mandatory payout, and other rules that begin to apply, delaying the conversion date is desirable. Due to its revenue sources during the time it operated as a hospital or school, it is likely it can qualify as a public charity for at least one, if not two, years after the sale of its assets.[25]
- *Record-keeping problems* may confront the ill-prepared charitable organization that follows Statement of Financial Accounting Standard (SFAS) No. 116[26] when completing Schedule A. Revenues are reported on a cash basis on Schedule A, rather than the accrual method. Pledge revenues booked for financial statement purposes, and thereby reported as revenue in Part I of Form 990, are not counted as public support until the pledge is collected. A system for reconciling the cash-to-accrual contributions must be designed by those organizations that qualify as public charities under IRC §509(a)(1) or (2) on the basis of their revenue sources. Considerable organizational time, as well as the time of outside accountants, can be saved if year-end reports are prepared in view of this reporting requirement. Lines 15 through 22 on Part IV-A—contributions, exempt function revenues, investment income, net income from unrelated businesses, and all other revenues—are all reported on a cash basis for the four years preceding the filing year.

Coordination of the reporting functions can be particularly important for an organization with major contributors. Schedule A, line 26a, asks §509(a)(1) organizations for the total amount received for the past four years from individual donors in excess of 2 percent of line 24. For §509(a)(2) organizations, similar details for its disqualified persons[27] (major donors, board members, and their families) are completed on line 27. To complete this report, each donor's total annual cash gifts for four years must be available. An organization's donor databases may need retooling to track pledges on both a cash and accrual system. For accrual purposes, the present value increments of unpaid pledges is reported. These numbers bear no relation to the required Schedule A details. An organization does not necessarily know in any one year which donors will, over the succeeding four-year period, fall into this special reporting category. Alas, the cash-to-accrual details certainly must be maintained on those donors potentially capable of becoming major donors—and to be safe, on all donors.

3.8 PART V—PRIVATE SCHOOL QUESTIONNAIRE

Part V requests information about the nondiscrimination policies of private schools. Schools must adopt and practice policies prohibiting racial discrimination. A statement that it has a racially nondiscriminatory policy must also be included in its charter, bylaws, or other governing instrument, or be effective by resolution of its governing body. School brochures, catalogs, and other printed matter used to inform prospective students of the school's programs must state the policy as it relates to admission applications, scholarships, and program participation. The following words are acceptable: "The (name) school admits students of any race, color, and national or ethnic origin." A school must also make its racially nondiscriminatory policy known to all segments of the general community served by the school using one of the following methods:

- *Method 1.* A statement of a school's policy must be published each year in an area newspaper during the period of the school's solicitation of students. The notice must appear in a section of the newspaper likely to be read by prospective students and their families and must occupy at least three column inches.
- *Method 2.* The school may instead use broadcast media to make its nondiscriminatory policy known to the general community the school serves. A tape of the announcement must be maintained, as well as keeping evidence that there were an adequate number of announcements broadcast during a time when the necessary audience could be reached.

- *Method 3.* A parochial or other church-related school the student body 75 percent of which consists of members of the sponsoring religious denomination may publish its notice in newspapers or circulars of the religious organization serving the same community the school serves.
- *Method 4.* A school that customarily draws a substantial percentage of its students nationally or worldwide, or from a large geographic section of the United States and actually follows a racially nondiscriminatory policy, can simply announce its policy in its brochures and catalogs dealing with student admissions, programs, and scholarships.

Action taken to publicize the school's antidiscrimination policies to its constituency are reported in this part. Form 5578 can be used to furnish the requested information but is not specifically required. Form 5578 is designed to be filed by schools that are not required to file Form 990, including primarily government schools and church schools that qualify as an integrated auxiliary of a church. The questions in this part reflect the school discrimination policy adopted by the IRS in 1975.[28] It is imperative that all private schools correctly answer them to ensure continued qualification for exemption. Questions 29 through 32 need a "yes" answer. All parts of question 33 must be answered "no." Because of its specific and in-depth directions, the author recommends that a preparer of this part actually review the IRS instructions for this part that reprint the 1975 IRS procedure.

3.9 PART VI-A—LOBBYING EXPENDITURES BY ELECTING PUBLIC CHARITIES—AND PART VI-B—LOBBYING ACTIVITY BY NONELECTING PUBLIC CHARITIES

Part VI is completed to allow the IRS to evaluate the levels of an organization's lobbying efforts. From the outset it is important to emphasize that public charities are permitted to conduct efforts to influence legislation, referred to as *lobbying*. Though they are absolutely prohibited from taking any steps to influence or otherwise intervene in the election of those that make the laws, contacting them or urging others to do so after election is allowed. The portion of a public charity's total effort spent on lobbying, however, is limited and governed by one of two very different sets of rules. One test, called the *expenditure test*, is based on money spent with separate limits for direct and grassroots efforts as described below. This test is applied for public charities that make an IRC §501(h) election by filing Form 5768 (Appendix 3B) within the year for which it is to be effective. The election can also be revoked at any time. There are two advantages to making the election:

1. The allowable spending for lobbying is based on a precise mathematical percentage of the organization's overall expenditures.
2. The definition of what constitutes lobbying is both specific and broad.

A "substantial part" test is instead applied to those public charities that do not lobby. This test is based on the fact that the regulations require a §501(c)(3) organization to operate exclusively for charitable purposes. While some would argue that lobbying advances their mission, lobbying is not considered an exempt function activity for a tax-exempt organization. The big disadvantage of this test is that the permissible amount of lobbying for organizations that do not elect is not specified. Instead, all of the facts and circumstances are taken into account to determine whether the overarching (c)(3) test is satisfied. Overall lobbying efforts are not only evidenced by spending, but also by involvement of volunteers and board members, by use of the organization's name to promote an effort, and a host of similar intangible factors that may be taken into account if the IRS wants to challenge an organization's tax-exempt status. The nationwide organization, Independent Sector, conducted a public information campaign in recent years and encouraged charities to participate in public affairs as well as informing them about the advantages of making the election. There is no enhanced risk of IRS scrutiny for organizations that elect.

(a) Part VI-A

Those charities that elect the mathematical lobbying limitations complete Part VI-A, which reflects the specific numerical test that is applied. Successful completion of this part depends on good accounting and an ability to identify direct expenses and to allocate indirect ones as discussed in Chapter 1§4. The terms are defined in Chapter 23. Form 5768 is to be used for making or revoking the election during the reporting period. Capital expenses are not included in the calculation of lobbying expense limitations. Only straight-line depreciation on assets directly used in connection with lobbying efforts are included as lobbying expenses. No explanation of the activity, nor details of expenditures is required.

(b) Part VI-B

Nine questions are asked of organizations that do not elect to conduct limited lobbying. Such organizations face a subjective and qualitative measure to ascertain if the lobbying comprises a substantial part of their activities, as discussed in Chapter 23§4(a). There are over 21 pages of IRS instructions to this part of Schedule A, and they should be read in detail if the answer to any of the items (a) through (h) is "yes."

Chapter 23 of *Tax Planning and Compliance* also details the rules, with full citations to historical cases and rulings.

3.10 PART VII—INFORMATION REGARDING TRANSFERS, TRANSACTIONS, AND RELATIONSHIPS WITH OTHER ORGANIZATIONS

Part VII was added in 1988 in response to a congressional mandate to the IRS to search for connections between public charities and non–501(c)(3) organizations. Particularly in regard to organizations that lobby or enter the political arena, the IRS is scouting for relationships that allow benefits to the noncharitable organization. This part looks for use of exempt organization assets to benefit non–(c)(3) organizations and asks the exempt organization to report any financial transactions, such as sales, transfers, or rentals of assets to or from another organization. The reportable transactions are those with affiliated or related organizations. The instructions are very specific and should be consulted if transactions are to be reported. To answer, consider that the following factors must be present to have a related organization:

- A historic and continuing relationship between two organizations evidenced by sharing of facilities, staff, joint effort, or other work in concert toward accomplishing a common goal.
- Common control whereby one or more of the officers, directors, or trustees (managers) of one organization is elected or appointed by those of the other. Similarly, common control is found when 25 percent or more of the managers are interlocking.

The few transactions that need not be reported include:

- Any transaction totaling $500 or less annually
- Specific transactions totaling less than 1 percent of the organization's annual gross receipts involving subscriptions, conferences, seminars, or other functionally related services or goods

This part indicates yet another type of special records an exempt organization might need to maintain in order to accurately complete annual IRS reports. To answer this part correctly, an organization having the described relationship will want to establish subcodes or new departments in its chart of accounts to tabulate the answers. See Chapter 22 of *Tax Planning and Compliance* for more discussion of such relationships.

Appendix 3A

SCHEDULE A
(Form 990 or 990-EZ)

Department of the Treasury
Internal Revenue Service

Organization Exempt Under Section 501(c)(3)

(Except Private Foundation) and Section 501(e), 501(f), 501(k), 501(n), or Section 4947(a)(1) Nonexempt Charitable Trust

Supplementary Information - (See separate instructions.)

MUST be completed by the above organizations and attached to their Form 990 or 990-EZ.

OMB No. 1545-0047

2000

Name of the organization	Employer identification number
Hometown Chapter, Campaign to Clean Up America	44-4444444

Part I Compensation of the Five Highest Paid Employees Other Than Officers, Directors, and Trustees
(See page 1 of the instructions. List each one. If there are none, enter "None.")

(a) Name and address of each employee paid more than $50,000	(b) Title and average hours per week devoted to position	(c) Compensation	(d) Contributions to employee benefit plans & deferred compensation	(e) Expense account and other allowances
None				
Total number of other employees paid over $50,000	None			

Part II Compensation of the Five Highest Paid Independent Contractors for Professional Services
(See page 1 of the instructions. List each one (whether individuals or firms.) If there are none, enter "None.")

(a) Name and address of each independent contractor paid more than $50,000	(b) Type of service	(c) Compensation
None		
Total number of others receiving over $50,000 for professional services	None	

For Paperwork Reduction Act Notice, see page 1 of the Instructions to Form 990 and Form 990-EZ. (HTA) Schedule A (Form 990 or 990-EZ) 2000

Schedule A (Form 990 or 990-EZ) 2000 — Hometown Chapter, Campaign to Clean Up America — 44-4444444 — Page 2

Part III Statements About Activities

			Yes	No
1	During the year, has the organization attempted to influence national, state, or local legislation, including any attempt to influence public opinion on a legislative matter or referendum? If "Yes," enter the total expenses paid or incurred in connection with the lobbying activities. 10,000. Organizations that made an election under section 501(h) by filing Form 5768 must complete Part VI-A. Other organizations checking "Yes," must complete Part VI-B AND attach a statement giving a detailed description of the lobbying activities.	1	X	
2	During the year, has the organization, either directly or indirectly, engaged in any of the following acts with any of its trustees, directors, officers, creators, key employees, or members of their families, or with any taxable organization with which any such person is affiliated as an officer, director, trustee, majority owner, or principal beneficiary:			
a	Sale, exchange, or leasing of property?	2a		X
b	Lending of money or other extension of credit?	2b		X
c	Furnishing of goods, services, or facilities?	2c		X
d	Payment of compensation (or payment or reimbursement of expenses if more than $1,000)? See Form 990 Part V	2d	X	
e	Transfer of any part of its income or assets? If the answer to any question is "Yes, " attach a detailed statement explaining the transactions.	2e		X
3	Does the organization make grants for scholarships, fellowships, student loans, etc.?	3	X	
4a	Do you have a section 403(b) annuity plan for your employees?	4a		X
b	Attach a statement to explain how the organization determines that individuals or organizations receiving grants or loans from it in furtherance of its charitable programs qualify to receive payments. (See page 2 of the instructions.) See attachment			

Part IV Reason for Non-Private Foundation Status (See pages 2 through 4 of the instructions.)

The organization is not a private foundation because it is (please check only ONE applicable box):

5 [ ] A church, convention of churches, or association of churches. Section 170(b)(1)(A)(i).

6 [ ] A school. Section 170(b)(1)(A)(ii). (Also complete Part V, page 5.)

7 [ ] A hospital or a cooperative hospital service organization. Section 170(b)(1)(A)(iii).

8 [ ] A Federal, state, or local government or governmental unit. Section 170(b)(1)(A)(v).

9 [ ] A medical research organization operated in conjunction with a hospital. Section 170(b)(1)(A)(iii). Enter the hospital's name, city, and state --

10 [ ] An organization operated for the benefit of a college or university owned or operated by a governmental unit. Section 170(b)(1)(A)(iv). (Also complete the Support Schedule in Part IV-A.)

11a [X] An organization that normally receives a substantial part of its support from a governmental unit or from the general public. Section 170(b)(1)(A)(vi). (Also complete the Support Schedule in Part IV-A.)

11b [ ] A community trust. Section 170(b)(1)(A)(vi). (Also complete the Support Schedule below.)

12 [ ] An organization that normally receives: (1) more than 33 1/3% of its support from contributions, membership fees, and gross receipts from activities related to its charitable, etc., functions- subject to certain exceptions, and (2) no more than 33 1/3% of its support from gross investment income and unrelated business taxable income (less section 511 tax) from businesses acquired by the organization after June 30, 1975. See section 509(a)(2). (Also complete the Support Schedule in Part IV-A.)

13 [ ] An organization that is not controlled by any disqualified persons (other than foundation managers) and supports organizations described in: (1) lines 5 through 12 above; or (2) section 501(c)(4), (5), or (6), if they meet the test of section 509(a)(2). (See section 509(a)(3).)

Provide the following information about the supported organizations. (See page 5 of the instructions.)

(a) Name(s) of supported organization(s)	(b) Line number from above

14 [ ] An organization organized and operated to test for public safety. Section 509(a)(4). (See page 5 of the instructions.)

Schedule A (Form 990 or 990-EZ) 2000

Schedule A (Form 990 or 990-EZ) 2000 Hometown Chapter, Campaign to Clean Up America 44-4444444 Page 3

Part IV-A Support Schedule (Complete only if you checked a box on line 10, 11, or 12.) Use cash method of accounting.

NOTE: You may use the worksheet in the instructions for converting from the accrual to the cash method of accounting.

Calendar year (or fiscal year beginning in)	(a) 1999	(b) 1998	(c) 1997	(d) 1996	(e) Total
15 Gifts, grants, and contributions received. (Do not include unusual grants. See line 28.)	260,000	150,000	68,700	52,500	531,200
16 Membership fees received					
17 Gross receipts from admissions, merchandise sold or services performed, or furnishing of facilities in any activity that is not a business unrelated to the organization's charitable, etc., purpose	22,500				22,500
18 Gross income from interest, dividends, amounts received from payments on securities loans (section 512(a)(5)), rents, royalties, and unrelated business taxable income (less section 511 taxes) from businesses acquired by the organization after June 30, 1975	10,000	600	400	200	11,200
19 Net income from unrelated business activities not included in line 18					
20 Tax revenues levied for the organization's benefit and either paid to it or expended on its behalf					
21 The value of services or facilities furnished to the organization by a governmental unit without charge. Do not include the value of services or facilities generally furnished to the public without charge					
22 Other income. Attach a schedule. Do not include gain or (loss) from sale of capital assets					
23 Total of lines 15 through 22	292,500	150,600	69,100	52,700	564,900
24 Line 23 minus line 17	270,000	150,600	69,100	52,700	542,400
25 Enter 1% of line 23	2,925	1,506	691	527	

26 Organizations described in lines 10 or 11: a Enter 2% of amount in column (e), line 24 . . . **26a** 10,848

b Attach a list (which is not open to public inspection) showing the name of and amount contributed by each person (other than a governmental unit or publicly supported organization) whose total gifts for 1996 through 1999 exceeded the amount shown in line 26a. Enter the sum of all these excess amounts . . . **26b** 195,682

c Total support for section 509(a)(1) test: Enter line 24, column (e) . . . **26c** 542,400

d Add: Amounts from column (e) for lines: 18 11,200 19 ______ 22 ______ 26b 195,682 **26d** 206,882

e Public support (line 26c minus line 26d total) . . . **26e** 335,518

f Public support percentage (line 26e (numerator) divided by line 26c (denominator)) . . . **26f** 61.86%

27 Organizations described on line 12: a For amounts included in lines 15, 16, and 17 that were received from a "disqualified person," attach a list (which is not open to public inspection) to show the name of, and total amounts received in each year from, each "disqualified person." Enter the sum of such amounts for each year:

(1999) ________ (1998) ________ (1997) ________ (1996) ________

b For any amount included in line 17 that was received from a nondisqualified person, attach a list to show the name of, and amount received for each year, that was more than the larger of (1) the amount on line 25 for the year or (2) $5,000. (Include in the list organizations described in lines 5 through 11, as well as individuals.) After computing the difference between the amount received and the larger amount described in (1) or (2), enter the sum of all these differences (the excess amounts) for each year:

(1999) ________ (1998) ________ (1997) ________ (1996) ________

c Add: Amounts from column (e) for lines: 15 ______ 16 ______ 17 ______ 20 ______ 21 ______ . . . **27c**

d Add: Line 27a total ______ and line 27b total ______ . . . **27d**

e Public support (line 27c minus line 27d total) . . . **27e**

f Total support for section 509(a)(2) test: Enter amount on line 23, column (e) . . . **27f**

g Public support percentage (line 27e (numerator) divided by line 27f (denominator)) . . . **27g**

h Investment income percentage (line 18, column (e) (numerator) divided by line 27f (denominator)) . . . **27h**

28 Unusual Grants: For an organization described in line 10, 11, or 12 that received any unusual grants during 1996 through 1999, attach a list (which is not open to public inspection) for each year showing the name of the contributor, the date and amount of the grant, and a brief description of the nature of the grant. Do not include these grants in line 15. (See page 5 of the instructions.)

Schedule A (Form 990 or 990-EZ) 2000

Schedule A (Form 990 or 990-EZ) 2000 Hometown Chapter, Campaign to Clean Up America 44-4444444 Page 4

Part V Private School Questionnaire (See page 5 of the instructions.)
(To be completed ONLY by schools that checked the box on line 6 in Part IV) **Not Applicable**

		Yes	No
29 Does the organization have a racially nondiscriminatory policy toward students by statement in its charter, bylaws, other governing instrument, or in a resolution of its governing body?	29		
30 Does the organization include a statement of its racially nondiscriminatory policy toward students in all its brochures, catalogues, and other written communications with the public dealing with student admissions, programs, and scholarships?	30		
31 Has the organization publicized its racially nondiscriminatory policy through newspaper or broadcast media during the period of solicitation for students, or during the registration period if it has no solicitation program, in a way that makes the policy known to all parts of the general community it serves?	31		
If "Yes," please describe; if "No," please explain. (If you need more space, attach a separate statement.)			
32 Does the organization maintain the following:			
a Records indicating the racial composition of the student body, faculty, and administrative staff?	32a		
b Records documenting that scholarships and other financial assistance are awarded on a racially nondiscriminatory basis?	32b		
c Copies of all catalogues, brochures, announcements, and other written communications to the public dealing with student admissions, programs, and scholarships?	32c		
d Copies of all material used by the organization or on its behalf to solicit contributions?	32d		
If you answered "No" to any of the above, please explain. (If you need more space, attach a separate statement.)			
33 Does the organization discriminate by race in any way with respect to:			
a Students' rights or privileges?	33a		
b Admissions policies?	33b		
c Employment of faculty or administrative staff?	33c		
d Scholarships or other financial assistance?	33d		
e Educational policies?	33e		
f Use of facilities?	33f		
g Athletic programs?	33g		
h Other extracurricular activities?	33h		
If you answered "Yes" to any of the above, please explain. (If you need more space, attach a statement.)			
34a Does the organization receive any financial aid or assistance from a governmental agency?	34a		
b Has the organization's right to such aid ever been revoked or suspended?	34b		
If you answered "Yes" to either 34a or b, please explain using an attached statement.			
35 Does the organization certify that it has complied with the applicable requirements of sections 4.01 through 4.05 of Rev. Proc. 75-50, 1975-2 C.B. 587, covering racial nondiscrimination? If "No," attach an explanation	35		

Schedule A (Form 990 or 990-EZ) 2000

Schedule A (Form 990 or 990-EZ) 2000 Hometown Chapter, Campaign to Clean Up America 44-4444444 Page 5

Part VI-A Lobbying Expenditures by Electing Public Charities (See page 7 of the instructions.)

(To be completed ONLY by an eligible organization that filed Form 5768)

Check here a ☐ If the organization belongs to an affiliated group.

Check here b ☐ If you checked "a" and "limited control" provisions apply.

	Limits on Lobbying Expenditures (The term "expenditures" means amounts paid or incurred)		(a) Affiliated group totals	(b) To be completed for ALL electing organizations
36	Total lobbying expenditures to influence public opinion (grassroots lobbying)	36		
37	Total lobbying expenditures to influence a legislative body (direct lobbying)	37		10,000
38	Total lobbying expenditures (add lines 36 and 37)	38		10,000
39	Other exempt purpose expenditures	39		701,000
40	Total exempt purpose expenditures (add lines 38 and 39)	40		711,000
41	Lobbying nontaxable amount. Enter the amount from the following table -			
	If the amount on line 40 is - / **The lobbying nontaxable amount is -**			
	Not over $500,000 . . . 20% of the amount on line 40			
	Over $500,000 but not over $1,000,000 . . . $100,000 plus 15% of the excess over $500,000			
	Over $1,000,000 but not over $1,500,000 . . . $175,000 plus 10% of the excess over $1,000,000	41		131,650
	Over $1,500,000 but not over $17,000,000 . . . $225,000 plus 5% of the excess over $1,500,000			
	Over $17,000,000 . . . $1,000,000			
42	Grassroots nontaxable amount (enter 25% of line 41)	42		32,913
43	Subtract line 42 from line 36. Enter -0- if line 42 is more than line 36	43		
44	Subtract line 41 from line 38. Enter -0- if line 41 is more than line 38	44		
	Caution: If there is an amount on either line 43 or line 44, file Form 4720.			

4 - Year Averaging Period Under Section 501(h)

(Some organizations that made a section 501(h) election do not have to complete all of the five columns below. See the instructions for lines 45 through 50 on page 9 of the instructions.)

	Lobbying Expenditures During 4-Year Averaging Period				
Calendar year (or fiscal year beginning in)	**(a)** 2000	**(b)** 1999	**(c)** 1998	**(d)** 1997	**(e)** Total
45 Lobbying nontaxable amount	131,650	42,000			173,650
46 Lobbying ceiling amount (150% of line 45(e))					260,475
47 Total lobbying expenditures	10,000	5,000			15,000
48 Grassroots nontaxable amount	32,913	10,500			43,413
49 Grassroots ceiling amount (150% of line 48(e))					65,120
50 Grassroots lobbying expenditures	None	None			None

Part VI-B Lobbying Activity by Nonelecting Public Charities

(For reporting by organizations that did not complete Part VI-A) (See page 9 of the instruction **Not Applicable**

During the year, did the organization attempt to influence national, state or local legislation, including any attempt to influence public opinion on a legislative matter or referendum, through the use of:	Yes	No	Amount
a Volunteers			
b Paid staff or management (include compensation in expenses reported on lines c through h.			
c Media advertisements			
d Mailings to members, legislators, or the public			
e Publications, or published or broadcast statements			
f Grants to other organizations for lobbying purposes			
g Direct contact with legislators, their staffs, government officials, or a legislative body			
h Rallies, demonstrations, seminars, conventions, speeches, lectures, or any other means			
i Total lobbying expenditures (add lines c through h)			

If "Yes" to any of the above, also attach a statement giving a detailed description of the lobbying activities.

Schedule A (Form 990 or 990-EZ) 2000

Schedule A (Form 990 or 990-EZ) 2000 Hometown Chapter, Campaign to Clean Up America 44-4444444 Page 6

Part VII Information Regarding Transfers To and Transactions and Relationships With Noncharitable Exempt Organizations (See page 9 of the instructions.)

51 Did the reporting organization directly or indirectly engage in any of the following with any other organization described in section 501(c) of the Code (other than section 501(c)(3) organizations) or in section 527, relating to political organizations?

		Yes	No
a Transfers from the reporting organization to a noncharitable exempt organization of:			
(i) Cash	51a(i)		X
(ii) Other assets	a(ii)		X
b Other transactions:			
(i) Sales or exchanges of assets with a noncharitable exempt organization	b(i)		X
(ii) Purchases of assets from a noncharitable exempt organization	b(ii)		X
(iii) Rental of facilities, equipment, or other assets	b(iii)		X
(iv) Reimbursement arrangements	b(iv)		X
(v) Loans or loan guarantees	b(v)		X
(vi) Performance of services or membership or fundraising solicitations	b(vi)		X
c Sharing of facilities, equipment, mailing lists, other assets, or paid employees	c		X

d If the answer to any of the above is "Yes," complete the following schedule. Column (b) should always show the fair market value of the goods, other assets, or services given by the reporting organization. If the organization received less than fair market value in any transaction or sharing arrangement, show in column (d) the value of the goods, other assets, or services received.

(a) Line no.	(b) Amount involved	(c) Name of noncharitable exempt organization	(d) Description of transfers, transactions, and sharing arrangements
		Not Applicable	

52a Is the organization directly or indirectly affiliated with, or related to, one or more tax-exempt organizations described in section 501(c) of the Code (other than section 501(c)(3)) or in section 527? ☐ Yes ☒ No

b If "Yes," complete the following schedule.

(a) Name of organization	(b) Type of organization	(c) Description of relationship
	Not Applicable	

Schedule A (Form 990 or 990-EZ) 2000

Hometown Chapter, Campaign to Clean Up America **44-4444444**
2000 Form 990

Schedule A, Part III, Line 4b

Campaign to Clean Up America annually recognizes volunteers who have provided exemplary services in advancing the organization's mission.

Attachment to Schedule A, Part III, line 4b

Hometown Chapter, Campaign to Clean Up America 44-4444444
2000 Form 990

Schedule A, Part IV-A, Line 26b

Name	1999	1998	1997	1996	Total	Excess over $10,848
Clean Industries, Inc.	$ 25,000		5,020		30,020	19,172
John & Jane Environmentalist	50,000				50,000	39,152
Friendly Corporation	50,000	75,000			125,000	114,152
Becky Naturalist	7,500	5,000			12,500	1,652
Sanitation Foundation		7,500	7,500	8,000	23,000	12,152
Trees for Families Foundation			15,000	5,250	20,250	9,402
Donors of less than 2%	127,500	62,500	41,180	39,250	270,430	
	$ 260,000	150,000	68,700	52,500	531,200	$ 195,682

Not Open to Public Inspection Attachment to Schedule A, Part IV-A, Line 26b

Appendix 3B

Form **5768**

(Rev. December 1996)

Department of the Treasury
Internal Revenue Service

Election/Revocation of Election by an Eligible Section 501(c)(3) Organization To Make Expenditures To Influence Legislation

(Under Section 501(h) of the Internal Revenue Code)

For IRS Use Only ▶

Name of organization	**Employer identification number**
Number and street (or P.O. box no., if mail is not delivered to street address)	Room/suite
City, town or post office, and state	ZIP + 4

1 Election– As an eligible organization, we hereby elect to have the provisions of section 501(h) of the Code, relating to expenditures to influence legislation, apply to our tax year ending .... (Month, day, and year) and all subsequent tax years until revoked.

Note: *This election must be signed and postmarked within the first taxable year to which it applies.*

2 Revocation– As an eligible organization, we hereby revoke our election to have the provisions of section 501(h) of the Code, relating to expenditures to influence legislation, apply to our tax year ending .... (Month, day, and year)

Note: *This revocation must be signed and postmarked before the first day of the tax year to which it applies.*

Under penalties of perjury, I declare that I am authorized to make this (check applicable box) ▶ ☐ election ☐r evocation on behalf of the above named organization.

(Signature of officer or trustee)	(Type or print name and title)	(Date)

General Instructions

Section references are to the Internal Revenue Code.

Section 501(c)(3) states that an organization exempt under that section will lose its tax-exempt status and its qualification to receive deductible charitable contributions if a substantial part of its activities are carried on to influence legislation. Section 501(h), however, permits certain eligible 501(c)(3) organizations to elect to make limited expenditures to influence legislation. An organization making the election will, however, be subject to an excise tax under section 4911 if it spends more than the amounts permitted by that section. Also, the organization may lose its exempt status if its lobbying expenditures exceed the permitted amounts by more than 50% over a 4-year period. For any tax year in which an election under section 501(h) is in effect, an electing organization must report the actual and permitted amounts of its lobbying expenditures and grass roots expenditures (as defined in section 4911(c)) on its annual return required under section 6033. See Schedule A (Form 990). Each electing member of an affiliated group must report these amounts for both itself and the affiliated group as a whole.

To make or revoke the election, enter the ending date of the tax year to which the election or revocation applies in item **1** or **2,** as applicable, and sign and date the form in the spaces provided.

Eligible Organizations.– A section 501(c)(3) organization is permitted to make the election if it is not a disqualified organization (see below) and is described in:

1. Section 170(b)(1)(A)(ii) (relating to educational institutions),

2. Section 170(b)(1)(A)(iii) (relating to hospitals and medical research organizations),

3. Section 170(b)(1)(A)(iv) (relating to organizations supporting government schools),

4. Section 170(b)(1)(A)(vi) (relating to organizations publicly supported by charitable contributions),

5. Section 509(a)(2) (relating to organizations publicly supported by admissions, sales, etc.), or

6. Section 509(a)(3) (relating to organizations supporting certain types of public charities other than those section 509(a)(3) organizations that support section 501(c)(4), (5), or (6) organizations).

Disqualified Organizations.– The following types of organizations are not permitted to make the election:

a. Section 170(b)(1)(A)(i) organizations (relating to churches),

b. An integrated auxiliary of a church or of a convention or association of churches, or

c. A member of an affiliated group of organizations if one or more members of such group is described in **a** or **b** of this paragraph.

Affiliated Organizations.– Organizations are members of an affiliated group of organizations only if **(1)** the governing instrument of one such organization requires it to be bound by the decisions of the other organization on legislative issues, or **(2)** the governing board of one such organization includes persons (i) who are specifically designated representatives of another such organization or are members of the governing board, officers, or paid executive staff members of such other organization, and (ii) who, by aggregating their votes, have sufficient voting power to cause or prevent action on legislative issues by the first such organization.

For more details, see section 4911 and section 501(h).

Note: *A private foundation (including a private operating foundation) is not an eligible organization.*

Where To File.– Mail Form 5768 to the Internal Revenue Service Center, Ogden, UT 84201-0027.

Cat. No. 12125M

Form **5768** (Rev. 12-96)

CHAPTER FOUR

The Private Foundation Return

In addition to reporting financial activity for the year, the 12-page Form 990-PF enables the IRS to evaluate a private foundation's compliance with the special sanctions and limitations on activities of foundations. The significance the IRS places on Form 990-PF is indicated by the fact that all private foundations, even those with few, if any, assets, are technically required to file the form annually. Equally important, private foundations, just like public charities, are required to make the form available for inspection by anyone who asks to see it or is willing to pay for a copy of the return. The returns are now being posted on the Internet site of Guidestar.org. Additionally, the form must be furnished to any and all states in which the foundation is registered or qualified to operate. Therefore this chapter is devoted to explaining part by part and, sometimes, line by line the why and how of completing this important form.[1]

4.1 SUCCESSFUL COMPLETION OF FORM 990-PF

Before one can successfully prepare Form 990-PF, the definitions of the following terms must be understood:

- *Private foundation*: A nonprofit organization qualifying as an IRC §501(c)(3) organization that does not meet the definitions for public charities in IRC §509(a)(1),(2), or (3) outlined in Chapter 3§3.
- *Disqualified person*: A substantial contributor, a foundation manager, owners of more than 20 percent of a business owned by a substantial contributor, a family member of those three persons (spouse, children, spouses of children, grandchildren, ancestors, but not siblings or aunts and uncles), and a corporation or partnership owned more than 35 percent by a disqualified person. Financial transactions between the foundation and its disqualified persons are generally prohibited by the self-dealing rules.
- *Substantial contributor*: A person who has donated an aggregate amount of more than 2 percent of the total contributions and bequests received by the private foundation before the close of the year, or $5,000, whichever is higher. Once one becomes a disqualified person, he or she remains so forever as a general rule.
- *Foundation manager*: A director, trustee, officer, or other individual having similar powers or responsibilities are the foundation's managers. Managers have authority to make administrative and policy decisions; for public charities, these persons are also called *key employees*.
- *Self-dealing*: A private foundation is not allowed to have financial transactions with its disqualified persons. Even if the transaction benefits the foundation—say the founder sells property worth $1 million to the foundation for $100,000—it is prohibited. Disqualified persons can be paid reasonable compensation for the services they render for the foundation and, with limitations, a foundation can share office space and personnel. If any money changes hands between the foundation and its disqualified persons, IRC §4941 should be very carefully studied.[2]
- *Mandatory payout:* IRC §4942 requires that a private foundation make grants for charitable and administrative purposes that equal at least 5 percent of the fair market value of its investment assets for the past year, less any excess distributions carried over from a prior year.
- *Taxable expenditure*: A private foundation is penalized under IRC §4945 if it makes an expenditure for a noncharitable purposes, for lobbying or electioneering, for scholarship grants (unless prior IRS plan approval is in place), and certain grants to other private or foreign organizations.[3]
- *Jeopardizing investments*: A foundation's managers are penalized by IRC §4944 if the foundation's assets are invested in a fashion that violates the prudent investor rules. Purchasing stocks on margin and buying and selling puts and calls are among the examples provided in the reg-

ulations that were written in 1972 and have not been updated for contemporary investing practices.[4]

- *Excess business holdings*: A private foundation, when its holdings are combined with those of its disqualified persons, may not own more than 20 percent of a business—whether it is a corporation, partnership, or investment trust. Excess holdings that are acquired by gift can be disposed of over a five-year period. Purchased holdings creating an excess are taxed under IRC §4943 and must be disposed of immediately.[5]

Form 990-PF (Appendix 4A) is designed to accomplish a number of purposes. First, the basic financial information—the revenues, disbursements, assets, and liabilities—are classified into meaningful categories to allow the IRS to statistically evaluate the scope and type of foundation activity, to measure the foundation's taxable investment income, and to tally those disbursements counted in meeting the foundation's 5 percent payout requirement. Second, the form has special parts with information and questions that fish for failures to comply with the federal requirements for maintenance of tax-exempt status for private foundations. The issues addressed by the information presented include, among many others, matters such as:

- Are the officers' salaries reported in Part VIII reasonable in relation to the foundation's resources and scope of activity, and if not, has prohibited self-dealing occurred?
- Does Part XIII or Part XIV show that the foundation has made the required amount of qualifying distributions by the end of the year?
- Is the foundation required to pay its investment income tax in quarterly installments because the liability shown in Part VI exceeds $500?
- Does the difference between the book value and the fair market value of the assets reported in Part II indicate that the foundation made jeopardizing investments?
- Do the programs described in Part IX-A constitute direct charitable activity? For a private operating foundation, do the descriptions indicate that the programs are directly carried out by the foundation? Or, similarly, do the program-related investments described in Part IX-B serve a charitable purpose?

A hypothetical Form 990-PF is reproduced in Appendix 3A and illustrates the depth and girth of information provided with the form. The instructions for the Form 990-PF alone are 28 pages long and exemplify the complexity of reporting and compliance requirements for a private foundation.[6] The booklet sent to private foundations by the IRS contains over 100 pages in total and includes:

- Form 990-PF—Return of Private Foundation
- Form 990-T—Exempt Organization Business Income Tax Return
- Form 4720—Return of Certain Excise Taxes on Charities and Other Persons under Chapters 41 and 42 of the Internal Revenue Code
- Form 990-W—Estimated Tax on Unrelated Business Taxable Income for Tax-Exempt Organizations and on Investment Income for Private Foundations

Form 990-PF has evolved over nearly 30 years as the law of private foundations has developed, retaining original concepts and adding new ones. Certain interdependent calculations do not follow in logical order. The most efficient order in which to prepare the form is the following:

Order in Which Form 990-PF Must Be Completed

1. Parts I, II, III, and IV
2. Skip to Parts VII, VIII, IX-A and B, XV, XVI-A and B, XVII, and XVIII
3. Part X
4. Part XII
5. Part V
6. Part VI
7. Part XI
8. Part XIII or XIV

4.2 THE PART I COLUMNS

Part I of Form 990-PF may be the most challenging and difficult part because some discretion is involved in presenting the information, particularly the expenses. The instructions for this part, in a very helpful fashion, begin by informing the preparer that the three right-hand columns may not necessarily equal the total amount of expenses shown in the leftmost column. Each of the columns in Part I serves a different purpose in the IRS regulatory scheme for private foundations. Deciding what goes where and why is not a logical process. Different accounting methods are used for reporting information in the columns and some items are included in more than one column, while others are not. A good accounting system applying the concepts presented in Chapter 1§4 is critical to accurate preparation of this part.

(a) Column (a): Revenue and Expenses per Books

This column agrees with financial reports prepared for the board and for public dissemination by the organization, except in-kind contributions of services or the use of property or facilities are not included. The cash or accrual method of accounting is permitted following the system regularly used to prepare financial statements for other purposes. While the change is essentially automatic, Form 3115 must be file to seek IRS approval for changing the tax reporting method from a cash to an accrual basis. A foundation that adopts the accounting literature set out in Statement of Financial Accounting Standard (SFAS) No. 116 for reporting contributions received and paid out need not seek permission for the change.

(b) Column (b): Net Investment Income

Each and every private foundation and wholly charitable trust is required to pay an excise tax on certain investment income. Column (b) reports the four specific types of designated taxable income—interest, dividends, rents, and royalties—plus the capital gains from sale of property producing such current income, less associated deductions used to arrive at income subject to the excise tax. Column (b) does not include:

- Unrelated business income separately reported on Form 990-T
- Program service revenue received from performing an exempt function
- Gain from sale of exempt function assets
- Profits from fund-raising events
- Net losses from sale of investment assets
- Unrealized investment gains or losses recognized under SFAS No. 124

(c) Column (c): Adjusted Net Income

This column became obsolete for most private foundations in 1976, but it is still important for two types of foundations. Private operating foundations must spend 85 percent of their adjusted net income on charitable projects they conduct directly. This column calculates what is called *adjusted gross income* by adding up investment income plus net short-term capital gains in excess of losses (a net loss is not entered) and unrelated business income, less expenses attributable to producing the includible income.

Private foundations receiving program service revenues use column (c) to report the income from the performance of its exempt functions. Such revenues are not reported in column (b) because they are not taxable. This column is basically used to reduce charitable disbursements by any income so that only the excess expenses over the revenues from program services are reported in column (d).

(d) Column (d): Disbursements for Charitable Purposes

The cash method must be used for this column. Under SFAS No. 116, foundations following generally accepted accounting principles (GAAP) report grants approved or pledged for future payment when the promise is made, rather than when the grant is actually disbursed. Such foundations must maintain a parallel accounting system that can prepare a report of grants paid on both the cash (for column (d) and the accrual basis (for column (a)). For foundations with expenses for the conduct of active program, the same type of dual reporting is required.

As the title of this column indicates, amounts reported in this column are significant because they count toward calculation of the mandatory charitable payout rules. As a basic concept, any expenses claimed as allocable to investment income would not also be reportable in this column. Direct charitable expenditures such as medical care, food, clothing, or cash to indigents or other members of a charitable class, books for a literacy program, printing expenses for producing the books, or other expenses associated with direct program activities are included here. Grants paid to other charitable organization, fundraising costs, and administrative expenses not allocable to investment income nor to adjusted gross income are reported in this column.

4.3 LINE-BY-LINE INSTRUCTIONS FOR REVENUES

(a) Line 1: Contributions, Gifts, and Grants Received

The total amount of voluntary donations the foundation receives during the year are reported on this line. The name, address, amount, date, and, in the case of property other than cash, a description of such property must be attached for gifts of $5,000 or more. The present value of pledges for future support reported in accordance with SFAS No. 116 are reported on this line. Distributions from split-interest trusts are included here for column (a) purposes. In-kind donations of time, services, or the use of property are not reported as support on page 1. They are not reported even if the services are recorded for financial reporting purposes in accordance with GAAP. The new Schedule B is not completed by private foundations.

The instructions to this line remind the foundation it must adhere to certain disclosure rules if it solicits contributions of more than $75 for which it gives the donor in return something of value (note such a transaction might constitute self-dealing as described in Chapter 5). Similarly, to enable its donors to claim a charitable contribution deduction for gifts to it, the foundation must provide a receipt acknowledging all gifts of $250 or more and indicating whether or not it provided goods and services to the contributor.

(b) Line 2: Contributions from Split-Interest Trusts

Distributions of income earned on, or attributable to, amounts placed in a "split-interest trust"[7] after October 26, 1969, are treated as investment income subject to the excise tax. Income earned on trust assets owned prior to that date, when this tax was introduced in Congress, are not subject to the excise tax.

(c) Line 3: Interest on Savings and Temporary Cash Investments

This line is mostly self-explanatory. The interest on a bank money market checking, savings, or other investments of the type reported on line 2 of the balance sheet is reported on this line; interest on a money market mutual fund might instead be reported on line 4. Interest earned on a program-related investment, on a note receivable from the sale of a foundation asset, or on an employee loan would be reported as other income on line 11.

(d) Line 4: Dividends and Interest from Securities

Income payments from investments in stocks, bonds, security loans, and other financial instruments regulated by state or federal securities law (of the type reported on line 10 of the balance sheet) are reported here. Dividends paid by a subsidiary operated as a program related investment would be reported on line 11. Capital gain dividends paid by a mutual fund are reported on line 6. Amounts received on tax-exempt government obligations are included only in column (c), not in (b).

(e) Line 5: Gross and Net Rental Income

Gross rent received from investment real or personal property of the type reported on line 11 of the balance sheet are reported on this line. Rents produced through exempt function programs, such as low-income housing, are also included on line 11. Rental of office space to other unaffiliated exempt organizations are usually reportable as rents on this line. Such rents are reported on line 11 only if the rental rate is well below the fair rental value of the property and the rental activity is conducted for a charitable purpose. Expenses directly connected with the rental income are deducted on lines 13 through 23.

(f) Line 6: Net Gain (Loss) from Sale of Assets

The gains or losses reported by the foundation for financial purposes from sales or other dispositions of all types of capital assets, including those held for investment, those held for exempt purposes, and those that produce unrelated business income, are reported on line 6 in column (a) only. By comparison, line 7 reports, in column (b) only, the gain subject to investment income tax. The detail of sales reported also on line 7 are not reported here. For sales of program-related assets not subject to tax only, a detailed schedule is attached reflecting the date acquired and sold, gross sales price and selling expenses, cost basis, and any depreciation. Unrealized gains reported for financial statement purposes under SFAS No. 124 is not included here but instead is shown as a reconciling item in Part III.

(g) Line 7: Capital Gain Net Income

Gains (short and long term—no losses) from the sale of property that ordinarily produces interest, dividends, royalties, or rents are taxed even if the property produced no current income; thus, the gain on a growth stock producing no dividends is also taxed. Details of these sales are reported in Part IV. Gains on program-related investments, for example, are not taxed because they are not held for investment even though the interest, rent, dividends, and royalties received currently are taxed. Other exceptions apply for certain gains.

For planning purposes, it is important to note that property received by the foundation as a donation retains the donor's basis.[8] Since the wealth of a foundation's creator often comes from business interests that are highly appreciated, the foundation receiving such wealth through gifts ends up paying tax on its contributor's gains, albeit at a much lower rate. If such property is distributed to the foundation's grant recipients, rather than cash from sale of the property, the gain is not taxed. Gain on investment property sold immediately after its receipt and before the foundation received current income is also taxed. See §4.9 for tax reduction ideas.

A foundation with marketable securities may benefit from year-end tax planning because of the rule that does not permit deduction of net capital losses against other investment income. Capital losses are deductible only to the extent of gains, and a net loss expires at year end with no carryover.

Even though the foundation is instructed to follow its book method of reporting income and expense in column (a), the tax rules require different reporting in certain respects for tax purposes. The basis of property the foundation received as a donation may be different for tax purposes than for financial purposes, as reflected in the discussion for lines 6 and 7. Thus, the capital gains shown in column (a) calculated using "book basis" may be different than those shown in columns (b) and (c) using the "tax basis." Also, columns (b) and (c) reflect no losses, and there is no provision for carryover of a net loss for the year.

(h) Line 8: Net Short-Term Capital Gains

Foundations that complete column (c) separately report net short-term capital gains. The gain increases the "adjusted net income" of a private operating foundation. If line 27c of column (c) is more than line 6 of Part X, adjusted net income determines the required distributions for a private operating foundation.

(i) Line 9: Income Modifications

This line also pertains exclusively to column (c) and mostly affects the required distributions for private operating foundations: repayments of amounts previously treated as qualifying distributions; proceeds of sales of assets, the purchase of which were treated as qualifying distributions; and the unused portion of funds previously set aside and claimed as a funds must be added. Essentially such recouped funds must be redistributed.

(j) Line 10: Gross Sales

This line is used by a foundation conducting a self-initiated project(s) that generates sales of inventory, such as an educational bookstore or handicapped worker factory. Because the excess business holdings rules generally prohibit a foundation's operation of a business, it is important that such revenues be reported as program-related business income. The gross profit reported in columns (c) should be reported in Part XVI-A in column (e). Such revenue also increases a private operating foundation's annual distribution requirement. This income is not entered into column (b) because it is not subject to the excise tax. The instructions suggest reporting of inventory items sold during fund-raising events (contribution portion is reported on line 1) on this line.

(k) Line 11: Other Income

All other types of income, taxable and nontaxable, are reported on this line. The four types of investment income subject to excise tax and not reported on lines 2 through 7 are entered on this line in columns (a), (b), and (c). Examples of such investment income include mineral royalties; interest on student or economic development loans not reported on line 3 or 4; rentals from low-cost housing or historic property; and interest, dividends, rents, or royalties distributed from a partnership or Subchapter S corporation.

Other kinds of income that are not subject to the investment income tax are also entered on line 11, but only in columns (a) and (c). Fees for services generated in an exempt activity, such as student tuition, testing fees, and ticket sales for cultural events, are good examples of this type of income. This type of income is entered in column (e) of Part XVI-A, and its relationship to the foundation's exempt activities must be explained. Unrealized gains or losses on investments carried at market value are reported in Part III, not here.

4.4 LINE-BY-LINE INSTRUCTIONS FOR EXPENDITURES

Good accounting is the key to successful completion of the expense columns on page 1 of Form 990-PF. Proper identification of those expenses directly attributable to management of the foundation affairs in general, its investments, and its grant-making and active charitable programs is a significant aspect of preparing Form 990-PF. Since foundations must pay a 1 to 2 percent tax rate on its investment income and normal tax rates on its unrelated business income, expenditure allocations are extremely important.[9] Proper identification of allocable expenses is the goal. Documentation and cost accounting records should be developed to capture revenues and costs in categories and to report them by function. A foundation often incurs expenses that support both its investments and charitable activities, such as the salary of its executive director and its office space. The portion of the compensation and fees paid to those persons is allocable to each function they perform. A foundation must develop techniques that provide verifiable bases on which expenses may be related to its grant-making and active charitable programs, its investment management activity, and its support service functions. To maintain such a functional classification of expenses, a foundation needs to study the cost accounting rules and allocation concepts discussed in Chapter 1§4.

The ordinary and necessary expenses of managing, accounting for, and reporting on investments producing the four taxable types of investment income are deductible in column (b) to arrive at net investment income subject to the excise tax. Basically, the rules are the same as the tax code provisions pertaining to deductible business and investment expenses.[10] In the best situation, foundation personnel keep track of the time they spend performing different functions so that directly attributable expenses can be entered into the respective columns. At a minimum, a foundation can report a reasonable portion, such as one fourth to one half of the total expense of its personnel and advisors, as attributable to its investment income in columns (b) and (c). The other three quarters or half is reflected in column (d) and adds to the amount of the foundation's qualifying distributions for the year. Upon examination, the IRS will request substantiation of such allocations.

(a) Line 13: Compensation of Officers, Directors, Trustees, Etc.

Column (a) of this line must agree with the detailed information in column (c) of line 1 of Part VIII reporting compensation paid to each and every officer, trustee, director, and foundation manager. The foundation has a burden to prove that amounts on this line are reasonable and do not result in self-dealing. The amounts paid for compensation on lines 13 through 15 must be apportioned between that paid in connection with managing and collecting investment income (column (b)) and managing the foundation's charitable programs (columns (c) and (d)). The names, addresses, and compensation paid to employees other than officers and directors are also detailed in Part VIII for those paid more than $50,000.

(b) Line 16: Legal, Accounting, and Other Professional Fees

Fees paid for professional services to outside consultants that are not employees are entered here. Management fees paid to investment or property managers, writers, researchers, or other independent contractors typically are reported on these lines. An attachment describing the type of service performed for the foundation and amount of expense for each is requested and, in addition, the name and address plus description in amount is entered again on Part VIII for those contractors paid in excess of $50,000.

(c) Line 17: Interest

A private foundation that borrows money for any purpose reports the interest on this line. Allocation of the interest to columns is a challenge and depends on the reason why the PF borrowed money. The unrelated debt-financed rules[11] make interest used to acquire investment property an expense of unrelated business income reportable only in column (a), as is the corresponding income. The net income from the indebted property is subject to normal income tax and is, therefore, not reported in column (b). A foundation that borrows money to pay its operating expenses would report the interest in columns (b), (c), and (d) and possibly face a challenge regarding its motivation for the borrowing. The self-dealing rules prohibit interest payments to the foundation's insiders.

(d) Line 18: Taxes

All types of taxes are reported in column (a), including excise taxes on investment income, property taxes on real estate, unrelated business income tax (UBIT), and payroll taxes for employees. Only taxes paid in regard to investment property are reported in column (b). Private operating foundations include both excise taxes and taxes paid on investment property in column (c). Only taxes paid on exempt function employees and property are reported in column (d). For nonoperating foundations, the excise tax reduces the foundation's distributable amount in Part XI, line 2a.

(e) Line 19: Depreciation

Depreciation is reported in column (a) using the same method the foundation follows for financial reporting purposes. Columns (b) and (c) depreciation must be calculated using the straight-line method and for mineral properties cost, but not percentage, depletion is allowed. The basis of property for this purpose is the same as that for calculating gain. Depreciation is entered in columns (b) and (c) only for the depreciation attributable to investment properties, the income of which is reported in the column.

Depreciation cannot be entered in column (d). The total acquisition cost of an asset used in conducting the foundation's charitable programs is treated as a qualifying distribution in the year in which the asset is acquired. The purchase price of exempt function assets is reported in Part XII, line 2, and adds to amounts treated as qualifying distributions for the year.

(f) Line 21: Travel, Conferences, and Meetings

Transportation fares, hotels, meals, and other costs of officers, employees, or others participating in meetings and conferences is reported here. Only 50 percent of the cost of meals paid in connection with investment income management activities is deductible in columns (b) and (c), a limitation that parallels the income tax rules for deductible meals. Honoraria or other fees paid to persons for services rendered in connection with such meetings should be reported on line 13, 14, or 16, not here.

A foundation incurring travel expenses should use a system of documentation designed to prove the travel's exempt or investment-related purpose. Expense vouchers reflecting the programmatic nature of the expenditures and evidence the absence of any personal expenses are desirable. Staff members using a foundation's vehicles or being reimbursed for use of a personal auto should maintain a mileage log to prove that auto usage is devoted to foundation affairs. Auto allowances for officers, directors, managers, and key and highly paid employees are included in column (e) of Part VIII.

(g) Line 25: Contributions, Gifts, Grants Paid

The total contributions or grants paid to other charitable organizations are reported on this line and in column (d) if the payments are qualifying distributions. A detailed report of grant recipients, their addresses, the purpose for each grant, and other information is entered in Part XV, line 3, as explained later. Grants or other payments that are not counted in calculating the foundation's qualifying distributions are not reported in column (d), such as those paid to a controlled organization, another private foundation, and certain pass-through grants. The following types of grant transactions are also excluded from column (d):

- Returned grant funds are not entered as a reduction, but added back in calculating net qualifying distributions for the year in Part XII.
- Set-asides are also entered in Part XII.
- Write-off of a program-related investment is also omitted because such investments are reported in Part XII in the year the investment is made.

For column (a) of this line, the foundation reports contributions and grants on the accounting method used for financial purposes. Column (d) must be prepared on a cash basis. As a result of the SFAS No. 116 accounting standards, many foundations now book unconditional pledges of support to other organizations in the year the pledge is made; consequently, such foundations, may now have a significant difference between columns (a) and (c).

(h) Line 26: Total Expenses and Disbursements

The total disbursements for charitable purposes shown in column (d) are transferred to Part XII, line 1a, to measure compliance with the minimum distributions requirement test.

(i) Line 27a: Excess of Revenues over Expenses and Disbursements

The difference between revenues and expenses reported for financial purposes shown here is carried to Part III, the analysis of changes in net assets or fund balances.

(j) Line 27b: Net Investment Income

The amount shown in column (b) is the foundation's taxable income that is carried to Part VI to calculate the excise tax.

(k) Line 27c: Adjusted Net Income

Only private operating foundations reflect an amount in this box. This number, if it is more than the amount shown on line 6 of Part X, is carried to Part XIV, line 2a, to determine satisfaction of the income test.

4.5 PART II—BALANCE SHEETS

Both the book value of the foundation assets and liabilities and the ending fair market value are presented in Part II. The total in column (c), line 16, must agree with item I on page 1, top left side. A considerable amount of detail is requested. The instructions should be read carefully for the following lines on the balance sheet:

Line 6	Insider receivables
Line 10	Investments—securities
Line 11	Investments—land, buildings, and equipment
Line 13	Investments—other
Line 14	Land, buildings, and equipment (devoted to exempt purposes)
Line 15	Other assets
Line 19	Support and revenue designated for future periods
Line 20	Loans from officers, directors, trustees, or other disqualified persons
Line 21	Mortgages and other notes payable

Certain lines in this part alert the IRS to problem issues, and in those cases detailed schedules are requested. For most loans receivable by or payable by the foundation, 10 detailed items of information are required: borrower's name and title, original amount, balance due, date of note, maturity date, repayment terms, interest rate, security provided by borrower, purpose of the loan, and description and fair market value of consideration furnished by the lender. This information is submitted to enable the IRS to evaluate the presence of self-dealing.

Schedules for depreciable assets should be prepared to coordinate with the information required to be attached for Parts I and II. Likewise, receivable and payable information should bear a reasonable relationship to the amount reported on line 17 of Part I for interest expense.

The same method used by the foundation for maintaining its normal accounting books and records is followed in completing this part. The fair market value for each category of asset is reported in column (c) for all foundations with assets of $5,000 or more. Only a total is entered on line 16 for a foundation with less than $5,000. If detailed schedules are requested, they need only be furnished for the year-end numbers. The instructions for this part are quite good and need not be repeated here. Foundations following SFAS No. 124[12] that mark their assets up or down to market value may essentially have identical numbers in columns (b) and (c).

4.6 PART III—ANALYSIS OF CHANGES IN NET WORTH OR FUND BALANCES

The information reported on page 1 for Form 990-PF purposes is reconciled to the Part II balance sheet in this part. The information in Part II is reporting according to the accounting method under which the foundation keeps its financial records, which may not match the tax reporting rules applicable to Part I. Revenues and expenses of this type include:

- Donated services associated with a capitalized asset, such as fees donated by the architects in connection with a foundation building
- Unrealized gain or loss in carrying value of marketable securities and other investment assets under SFAS No. 124
- Change in accounting treatment of charitable pledges receivable or payable as required under SFAS No. 116
- A prior-period accounting adjustment not corrected on an amended return because it is immaterial

Sometimes, a foundation discovers a mistake was made in a prior-year return that requires correction. Dependent on the significance of the mistake, an amended return must be considered. An under- or overreporting of investment income calculated in Part VI signals a need for amendment. As a practical matter, a modest mistake can be adjusted in the currently filed return by increases or decreasing revenues or expenses. A prior-year mistake that affects a foundation's excess distribution carryover can also be corrected by attaching an explanation of the adjustment to the return and accurately reflecting the carryover in Part XIII. A change affecting the UBIT would necessitate the filing of an amended return. An automatic change of accounting method is allowed for a foundation that changes its accounting method to conform with SFAS No. 116 reporting of grants paid and received.

4.7 PART IV—CAPITAL GAINS AND LOSSES FOR TAX ON INVESTMENT INCOME

Capital gains and losses for excise tax purposes are, as a general rule, imposed on the sale or exchange of property capable of producing interest, dividends, rents, and royalties—the types of investment income also subject to the excise tax. Transactions involving other types of assets, particularly exempt function assets or program-related investments, are not reported in this part. Property that is distributed to charitable recipients, rather than sold, is not reported and any gain is not taxed. For a foundation with substantially appreciated property, this rule provides an important tax planning opportunity.[13]

The gain or loss is calculated by subtracting the amount of sales proceeds the foundation received less the amount the foundation paid to purchase the property, adjusted for depreciation reserves, amortization, and selling expenses.[14] However, basis for property the foundation received as a gift is equal to the amount the donor paid for the gifted property, or what is called the donor's tax or carryover basis. Property received through a bequest is valued as of the date of death or the alternate valuation date for the decedent.[15]

Only the total capital gain net income is carried from this schedule to column (b) and added to taxable investment income. The short-term portion of the gain is reported only in column (c) and increases the amount of adjusted gross income that affects the amount of direct charitable activity expenditures a private operating foundation is required to pay out for the year. A net capital loss for the year is not carried to Part I and is *not* deductible against other investment income, and no capital loss carryover to a subsequent year is allowed.[16]

4.8 REPORTS UNIQUE TO PRIVATE FOUNDATIONS

To measure compliance with and enforce the special rules unique to private foundations, Form 990-PF contains 15 parts. The first five, discussed above, essentially report the financial transactions for the year in a financial statement format. The other 10 parts explore particular issues and ask questions that indicate satisfaction of requirements and prompt attachments of additional information. Failure to furnish a complete report regarding an expenditure responsibility ageement, for example, results in a taxable expenditures. Each foundation should seek to clearly reflect its mission in completing these parts. Its charitable programs are described and detailed to furnish the reader a clear picture of the type of grants and activities it supports. Not only is the form available for all to see and request a copy of, the information is widely available in directories—paper and electronic—published throughout the country as an aid to grant seekers.[17] The volume and quality of grant requests the foundation receives is influenced by the manner in which information is presented on its Form 990-PF.

4.9 PART V—REDUCING THE TAX RATE

A private foundation can cut its tax in half (from 2 percent to 1 percent of net investment income) by essentially giving the tax to charity. If the foundation's current-year qualifying distributions (Part XII) exceed a hypothetical number (past five-year average payout percentage times average fair market value of assets for the year of calculation plus 1 percent tax for the current year), the tax is reduced to 1 percent. Achieving this reduction is complicated because the two most important factors are not known until the last day of the taxable year—line 4 (the average month-end value of investment assets) and probably line 8 (qualifying distributions). Except for the most generous foundations whose distributions continually increase year to year, reducing the excise tax requires very careful planning. A newly established private foundation cannot qualify for the reduced tax rate in its first year.[18]

4.10 PART VI—CALCULATING THE EXCISE TAX

Except for exempt private operating foundations and certain terminating foundations, private foundations pay a tax of 2 percent, or possibly 1 percent, on their net investment income reported in Part I, column (b), line 27b. Foreign foundations that receive more than 15 percent of their investment income from

U.S. sources pay a 4 percent tax on such income. A foundation converting itself to a public charity under the 60-month termination rules is excused from paying the excise tax. Such a foundation signs an agreement to extend the statute of limitations for collecting the excise tax in the event that it fails to receive sufficient amounts of public support. A copy of the signed consent agreement is attached to the return each year during the termination period, and Part VI, line 1, should refer to the attachment and state the tax is not applicable.[19]

If the annual tax is under $500, it can be paid with a check accompanying the return as it is filed. If the tax is over $500, it is paid in advance through the estimated tax system, using the depository receipt system at a banking institution. Form 990-W is used to compute the tax. Foundations with over $1 million of income must make quarterly payments based on actual income earned during the second, third, and fourth quarters, similar to the *large corporation* rules. Penalties are due for failure to pay a sufficient amount by the quarterly due dates.[20] Form 2220 is attached to Form 990-PF to calculate the penalty. Penalties are also imposed for failure to deposit taxes with a federal tax deposit coupon (Form 8109) at a qualified bank or federal reserve bank.

4.11 PART VII-A—PROOF OF ONGOING QUALIFICATION FOR EXEMPTION

The information desired by the IRS to evaluate a private foundation's qualification for ongoing tax exemption is solicited by 13 questions in this part and the five in Part B. Certain answers can cause serious problems for the foundation, as described below. The questions essentially "fish," or look for failures to comply with the tax code and regulations and IRS policy rules pertaining to private foundations. The IRS is reportedly guided by the answers to certain questions in choosing suitable candidates for examination. Certain answers must be "no," as described below. Other questions, like 2 and 4, indicate that other filings are required. Attention to the impact of the answer to each question is desirable. The IRS instructions to the form provide no guidance regarding the answers to questions 2, 4, 5, 7, 11, or 12.

(a) Line 1: Did the Foundation Intervene in an Election or Conduct Any Lobbying?

Answering any of the three parts of this question "yes" is tantamount to admitting that the exempt status should be questioned and certainly a taxable expenditure has occurred. All §501(c)(3) organizations are strictly prohibited from seeking to influence an election.[21] Though public charities may spend a limited amount of money on lobbying efforts, private foundations may spend nothing to attempt to influence legislation. All of the parts of this question, including (c), should be "no."

(b) Line 2: Did the Foundation Have Activities Not Previously Reported to the IRS?

A "yes" answer to this question alerts the IRS to review organizational changes that the form instructs the foundation to explain in a detailed attachment. The question is sometimes hard to answer when the foundation's activity has evolved or expanded, but has not necessarily dramatically or totally changed in its focus or overall purpose. As an example, assume a grant-making foundation previously supported soup kitchen programs to feed the poor and has begun to redirect its grants to community gardens that teach the poor to raise their own food.

The question requests detailed disclosure for any new foundation activities. A "yes" response does not constitute a request for IRS approval for the new activity, but simply a mechanism to keep the IRS informed with a detailed description of the changes that is attached. In fact, a "yes" answer does not customarily result in an IRS response. If the foundation board or trustees desire written IRS approval for conduct of the new projects or change in purpose, a formal ruling request must be filed with the Key District Office.[22] Such a submission, however, is not required or encouraged by the IRS.

(c) Line 3: Have the Organizational Documents Been Changed?

A conformed copy, meaning one accompanied by a foundation official's sworn statement that it is a "true and correct copy of the original," of any nonprofit charter, trust instrument, or bylaw changes must be attached. The same issues regarding a desire for IRS positive approval for such changes, as discussed under line 2, are raised by a "yes" answer to this question.

(d) Line 4: Did the Foundation Have More Than $1,000 of Unrelated Business Gross Income?

If question 4(a) is answered "yes," question 4(b) must also be answered "yes." The answer to this question should be coordinated with Part XVI-A. If an amount in excess of $1,000 appears in column (b), the answer to this question should be "yes." This question can be confusing since the investment income private foundations earn is technically defined as unrelated trade or business income.[23] Most investment income, however, is modified or excluded from unrelated business taxable income, is not required to be reported on Form 990-T, and should appear in column (d) of Part XVI-A.

(e) Line 5: Did the Foundation Liquidate, Terminate, Dissolve, or Substantially Contract?

The tax code specifically requires a private foundation to notify the Secretary of the Treasury of its intention to, and the fashion in which it plans to, cease to operate.[24] A statement explaining the facts and circumstances of any of the four named situations must be attached. For a full liquidation or termination, a certified copy of the plan with a schedule listing the names and addresses of all recipients of assets, along with a description of the nature and value of such assets, is required. According to the IRS instructions, disposition of 25 percent or more of the fair market value of the foundation's assets is a substantial contraction. Prior permission to make a substantial contraction, short of totally terminating the foundation, is not literally required by the tax code or the IRS instructions, although the foundation managers may deem it prudent to seek such approval.

(f) Line 6: Does the Foundation's Governing Instrument Satisfy §508(e) Requirements?

This question must be answered "yes." A private foundation cannot qualify and be recognized as an exempt organization by the IRS unless its governing instruments prohibit its engaging in transactions that would cause it to incur excise taxes for entering into a self-dealing transaction, making taxable expenditures, maintaining excess business holdings, or buying a jeopardizing investment. The requirement can be met in two ways. Many foundations' governing instruments actually contain required language. Instead, some foundations rely on local law. Most states passed legislation in the early 1970s to automatically incorporate the required language for private foundations based in the state.

(g) Line 7: Did the Foundation Have at Least $5,000 in Assets During the Year?

If the answer to this question is "yes," the foundation must report the fair market value of its assets in Part II by completing column (c). Such a modestly sized foundation is also excused from completing Part XV. The data submitted in Part XV is compiled and published in directories containing information for grant seekers.

(h) Line 8: Submit Information Regarding State Filings

This question has two parts. The foundation must enter the name(s) of state(s) to which the foundation reports and in which the foundation is registered as a charitable organization. Note that even if a private foundation is not registered to do business in a particular state, state filings may be required if the foundation has solicited and received donations from persons residing in the state. A foundation with assets of $5,000 or more (answers question 7 "yes") is required to furnish a copy of Form 990-PF and Form 4720, if any, to the attorney general of:

- Each state listed in the answer to question 8(a)
- The state in which its principal office is located
- The state in which the foundation was incorporated or created

The state copy must be submitted at the same time the federal form is filed. The foundation must also furnish a copy of its Form 990-PF to the attorney general of any state that requests it whether or not it is registered in that state.

(i) Line 9: Is this Organization a Private Operating Foundation?

A "yes" answer to this question alerts the IRS that the foundation will complete Part XIV, instead of Part XIII, to determine satisfaction of charitable pay out tests *and* that the foundation must complete column (c) of Part I. A private operating foundation spends its money to conduct its own active programs, rather than granting money to other organizations.

(j) Line 10: Did Any Person(s) Become Substantial Contributors During the Year?

If the answer to this question is "yes," the foundation is prompted to attach a schedule listing their names and addresses. Note for those contributing $5,000 or more during the year, the same information plus details regarding the gift are attached to Part I, line 1. Also their names are listed in Part XI.

(k) Line 11(a): Did Anyone Request to See the Foundation's Form 990-PF?

(l) Line 11(b): If the Answer to 11(a) is "Yes," Did the Foundation Cooperate?

The answer to Question 11(b) should never be "no." A penalty is imposed for failure to comply with the return disclosure rules outlined in Chapter 1.3.

4.12 QUESTIONS SEEKING EVIDENCE THAT NO SANCTIONS APPLY

A "yes" answer to a question in this part signals the IRS that the foundation may have violated one of the rules in §§4941 through 4945. An entry in the "yes" column requires that the foundation file Form 4720 and possibly an excise tax for the forbidden act. A "yes" answer to question 5c requires attachment of an Expenditure Responsibility Report.

The labyrinth of don'ts (but it may be okay if you do's) regarding self-dealing should be studied carefully if any of the question 1 answers are "yes." To avoid an excise tax for self-dealing, the foundation must be able to answer "no" to question 1b. Similarly, any "yes" answers to the (a) portions of questions 2, 3, or 5 need to be answered with a "no" in 2b, 3b, and 5b to signal that, though a potential violation of the rules occurred, an exception applied. The answer to both questions 4a and 4b should be "no." Readers might find it useful to study Chapter 6 of *Private Foundations*[25] to aid in answering question 2,

Chapter 7 for question 3, Chapter 8 for question 4, and Chapter 9 for question 5.

4.13 PART VIII—INFORMATION ABOUT OFFICERS, DIRECTORS, TRUSTEES, FOUNDATION MANAGERS, HIGHLY PAID EMPLOYEES, AND CONTRACTORS

To assist the IRS in detecting self-dealing and private inurement, details of compensation are to be reported. Line 1 of this part must be completed to list all of the foundation's officials, regardless of the number, and whether or not they receive any compensation or expense reimbursements. Foundation managers are those persons who have responsibilities or powers similar to those of officers, directors, and trustees. A foundation's executive director and chief financial officer are usually considered managers. The address at which officials would prefer the IRS contact them (can be the foundation's address) is requested.

For a foundation that lacks precise time records regarding its volunteer officials, it is suitable to note that they spent "part time" attending to foundation affairs. For an official that is compensated, the entry in column (b) has other import and should, if possible, be entered with some precision. The relationship between the amount of time spent and the compensation paid could indicate that the foundation has made a taxable expenditure and a self-dealing transaction.

Total compensation paid to persons serving on the governing board, for all services rendered, is to be reported, whether they are employees or independent contractors. For persons serving in more than one position (e.g., both as a director and officer or staff member), the compensation for each respective position should be separately presented. The instructions for preparation of this part are the same as those for Part V of Form 990 discussed in Chapter 2§6.

4.14 PART IX-A AND B—SUMMARY OF CHARITABLE ACTIVITIES AND PROGRAM-RELATED INVESTMENTS

In this part, the foundation has the opportunity to describe its exempt purposes and the achievements of the programs it conducts. To describe its accomplishments, the services provided are summarized along with numerical data. How many children were counseled, classes taught, meals served, patients healed, sites restored, books published, conferences convened, research papers produced, or similar data is reported for the foundation's four major projects.

If numerical results are not pertinent or available, the project objectives and the long-range plans can be described. Reasonable estimates can be furnished if the exact number of recipients is not known. A foundation conducting research on heart disease and testing a controlled group of 100 women over a five-year period would say so. Similarly, assuming the foundation commissions a study of an area's history and expects the project to take 10 years, it could report four scholars have been hired to annually deliver a minimum of 100 pages each, with citations and appropriate photographic documentation or other archival materials. How the documents will be eventually published is not known, so the number of copies and eventual public benefit cannot be measured. However, the research modality can be described to evidence the work's educational nature.

Program-related investments made during the year are reported in Part IX-B. For a foundation with ongoing investments, this report should be coordinated with the balance sheet reporting and expenditure responsibility reporting requirements.

4.15 PART X—MINIMUM INVESTMENT RETURN

This part calculates the first factor used to determine the foundation's required amount of annual charitable giving—the average fair value of the foundation's investment assets times 5 percent. Cash and marketable securities for which market quotes are available are valued monthly and average for the year. Partnership interests and unlist securities are valued annually. Land and mineral properties are valued every five years. Assets used in conducting the foundation's charitable programs are not included. Assets held for less than a full year are prorated. The 5 percent rate is also prorated on a daily basis for a foundation filing for less than a full year.

4.16 PART XI—DISTRIBUTABLE AMOUNT

This part begins with the calculated minimum investment return from Part X. The excise tax on investment income is next allowed to reduce the required charitable payout. Recoveries of grants claimed as a distribution in a past year are added back. A controversial add-on of split-interest trust income is reflected on line 4b. Private operating foundations do not complete this part. The resulting sum is the amount required to be distributed in the next fiscal year that is carried to Part XIII.

4.17 PART XII—QUALIFYING DISTRIBUTIONS

Finally, in this part, the foundation tallies up the amount of its current-year disbursements that are counted toward its mandatory distribution requirement that is calculated in Part XIII or XIV (for private operating foundations). Expenditures that count for this test are reported in column (d) on page 1, as discussed in §4.2, and mostly include grants paid out to other charitable organizations. Certain commitments to spend money in the future, called *set-asides*, may be counted. Acquisition of assets used for charitable purposes and program-related investments are counted. Returned grants and sales of assets previously counted as charitable disbursements are added to the requirement. The number on line 4 carries to Part V, line 8; Part XIII, line 4; and Part XIV, line 2c.

4.18 PART XIII—UNDISTRIBUTED INCOME

This part surveys five years of grant-making history to determine if the foundation has expended sufficient funds on charitable giving to meet the IRC §4942 tests. If this schedule reflects a balance remaining on line 2(b), 6(d), or 6(e), Form 4720 should be filed to calculate the penalty on underdistributions. The order in which distributions are applied is important.[26]

Qualifying distributions entered on line 4 should be the same as on line 4 of Part XII, but the trick is knowing how to apply the total among the four columns and when a distribution is charged to corpus. As the form's design indicates, current-year distributions are first applied to column (c), the remaining undistributed income from the immediately preceding year. This can create a cash flow problem when a foundation (or the IRS) finds that deficient distributions from the past must be corrected. The current-year required payments must be paid before the correction can be made. Next, corrections of prior-year deficiencies are applied to line 4(b) (not required).

A foundation might elect to apply current-year grants to corpus on line

4c, column (a), under certain circumstances. For example, the corpus election is appropriate for a foundation redistributing a donation for which the contributor desires the maximum deduction. The point is that the private foundation cannot count a gift attributable to a pass-through contribution as part of its qualifying distributions. Other instances in which a corpus election is appropriate involve grants paid to a controlled public charity and pass-through grants to another foundation. To make the corpus election, a foundation manager signs a statement declaring that the foundation is making an election and designating whether it is out of a specific year's prior income or corpus.

4.19 PART XIV—PRIVATE OPERATING FOUNDATIONS

Private operating foundations submit information to calculate their ongoing qualification based on four years of their qualifying distributions, income, and assets. The terms and rules applicable to this special type of foundation are somewhat complex and should be carefully studied before this part is completed.[27]

4.20 PART XV—SUPPLEMENTARY INFORMATION

Lines 1 and 2 of this part are completed for foundations with assets of $5,000 or more, except those foreign foundations whose U.S. source income is entirely investment income. The name of any foundation manager who is also a substantial contributor who has donated more than $5,000 to the foundation is listed. Those foundation managers who own 10 percent or more of the stock of a corporation in which the foundation also has a 10 percent or greater interest is listed.

The foundation reveals information regarding its grant programs: to whom a request is addressed, the form (if any) in which applications should be submitted, what should be attached, the deadlines, and any restrictions and limitations on awards, such as geographic area, subject, kinds of institutions, and so on. Grant seekers use the information submitted in this part to select the PFs to whom they will make applications for funding. Because the return is now going onto the Internet at Guidestar.org, this part should be very carefully prepared. The Foundation Center and other organizations publish books and electronic media that also contain this information. Public libraries in many cities cooperate in making Forms 990-PF available for public inspection. Most often, inspectors look at this and the following part to find out what kind of grants a PF makes.

Foundations that make grants only to preselected charities and do not accept unsolicited requests for funds can check the blank on line 2. Because the paper load for some foundations is immense, there is a temptation in some cases to check the box although it does not necessarily apply. There are ongoing philosophical discussions about the pros and cons of the box: Should a private foundation with unrestricted funds close the door to grant applicants by checking the blank?

4.21 PART XV—GRANTS AND CONTRIBUTIONS PAID DURING THE YEAR OR APPROVED FOR FUTURE PAYMENT

Line 3 of this part lists grants paid during the year and approved for future payment. The total under 3a should agree with the amount reported on line 25, column (d). The line 3b total of future grant commitments is provided for public inspection purposes only, and does not necessarily carry to any other part of the form. A foundation using generally accepted accounting principles would reflect a liability on the balance sheet in Part II, line 18, for grants payable with which the number should agree. Note that this amount for SFAS No. 116 financial purposes will be equal to the discounted present value of the pledges, not necessarily the gross face amount of the pledge.

The presentation of this information is extremely important for several reasons. Grant information is contained in the widely circulated local, state, and national directories published for grant seekers, in books and electronic media, and now on the Internet. The foundation has an opportunity to paint a picture of its mission and reflect the scope and depth of its grant making. Organizing the grant payments to arrive at subtotals for categories, such as feeding the poor, crime prevention, education, culture, and so on, for example, can result in improved grant applications. At the same time, it satisfies the IRS request that the purpose of the grant be described in the second-from-the-left column.

From a tax standpoint, the middle column in this part is very important and informs the IRS of the "foundation status of the recipient." What this means is the grantee's classification as a public or private charity under IRC §509, as defined in Chapter 3§3. If the grantee is a public charity, no other information is reported in Form 990-PF concerning the grant. If, instead, the grantee is another private foundation, question 5a(4) in Part VII-B will be answered "yes." Additionally, the foundation must exercise "expenditure responsibility," answer question 5a(c) "yes," and attach a detailed report to the return.

The relationship, if any, between individual grant recipients and any foundation manager or substantial contributor is also revealed. Any answer other than "none" raises several issues. The first question is whether self-dealing might have occurred because a payment was made to a disqualified person. Additionally, payment to related individuals might indicate that the foundation's scholarship payments are not made on the required "objective and nondiscriminatory basis." Finally, a grant to a controlled organization may not be a qualifying distribution.

4.22 PART XVI-A—ANALYSIS OF INCOME-PRODUCING ACTIVITY

At the behest of Congress, Part XVI-A was added to Form 990-PF in 1989 as an audit trail to find unrelated business income. Unrelated income is reported alongside related income in Part I, and this part is designed to fragment the two different types and alert the IRS when Form 990-T should be filed to report and identify. The IRS instructions contain a helpful chart comparing the lines of Part I to the lines for entry on this part. Suggestions for completing this part can be found in Chapter 2§8.

4.23 PART XVII—INFORMATION REGARDING TRANSFERS TO AND TRANSACTIONS AND RELATIONSHIPS WITH NONCHARITABLE EXEMPT ORGANIZATIONS

This part was designed for Form 990, does not apply to many private foundations, and was added in 1988 in response to a congressional mandate that the IRS search for connections between private foundations and non–501(c)(3) organizations. The IRS is scouting for relationships that allow benefits, or the use of a foundation's assets, to flow from the foundation to a noncharitable exempt organization. Instructions for its completion can be found in Chapter 3§10.

Part XVIII has been dropped from the return for 2000 because a newspaper notice is no longer required as explained in Chapter 1§3.

Appendix 4A

Form **990-PF**

Department of the Treasury
Internal Revenue Service

Return of Private Foundation

or Section 4947(a)(1) Nonexempt Charitable Trust
Treated as a Private Foundation

Note: The organization may be able to use a copy of this return to satisfy state reporting requirements.

OMB No. 1545-0052

2000

For the calendar year 2000, or tax year beginning , and ending

G Check all that apply: ☐ Initial return ☐ Final return ☐ Amended return ☐ Address change ☐ Name change

Use the IRS label. Otherwise, please print or type.

Name of organization: **Environmentalist Fund**

Number and street (or P.O. box number if mail is not delivered to street address): **1111 Any Street**

City or town: **Hometown** State: **Texas** Zip + 4: **77777-7777**

A Employer identification number: **77-7777777**

B Telephone number (see page 9 of the instr.): **(444) 444-4466**

C If exemption application is pending, check here ☐

D 1. Foreign organizations, check here ☐

2. Organizations meeting the 85% test, check ☐

E If private foundation status was terminated under section 507(b)(1)(A), check here ☐

F If the foundation is in a 60-month termination under section 507(b)(1)(B), check here ☐

H Check organization: ☒ Section 501(c)(3) exempt private foundation ☐ Section 4947(a)(1) nonexempt charitable trust ☐ Other taxable private foundation

I Fair market value of all assets at end of year (from Part II, column (c), line 16) 2,281,200

J Accounting method: ☒ Cash ☐ Accrual ☐ Other (specify) ________ (Part I, col. (d) must be on cash basis.)

	Part I Analysis of Revenue and Expenses (The total of amounts in columns (b), (c), and (d) may not necessarily equal the amounts in column (a).)	(a) Revenue and expenses per books	(b) Net investment income	(c) Adjusted net income	(d) Disbursements for charitable purposes (cash basis only)
Revenue	1 Contributions, gifts, grants, etc., received	300,000			
	2 Distributions from split-interest trusts				
	3 Interest on savings and temporary cash investments	4,000	4,000	Not	
	4 Dividends and interest from securities	160,000	160,000	Applicable	
	5a Gross rents				
	b (Net rental income/loss ________)				
	6 Net gain or (loss) from sale of assets not on line 10	30,000			
	7 Capital gain net income (Part IV, line 2)		50,000		
	8 Net short-term capital gain				
	9 Income modifications				
	10a Gross sales less returns				
	b Less: C.O.G.S.				
	c Gross profit or (loss) (attach schedule)				
	11 Other income (attach schedule)				
	12 Total. Add lines 1 through 11	494,000	214,000		
Expenses	13 Compensation of officers, directors, trustees, etc.				
	14 Other employee salaries and wages				
	15 Pension plans, employee benefits				
	16a Legal fees (attach schedule)	5,000	2,500		2,500
	b Accounting fees (attach schedule)	5,000	2,500		2,500
	c Other professional fees	6,000	6,000		
	17 Interest				
	18 Taxes (attach schedule)	4,000			
	19 Depreciation and depletion				
	20 Occupancy				
	21 Travel, conferences, and meetings	2,000	500		1,500
	22 Printing and publications	2,800	600		2,200
	23 Other expenses (attach schedule)				
	24 Total operating and administrative expenses. Add lines 13 through 23	24,800	12,100		8,700
	25 Contributions, gifts, grants paid	310,000			310,000
	26 Total expenses and disbursements. Add lines 24 and 25	334,800	12,100		318,700
	27 Subtract line 26 from line 12:				
	a Excess of revenue over expenses and disbursements	159,200			
	b Net investment income (if negative, enter -0-)		201,900		
	c Adjusted net income (if negative, enter -0-)				

For Paperwork Reduction Act Notice, see the instructions. (HTA) Form 990-PF (2000)

Form 990-PF (2000) Environmentalist Fund 77-7777777 Page 2

Part II Balance Sheets	Attached schedules and amounts in the description column should be for end-of-year amounts only.	Beginning of year (a) Book Value	End of year (b) Book Value	(c) Fair Market Value
Assets	1 Cash - non-interest bearing			
	2 Savings and temporary cash investments	82,000	111,200	111,200
	3 Accounts receivable			
	Less: allowance for doubtful accounts			
	4 Pledges receivable			
	Less: allowance for doubtful accounts			
	5 Grants receivable			
	6 Receivables due from officers, directors, trustees, and other disqualified persons (attach schedule) (see page 15 of the instructions)			
	7 Other notes and loans receivable			
	Less: allowance for doubtful accounts			
	8 Inventories for sale or use			
	9 Prepaid expenses and deferred charges			
	10a Investments - U.S. and state government obligations			
	b Investments - corporate stock (attach schedule)	535,555	665,555	2,170,000
	c Investments - corporate bonds (attach schedule)			
	11 Investments - land, buildings, and equipment: basis			
	Less: accumulated depreciation			
	12 Investments - mortgage loans			
	13 Investments - other (attach schedule)			
	14 Land, buildings, and equipment: basis			
	Less: accumulated depreciation			
	15 Other assets (describe)			
	16 Total assets (to be completed by all filers-see page 16 of the instructions. Also, see page 1, item I)	617,555	776,755	2,281,200
Liabilities	17 Accounts payable and accrued expenses			
	18 Grants payable			
	19 Deferred revenue			
	20 Loans from officers, directors, trustees, and other disqualified persons			
	21 Mortgages and other notes payable (attach schedule)			
	22 Other liabilities (describe)			
	23 Total liabilities (add lines 17 through 22)			
Net Assets	**Organizations that follow SFAS 117, check here and complete lines 24 through 26 and lines 30 and 31.** ☐			
	24 Unrestricted			
	25 Temporarily restricted			
	26 Permanently restricted			
	Organizations that do not follow SFAS 117, check here and complete lines 27 through 31. X			
	27 Capital stock, trust principal, or current funds	617,555	776,755	
	28 Paid-in or capital surplus, or land, bldg., and equipment fund			
	29 Retained earnings, accumulated income, endowment, or other funds			
	30 Total net assets or fund balances (see page 17 of the instructions)	617,555	776,755	
	31 Total liabilities and net assets/fund balances (see page 17 of the instructions)	617,555	776,755	

Part III Analysis of Changes in Net Assets or Fund Balances

1	Total net assets or fund balances at beginning of year - Part II, column (a), line 30 (must agree with end-of-year figure reported on prior year's return)	1	617,555
2	Enter amount from Part I, line 27a	2	159,200
3	Other increases not included in line 2 (itemize)	3	
4	Add lines 1, 2, and 3	4	776,755
5	Decreases not included in line 2 (itemize)	5	
6	Total net assets or fund balances at end of year (line 4 minus line 5) - Part II, column (b), line 30	6	776,755

Form 990-PF (2000)

Form 990-PF (2000) Environmentalist Fund 77-7777777 Page 3

Part IV Capital Gains and Losses for Tax on Investment Income

	(a) List and describe the kind(s) of property sold (e.g., real estate, 2-story brick warehouse; or common stock, 200 shs. MLC Co.)	(b) How acquired P - Purchase D - Donation	(c) Date acquired (mo., day, yr.)	(d) Date sold (mo., day, yr.)
1a	1,700 shares Clean Air Industries	D	December 1, 19xx	July 1, 20xx
b				
c				
d				
e				

	(e) Gross sales price	(f) Depreciation allowed (or allowable)	(g) Cost or other basis plus expense of sale	(h) Gain or (loss) (e) plus (f) minus (g)
a	50,000		-0-	50,000
b				
c				
d				
e				

Complete only for assets showing gain in column (h) and owned by the foundation on 12/31/69

	(i) F.M.V. as of 12/31/69	(j) Adjusted basis as of 12/31/69	(k) Excess of col. (i) over col. (j), if any	(l) Gains (Col. (h) gain minus col. (k), but not less than -0-) or Losses (from col.(h))
a				50,000
b				
c				
d				
e				

2 Capital gain net income or (net capital loss). If gain, also enter in Part I, line 7. If (loss), enter -0- in Part I, line 7 — 2 — 50,000

3 Net short-term capital gain or (loss) as defined in sections 1222(5) and (6): If gain, also enter in Part I, line 8, column (c) (see pages 13 and 17 of the instructions). If (loss), enter -0- in Part I, line 8 3

Part V Qualification Under Section 4940(e) for Reduced Tax on Net Investment Income

(For optional use by domestic private foundations subject to the section 4940(a) tax on net investment income.)

If section 4940(d)(2) applies, leave this part blank.

Was the organization liable for the section 4942 tax on the distributable amount of any year in the base period? . . . . Yes [ ] No [X]

If "Yes," the organization does not qualify under section 4940(e). Do not complete this part.

1 Enter the appropriate amount in each column for each year; see page 16 of the instructions before making any entries.

(a) Base period years Calendar year (or tax year beginning in)	(b) Adjusted qualifying distributions	(c) Net value of noncharitable-use assets	(d) Distribution ratio (col. (b) divided by col. (c))
1999	278,200	1,800,000	.154600000
1998	212,800	1,600,000	.133000000
1997	221,800	1,400,000	.158400000
1996	109,200	1,200,000	.091000000
1995	90,000	1,000,000	.090000000

2	Total of line 1, column (d)	2	0.627
3	Average distribution ratio for the 5-year base period - divide the total on line 2 by 5, or by the number of years the foundation has been in existence if less than 5 years	3	0.1254
4	Enter the net value of noncharitable-use assets for 2000 from Part X, line 5	4	2,019,250
5	Multiply line 4 by line 3	5	253,214
6	Enter 1% of net investment income (1% of Part I, line 27b)	6	2,019
7	Add lines 5 and 6	7	255,233
8	Enter qualifying distributions from Part XII, line 4	8	318,700

If line 8 is equal to or greater than line 7, check the box in Part VI, line 1b, and complete that part using a 1% tax rate. See the Part VI instructions on page 18.

Form 990-PF (2000)

Form 990-PF (2000) Environmentalist Fund 77-7777777 Page 4

Part VI Excise Tax on Investment Income (Section 4940(a), 4940(b), 4940(e), or 4948 - see page 16)

1a	Exempt operating foundations described in section 4940(d)(2), check here and [ ] enter "N/A" on line 1. Date of ruling letter: ________ (attach copy of ruling letter if necessary)		
b	Domestic organizations that meet the section 4940(e) requirements in Part V, check here [X] and enter 1% of Part I, line 27b	1	2,019
c	All other domestic organizations enter 2% of line 27b. Exempt foreign organizations enter 4% of Part I, line 12, col. (b)		
2	Tax under section 511(domestic section 4947(a)(1) trusts and taxable foundations only. Others enter -0-)	2	
3	Add lines 1 and 2	3	2,019
4	Subtitle A (income) tax (domestic section 4947(a)(1) trusts and taxable foundations only. Others enter -0-)	4	
5	Tax based on investment income. Subtract line 4 from line 3. If zero or less, enter -0-	5	2,019
6	Credits/Payments:		
a	2000 estimated tax payments and 1999 overpayment credited to 2000 — 6a: 2,400		
b	Exempt foreign organizations - tax withheld at source — 6b		
c	Tax paid with application for extension of time to file (Form 2758) — 6c		
d	Backup withholding erroneously withheld — 6d		
7	Total credits and payments. Add lines 6a through 6d	7	2,400
8	Enter any PENALTY for underpayment of estimated tax. Check here if Form 2220 [ ] is attached.	8	
9	TAX DUE. If the total of lines 5 and 8 is more than line 7, enter AMOUNT OWED	9	
10	OVERPAYMENT. If line 7 is more than the total of lines 5 and 8, enter the AMOUNT OVERPAID	10	381
11	Enter the amount of line 10 to be: Credited to 2001 estimated tax 381 Refunded	11	

Part VII-A Statements Regarding Activities

			Yes	No
1a	During the tax year, did the organization attempt to influence any national, state, or local legislation or did it participate or intervene in any political campaign?	1a		X
b	Did it spend more than $100 during the year (either directly or indirectly) for political purposes (see page 17 of the instructions for definition)?	1b		X
	If the answer is "Yes" to 1a or 1b, attach a detailed description of the activities and copies of any materials published or distributed by the organization in connection with the activities.			
c	Did the organization file Form 1120-POL for this year?	1c		X
d	Enter the amount (if any) of tax on political expenditures (section 4955) imposed during the year: (1) On the organization. -0- (2) On organization managers. -0-			
e	Enter the reimbursement (if any) paid by the organization during the year for political expenditure tax imposed on organization managers. -0-			
2	Has the organization engaged in any activities that have not previously been reported to the IRS? If "Yes," attach a detailed description of the activities.	2		X
3	Has the organization made any changes, not previously reported to the IRS, in its governing instrument, articles of incorporation, or bylaws, or other similar instruments? If "Yes," attach a conformed copy of the changes	3		X
4a	Did the organization have unrelated business gross income of $1,000 or more during the year?	4a		X
b	If "Yes," has it filed a tax return on Form 990-T for this year? N/A	4b		
5	Was there a liquidation, termination, dissolution, or substantial contraction during the year? If "Yes," attach the statement required by General Instruction T.	5		X
6	Are the requirements of section 508(e) (relating to sections 4941 through 4945) satisfied either: * By language in the governing instrument; or * By state legislation that effectively amends the governing instrument so that no mandatory directions that conflict with the state law remain in the governing instrument?	6	X	
7	Did the organization have at least $5,000 in assets at any time during the year? If "Yes," complete Part II, column (c), and Part XV	7	X	
8a	Enter the states to which the foundation reports or with which it is registered (see page 19 of the instructions) Texas			
b	If the answer is "Yes" to line 7, has the organization furnished a copy of Form 990-PF to the Attorney General (or designate) of each state as required by General Instruction G? If "No," attach explanation	8b	X	
9	Is the organization claiming status as a private operating foundation within the meaning of section 4942(j)(3) or 4942(j)(5) for calendar year 2000 or the taxable year beginning in 1999 (see instructions for Part XIV on page 23)? If "Yes," complete Part XIV	9		X
10	Did any persons become substantial contributors during the tax year? If "Yes," attach a schedule listing their names and addresses	10		X
11a	Did anyone request to see either the organization's annual return or its exemption application (or both)?	11a		X
b	If "Yes," did the organization comply pursuant to the instructions? (See General Instruction Q.) N/A	11b		

12 The books are in care of Mary Goodbooks Telephone no. (444) 444-4555
Located at 1011 Main Street, Hometown Texas ZIP+4 77777-7777

13 Section 4947(a)(1) nonexempt charitable trusts filing Form 990-PF in lieu of Form 1041. - Check here [ ] and enter the amount of tax-exempt interest received or accrued during the year | 13 |

Form 990-PF (2000)

Form 990-PF (2000) Environmentalist Fund 77-7777777 Page 5

Part VII-B Statements Regarding Activities for Which Form 4720 May Be Required

File Form 4720 if any item is checked in the "Yes" column, unless an exception applies. | Yes | No

1a During the year did the organization (either directly or indirectly):

(1) Engage in the sale or exchange, or leasing of property with a disqualified person? . . No

(2) Borrow money from, lend money to, or otherwise extend credit to (or accept it from) a disqualified person? . . . . No

(3) Furnish goods, services, or facilities to (or accept them from) a disqualified person? No

(4) Pay compensation to, or pay or reimburse the expenses of, a disqualified person? . . No

(5) Transfer any income or assets to a disqualified person (or make any of either available for the benefit or use of a disqualified person)? . . . . No

(6) Agree to pay money or property to a government official? (Exception. Check "No" if the organization agreed to make a grant to or to employ the official for a period after termination of government service, if terminating within 90 days.) . . . . . No

b If any answer is "Yes" to 1a(1) - (6), did ANY of the acts fail to qualify under the exceptions described in Regulations section 53.4941(d)-3 or in a current notice regarding disaster assistance (see page 20 of the instructions)? . . . . N/A **1b**

Organizations relying on a current notice regarding disaster assistance check here ☐

c Did the organization engage in a prior year in any of the acts described in 1a, other than excepted acts, that were not corrected before the first day of the tax year beginning in 2000? . . . . **1c** No: X

2 Taxes on failure to distribute income (section 4942) (does not apply for years the organization was a private operating foundation defined in section 4942(j)(3) or 4942(j)(5)):

a At the end of tax year 2000, did the organization have any undistributed income (lines 6d and 6e, Part XIII) for tax year(s) beginning before 2000? . . . . No

If "Yes," list the years ______ , ______ , ______ , ______

b Are there any years listed in 2a for which the organization is NOT applying the provisions of section 4942(a)(2) (relating to incorrect valuation of assets) to the year's undistributed income? (If applying section 4942(a)(2) to all years listed, answer "No" and attach statement-see page 20 of the instructions.) . . . . N/A **2b**

c If the provisions of section 4942(a)(2) are being applied to ANY of the years listed in 2a, list the years here. ______ , ______ , ______ , ______

3a Did the organization hold more than a 2% direct or indirect interest in any business enterprise at any time during the year? . . . . No

b If "Yes," did it have excess business holdings in 2000 as a result of (1) any purchase by the organization or disqualified persons after May 26, 1969; (2) the lapse of the 5-year period (or longer period approved by the Commissioner under section 4943(c)(7)) to dispose of holdings acquired by gift or bequest; or (3) the lapse of the 10-, 15-, or 20-year first phase holding period? (Use Schedule C, Form 4720, to determine if the organization had excess business holdings in 2000.) . . . . N/A **3b**

4a Did the organization invest during the year any amount in a manner that would jeopardize its charitable purposes? **4a** No: X

b Did the organization make any investment in a prior year (but after December 31, 1969) that could jeopardize its charitable purpose that had not been removed from jeopardy before the first day of the tax year beginning in 2000? . . . . **4b** No: X

5a During the year did the organization pay or incur any amount to:

(1) Carry on propaganda, or otherwise attempt to influence legislation (section 4945(e))? . No

(2) Influence the outcome of any specific public election (see section 4955); or to carry on, directly or indirectly, any voter registration drive? . . . . No

(3) Provide a grant to an individual for travel, study, or other similar purposes? . . . . . No

(4) Provide a grant to an organization other than a charitable, etc., organization described in section 509(a)(1), (2), or (3), or section 4940(d)(2)? . . . . Yes

(5) Provide for any purpose other than religious, charitable, scientific, literary, or educational purposes, or for the prevention of cruelty to children or animals? . . . . No

If any answer is "Yes" to 5a(1) - (5), did ANY of the transactions fail to qualify under the exceptions described in Regulations section 53.4945 or in a current notice regarding disaster assistance (see page 20 of the instructions)? . . . . **5b** No: X

Organizations relying on a current notice regarding disaster assistance check here ☐

c If the answer is "Yes" to question 5a(4), does the organization claim exemption from the tax because it maintained expenditure responsibility for the grant? . . . . Yes

If "Yes," attach the statement required by Regulations section 53.4945-5(d).

6a Did the organization, during the year, receive any funds, directly or indirectly, to pay premiums on a personal benefit contract? No

b Did the organization, during the year, pay premiums, directly or indirectly, on a personal benefit contract? . . . . **6b** No: X

If you answered "Yes" to 6b, also file Form 8870.

Form 990-PF (2000)

Form 990-PF (2000) Environmentalist Fund 77-7777777 Page 6

Part VIII Information About Officers, Directors, Trustees, Foundation Managers, Highly Paid Employees, and Contractors

1 List all officers, directors, trustees, foundation managers and their compensation (see instructions):

(a) Name and address	(b) Title, and average hours per week devoted to position	(c) Compensation (If not paid, enter -0-)	(d) Contributions to employee benefit plans & deferred compensation	(e) Expense account, other allowances
Jane Environmentalist	President 10 hours per week	-0-	-0-	-0-
John J. Environmentalist	Vice-President 10 hours per week	-0-	-0-	-0-
John J. Environmentalist, Jr.	Secretary/Treasurer 8 hours per week	-0-	-0-	-0-
All the officers can be contacted at: 1111 Any Street, Hometown, Texas 77777				

2 Compensation of five highest-paid employees (other than those included on line 1 - see page 21 of the instructions). If none, enter "NONE."

(a) Name and address of each employee paid more than $50,000	(b) Title and average hours per week devoted to position	(c) Compensation	(d) Contributions to employee benefit plans & deferred compensation	(e) Expense account, other allowances
The Foundation has no employees.				

Total number of other employees paid over $50,000 . . . . None

3 Five highest-paid independent contractors for professional services - (see page 21 of the instructions). If none, enter "NONE."

(a) Name and address of each person paid more than $50,000	(b) Type of service	(c) Compensation
The Foundation pays no one $50,000 or more.		

Total number of others receiving over $50,000 for professional services . . . . None

Part IX-A Summary of Direct Charitable Activities

List the foundation's four largest direct charitable activities during the tax year. Include relevant statistical information such as the number of organizations and other beneficiaries served, conferences convened, research papers produced, etc.	Expenses
1 Not Applicable	
2	
3	
4	

Form 990-PF (2000)

Form 990-PF (2000) Environmentalist Fund 77-7777777 Page 7

Part IX-B Summary of Program-Related Investments (see page 22 of the instructions)

	Describe the two largest program-related investments made by the foundation during the tax year on lines 1 and 2	Amount
1	Not Applicable	
2		
3	All other program-related investments. See page 22 of the instructions.	

Part X Minimum Investment Return (All domestic foundations must complete this part. Foreign foundations, see page 22 of the instructions.)

1	Fair market value of assets not used (or held for use) directly in carrying out charitable, etc., purposes:			
a	Average monthly fair market value of securities		1a	1,995,000
b	Average of monthly cash balances		1b	55,000
c	Fair market value of all other assets (see page 23 of the instructions)		1c	
d	Total (add lines 1a, b, and c)		1d	2,050,000
e	Reduction claimed for blockage or other factors reported on lines 1a and 1c (attach detailed explanation)	1e		
2	Acquisition indebtedness applicable to line 1 assets		2	
3	Subtract line 2 from line 1d		3	2,050,000
4	Cash deemed held for charitable activities. Enter 1 1 /2% of line 3 (for greater amount, see page 23 of the instructions)		4	30,750
5	Net value of noncharitable-use assets. Subtract line 4 from line 3. Enter here and on Part V, line 4		5	2,019,250
6	Minimum investment return. Enter 5% of line 5		6	100,963

Part XI Distributable Amount (see page 23 of the instructions) (Section 4942(j)(3) and (j)(5) private operating foundations and certain foreign organizations check here ☐ and do not complete this part.)

1	Minimum investment return from Part X, line 6			1	100,963
2a	Tax on investment income for 2000 from Part VI, line 5	2a	2,019		
b	Income tax for 2000. (This does not include the tax from Part VI.)	2b			
c	Add lines 2a and 2b			2c	2,019
3	Distributable amount before adjustments. Subtract line 2c from line 1			3	98,944
4a	Recoveries of amounts treated as qualifying distributions	4a			
b	Income distributions from section 4947(a)(2) trusts	4b			
c	Add lines 4a and 4b			4c	
5	Add lines 3 and 4c			5	98,944
6	Deduction from distributable amount (see page 23 of the instructions)			6	
7	Distributable amount as adjusted. Subtract line 6 from line 5. Enter here and on Part XIII, line 1			7	98,944

Part XII Qualifying Distributions (see page 24 of the instructions)

1	Amounts paid (including administrative expenses) to accomplish charitable, etc., purposes:		
a	Expenses, contributions, gifts, etc. - total from Part I, column (d), line 26	1a	318,700
b	Program-related investments - total of lines 1-3 of Part IX-B	1b	
2	Amounts paid to acquire assets used (or held for use) directly in carrying out charitable, etc., purposes	2	
3	Amounts set aside for specific charitable projects that satisfy the:		
a	Suitability test (prior IRS approval required)	3a	
b	Cash distribution test (attach the required schedule)	3b	
4	Qualifying distributions. Add lines 1a through 3b. Enter here and on Part V, line 8, and Part XIII, line 4	4	318,700
5	Organizations that qualify under section 4940(e) for the reduced rate of tax on net investment income. Enter 1% of Part I, line 27b (see page 24 of the instructions)	5	2,019
6	Adjusted qualifying distributions. Subtract line 5 from line 4	6	316,681

NOTE: The amount on line 6 will be used in Part V, column (b), in subsequent years when calculating whether the foundation qualifies for the section 4940(e) reduction of tax in those years.

Form 990-PF (2000)

Form 990-PF (2000) Environmentalist Fund 77-7777777 Page 8

Part XIII Undistributed Income (see page 24 of the instructions)

	(a) Corpus	(b) Years prior to 1999	(c) 1999	(d) 2000
1 Distributable amount for 2000 from Part XI, line 7				98,944
2 Undistributed income, if any, as of the end of 1999:				
a Enter amount for 1999 only				
b Total for prior years: 19__, 19__, 19__				
3 Excess distributions carryover, if any, to 2000:				
a From 1995 . . . 10,000				
b From 1996 . . . 9,200				
c From 1997 . . . 102,000				
d From 1998 . . . 146,000				
e From 1999 . . . 163,000				
f Total of lines 3a through e	430,200			
4 Qualifying distributions for 2000 from Part XII, line 4: $ 318,700				
a Applied to 1999, but not more than line 2a				
b Applied to undistributed income of prior years (Election required - see instructions)				
c Treated as distributions out of corpus (Election required - see instructions)				
d Applied to 2000 distributable amount				98,944
e Remaining amount distributed out of corpus	219,756			
5 Excess distributions carryover applied to 2000 (If an amount appears in column (d), the same amount must be shown in column (a).)				
6 **Enter the net total of each column as indicated below:**				
a Corpus. Add 3f, 4c, and 4e. Subtract line 5	649,956			
b Prior years' undistributed income. Subtract line 4b from line 2b				
c Enter the amount of prior years' undistributed income for which a notice of deficiency has been issued, or on which the section 4942(a) tax has been previously assessed				
d Subtract line 6c from line 6b. Taxable amount - see instructions				
e Undistributed income for 1999. Subtract line 4a from line 2a. Taxable amount				
f Undistributed income for 2000. Subtract lines 4d and 5 from line 1. This amount must be distributed in 2001				-0-
7 Amounts treated as distributions out of corpus to satisfy requirements imposed by section 170(b)(1)(E) or 4942(g)(3)				
8 Excess distributions carryover from 1995 not applied on line 5 or line 7 (see page 23 of the instructions)	10,000			
9 Excess distributions carryover to 2001 Subtract lines 7 and 8 from line 6a	639,956			
10 Analysis of line 9:				
a Excess from 1996 . . . 9,200				
b Excess from 1997. . . . 102,000				
c Excess from 1998 . . . 146,000				
d Excess from 1999 . . . 163,000				
e Excess from 2000 . . . 219,756				

Form 990-PF (2000)

Form 990-PF (2000) Environmentalist Fund 77-7777777 Page 9

Part XIV Private Operating Foundations (see page 25 of the instructions and Part VII-A, question 9) Not Applicable

1a If the foundation has received a ruling or determination letter that it is a private operating foundation, and the ruling is effective for 2000, enter the date of the ruling . . . . .

b Check box to indicate whether the organization is a private operating foundation described in section ☐ 4942(j)(3) or ☐ 4942(j)(5)

	Tax Year	Prior 3 years			
	(a) 2000	(b) 1999	(c) 1998	(d) 1997	(e) Total
2a Enter the lesser of the adjusted net income from Part I or the minimum investment return from Part X for each year listed . . .					
b 85% of line 2a . . .					
c Qualifying distributions from Part XII, line 4 for each year listed . . .					
d Amounts included in line 2c not used directly for active conduct of exempt activities . . .					
e Qualifying distributions made directly for active conduct of exempt activities Subtract line 2d from line 2c . . .					
3 Complete 3a, b, or c for the alternative test relied upon:					
a "Assets" alternative test - enter: (1) Value of all assets . . .					
(2) Value of assets qualifying under section 4942(j)(3)(B)(i) . . .					
b "Endowment" alternative test - Enter 2/3 of minimum investment return shown in Part X, line 6 for each year listed . . .					
c "Support" alternative test - enter: (1) Total support other than gross investment income (interest, dividends, rents, payments on securities loans (section 512(a)(5)), or royalties)					
(2) Support from general public and 5 or more exempt organizations as provided in section 4942(j)(3)(B)(iii)					
(3) Largest amount of support from an exempt organization . . .					
(4) Gross investment income . . .					

Part XV Supplementary Information (Complete this part only if the organization had $5,000 or more in assets at any time during the year - see page 26 of the instructions.)

1 Information Regarding Foundation Managers:

a List any managers of the foundation who have contributed more than 2% of the total contributions received by the foundation before the close of any tax year (but only if they have contributed more than $5,000). (See section 507(d)(2).)

Jane D. and John J. Environmentalist

b List any managers of the foundation who own 10% or more of the stock of a corporation (or an equally large portion of the ownership of a partnership or other entity) of which the foundation has a 10% or greater interest.

None

2 Information Regarding Contribution, Grant, Gift, Loan, Scholarship, etc., Programs:

Check here if the ☐ organization only makes contributions to preselected charitable organizations and does not accept unsolicited requests for funds. If the organization makes gifts, grants, etc. (see page 26 of the instructions) to individuals or organizations under other conditions, complete items 2a, b, c, and d.

a The name, address, and telephone number of the person to whom applications should be addressed:

Mary Goodbooks, 1011 Main Street, Hometown, Texas 77777-7777

b The form in which applications should be submitted and information and materials they should include:

Description of programs with budgets (no more than 6 pages); Form 990 and audit (if available) for most recent year; board list.

c Any submission deadlines:

March 1st and September 1st

d Any restrictions or limitations on awards, such as by geographical areas, charitable fields, kinds of institutions, or other factors:

The Foundation supports innovative programs to enhance protection of the environment.

Form 990-PF (2000)

Form 990-PF (2000) Environmentalist Fund 77-7777777 Page 10

Part XV Supplementary Information (continued)

3 Grants and Contributions Paid During the Year or Approved for Future Payment

Recipient Name and address (home or business)	If recipient is an individual show any relationship to any foundation manager or substantial contributor	Foundation status of recipient	Purpose of grant or contribution	Amount
a Paid during the year				
Municipal beautification				
Hometown Chapter, Campaign to Clean Up America 1111 Any Street, Hometown, Texas 77777		509(a)(1)	General support	160,000
National Campaign to Clean Up America 2525 Capital Street, Capital City, D.C. 01010		509(a)(1)	General support	50,000
Urban Planning				
Smart Growth Institute 404 Fourth Street, Hometown, Texas 77777		509(a)(2)	Support research and dissemination of educational materials regarding livable communities.	50,000
Save the Bay Project 5 Shoreline Drive, Beachville, Texas 77777		509(a)(1)	General support	25,000
Environmental Education				
Hometown Public Schools 303 Academic Row, Hometown, Texas 77777		170(b)(1)(A)(v)	To develop teacher curriculum and support field trips focused on environmental issues.	25,000
Total **3a**				310,000
b Approved for future payment				
Total **3b**				

Form 990-PF (2000)

Form 990-PF (2000) Environmentalist Fund 77-7777777 Page 11

Part XVI-A Analysis of Income-Producing Activities

Enter gross amounts unless otherwise indicated.	Unrelated business income		Excluded by sec. 512, 513, or 514		(e) Related or exempt function income
	(a) Business code	(b) Amount	(c) Exclusion code	(d) Amount	
1 Program service revenue:					
a					
b					
c					
d					
e					
f					
g Fees and contracts from government agencies					
2 Membership dues and assessments					
3 Interest on savings and temporary cash investments			14	4,000	
4 Dividends and interest from securities			14	160,000	
5 Net rental income or (loss) from real estate:					
a Debt-financed property					
b Not debt-financed property					
6 Net rental income or (loss) from personal property					
7 Other investment income					
8 Gain or (loss) from sales of assets other than inventory			18	30,000	
9 Net income or (loss) from special events					
10 Gross profit or (loss) from sales of inventory					
11 Other revenue: (a)					
b					
c					
d					
e					
12 Subtotal. Add cols. (b), (d), and (e)				194,000	

13 Total. Add line 12, columns (b), (d), and (e) 13 194,000

(See worksheet in line 13 instructions on page 25 to verify calculations.)

Part XVI-B Relationship of Activities to the Accomplishment of Exempt Purposes

Line No.	Explain below how each activity for which income is reported in column (e) of Part XVI-A contributed importantly to the accomplishment of the organization's exempt purposes (other than by providing funds for such purposes). (See page 27 of the instructions.)
	Not Applicable

Form 990-PF (2000)

Form 990-PF (2000) Environmentalist Fund 77-7777777 Page 12

Part XVII Information Regarding Transfers To and Transactions and Relationships With Noncharitable Exempt Organizations

		Yes	No
1 Did the organization directly or indirectly engage in any of the following with any other organization described in section 501(c) of the Code (other than section 501(c)(3) organizations) or in section 527, relating to political organizations?			
a Transfers from the reporting organization to a noncharitable exempt organization of:			
(1) Cash	**1a(1)**		X
(2) Other assets	**1a(2)**		X
b Other Transactions:			
(1) Sales of assets to a noncharitable exempt organization	**1b(1)**		X
(2) Purchases of assets from a noncharitable exempt organization	**1b(2)**		X
(3) Rental of facilities, equipment, or other assets	**1b(3)**		X
(4) Reimbursement arrangements	**1b(4)**		X
(5) Loans or loan guarantees	**1b(5)**		X
(6) Performance of services or membership or fundraising solicitations	**1b(6)**		X
c Sharing of facilities, equipment, mailing lists, other assets, or paid employees	**1c**		X

d If the answer to any of the above is "Yes ," complete the following schedule. Column (b) should always show the fair value of the goods, other assets, or services given by the reporting organization. If the organization received less than fair market value in any transaction or sharing arrangement, show in column (d) the value of the goods, other assets, or services received.

(a) Line no.	(b) Amount involved	(c) Name of noncharitable exempt organization	(d) Description of transfers, transactions, and sharing arrangements

2a Is the organization directly or indirectly affiliated with, or related to, one or more tax-exempt organizations described in section 501(c) of the Code (other than section 501(c)(3)) or in section 527? Yes ☐ No ☒

b If "Yes," complete the following schedule.

(a) Name of organization	(b) Type of organization	(c) Description of relationship
Not Applicable		

Please Sign Here

Under penalties of perjury, I declare that I have examined this return, including accompanying schedules and statements, and to the best of my knowledge and belief, it is true, correct, and complete. Declaration of preparer (other than taxpayer or fiduciary) is based on all information of which preparer has any knowledge.

Signature of officer or trustee	Date	Title
Jane D Environmentalist	5/1/01	President

Paid Preparer's Use Only

Preparer's signature: a Good, C.P.A.	Date 4/29/01	Check if self-employed ☒	Preparer's SSN or PTIN 400-00-0000
Firm's name (or yours if self-employed), address, and ZIP code	A Qualified CPA Firm 1001 Main Street Hometown, Te 77098-3013	EIN	45-5555555
		Phone	(444) 422-2222

Form 990-PF (2000)

Environmentalist Fund **77-7777777**
2000 Form 990-PF

Part I, line 1 - Contributions Received

Jane D. & John J. Environmentalist 333 First Street Hometown, Texas 77777	Gift of 10,000 shares of Clean Air Industries, Inc. NYSE average price on gift date 4/1/20xx	$300,000

	Column (a)	Column (b)	Column (d)
Part I, line 16a - Legal fees			
General corporate matters during the year	$5,000	2,500	$2,500
Part I, Line 16b - Accounting fees			
Preparation of Form 990-PF and tax planning consultations throughout the year	$5,000	2,500	$2,500
Part I, line 16c - Other professional fees			
Investment management services	$ 6,000	6,000	$0
Part I, line 18 - Taxes			
Excise tax on investment income	$ 4,000	0	$0

Part II, line 10b - Investments - corporate stocks

	Book Value	Market Value
700 shares ABC Securities, Inc.	$ 50,000	$ 200,000
500 shares DEF Incorported	65,000	200,000
400 shares GHI Company	80,000	200,000
600 shares JKL Inc.	95,000	200,000
300 shares MNO Enterprises	75,555	370,000
10,000 shares Clean Air Industries	300,000	1,000,000
Total investment in corporate stocks	$ 665,555	$ 2,170,000

Attachment to Part I, Lines 1, 16a, 16b, 16c, 18 and Part II, Line 10b

Appendix 4B

Form **4720**

Department of the Treasury
Internal Revenue Service

Return of Certain Excise Taxes on Charities and Other Persons Under Chapters 41 and 42 of the Internal Revenue Code

(Sections 170(f)(10), 4911, 4912, 4941, 4942, 4943, 4944, 4945, 4955, and 4958)

See separate instructions.

OMB No. 1545-0052

2000

For calendar year 2000 or other tax year beginning ________________, and ending ________________

Name of foundation or public charity	Employer identification number
Environmentalist Fund	77-7777777
Number, street, and room or suite no. (or P. O. box if mail is not delivered to street address) **1111 Any Street**	Check box for type of annual return: ☐ Form 990 ☐ Form 990-EZ
City or town, state, and ZIP code **Hometown , Texas 77777-7777**	☒ Form 990-PF ☐ Form 5227

		Yes	No
A	Is the organization a foreign private foundation within the meaning of section 4948(b)?		X
B	Has corrective action been taken on any taxable event that resulted in Chapter 42 taxes being reported on this form? (Enter "N/A" if not applicable)		X

If "Yes," attach a detailed documentation and description of the corrective action taken and, if applicable, enter the fair market value of any property recovered as a result of the correction $ N/A . If "No, " (i.e., any uncorrected acts, or transactions), attach an explanation (see page 3 of the instructions).

Part I Taxes on Organization (Sections 170(f)(10), 4911(a), 4912(a), 4942(a), 4943(a), 4944(a)(1), 4945(a)(1), and 4955(a)(1))

1	Tax on undistributed income - Schedule B, line 4	1	
2	Tax on excess business holdings - Schedule C, line 7	2	
3	Tax on investments that jeopardize charitable purpose - Schedule D, Part I, column (e)	3	
4	Tax on taxable expenditures - Schedule E, Part I, column (g)	4	None
5	Tax on political expenditures - Schedule F, Part I, column (e)	5	
6	Tax on excess lobbying expenditures - Schedule G, line 4	6	
7	Tax on disqualifying lobbying expenditures - Schedule H, Part I, column (e)	7	
8	Tax on premiums paid on personal benefit contracts	8	
9	Total (add lines 1-8)	9	

Part II-A Taxes on Self-Dealers, Disqualified Persons, Foundation Managers, and Organization Managers (Sections 4912(b), 4941(a), 4944(a)(2), 4945(a)(2), 4955(a)(2), and 4958(a))

	(a) Name and address of person subject to tax	(b) Taxpayer identification number
a		
b		
c		
d		

	(c) Tax on self-dealing - Schedule A, Part II, col. (d), and Part III, col. (d)	(d) Tax on investments that jeopardize charitable purpose-Schedule D, Part II, col. (d)	(e) Tax on taxable expenditures - Schedule E, Part II, col. (d)	(f) Tax on political expenditures-Sch. F, Part II, col. (d)
a				
b				
c				
d				
Total				

	(g) Tax on disqualifying lobbying expenditures - Sch. H, Part II, col. (d)	(h) Tax on excess benefit transactions - Schedule I, Part II, col. (d), and Part III, col (d)	(i) Total - Add cols. (c) through (h)
a			
b			
c			
d			
Total			

Part II-B Summary of Taxes (See TAX PAYMENTS on page 2 of the instructions)

1	Enter the taxes listed in Part II-A, column (i), that apply to self-dealers, disqualified persons, foundation managers, and organization managers who sign this form. If all sign, enter the total amount from Part II-A, column (i)	1	**See Abatement Request**
2	Total tax. Add Part I, line 9, and Part II-B, line 1. (Make check(s) or money order(s) payable to the United States Treasury.)	2	None

For Paperwork Reduction Act Notice, see the instructions. (HTA) Form 4720 (2000)

Form 4720 (2000) Environmentalist Fund 77-7777777 Page 2

SCHEDULE A - Initial Taxes on Self-Dealing (Section 4941)

Part I Acts of Self-Dealing and Tax Computation

(a) Act number	(b) Date of act	(c) Description of act
1		
2		
3		
4		
5		

(d) Question number from Form 990-PF, Part VII-B, or Form 5227, Part VI-B, applicable to the act	(e) Amount involved in act	(f) Initial tax on self-dealing (5% of col. (e))	(g) Tax on foundation managers (if applicable) (lesser of $10,000 or 2 1/2 % of col. (e))

Part II Summary of Tax Liability of Self-Dealers and Proration of Payments

(a) Names of self-dealers liable for tax	(b) Act no. from Part I, col. (a)	(c) Tax from Part I, col. (f), or prorated amount	(d) Self-dealer's total tax liability (add amounts in col. (c)) (see page 4 of the instructions)

Part III Summary of Tax Liability of Foundation Managers and Proration of Payments

(a) Names of foundation managers liable for tax	(b) Act no. from Part I, col. (a)	(c) Tax from Part I, col. (g), or prorated amount	(d) Manager's total tax liability (add amounts in col. (c)) (see page 4 of the instructions)

SCHEDULE B - Initial Tax on Undistributed Income (Section 4942)

1	Undistributed income for years before 1999 (from Form 990-PF for 2000, Part XIII, line 6d)	1	
2	Undistributed income for 1999 (from Form 990-PF for 2000, Part XIII, line 6e)	2	
3	Total undistributed income at end of current tax year beginning in 2000 and subject to tax under section 4942 (add lines 1 and 2)	3	
4	Tax - Enter 15% of line 3 here and on page 1, Part I, line 1	4	

Form 4720 (2000)

Form 4720 (2000) Environmentalist Fund 77-7777777 Page 3

SCHEDULE C - Initial Tax on Excess Business Holdings (Section 4943)

Business Holdings and Computation of Tax

If you have taxable excess holdings in more than one business enterprise, attach a separate schedule for each enterprise. Refer to the instructions on page 4 for each line item before making any entries.

Name and address of business enterprise

Employer identification number . . . .

Form of enterprise (corporation, partnership, trust, joint venture, sole proprietorship, etc.) . . .

			(a) Voting stock (profits interest or beneficial interest)	(b) Value	(c) Nonvoting stock (capital interest)
1	Foundation holdings in business enterprise . . .	1			
2	Permitted holdings in business enterprise	2			
3	Value of excess holdings in business enterprise	3			
4	Value of excess holdings disposed of within 90 days; or, other value of excess holdings not subject to section 4943 tax (attach explanation)	4			
5	Taxable excess holdings in business enterprise - line 3 minus line 4	5			
6	Tax - Enter 5% of line 5	6			
7	Total tax - Add amounts on line 6, columns (a), (b), and (c); enter total here and on page 1, Part I, line 2 . . .	7			

SCHEDULE D - Initial Taxes on Investments That Jeopardize Charitable Purpose (Section 4944)

Part I Investments and Tax Computation

(a) Investment number	(b) Date of investment	(c) Description of investment	(d) Amount of investment	(e) Initial tax on foundation (5% of col. (d))	(f) Initial tax on foundation managers (if applicable)-(lesser of $5,000 or 5% of col. (d))
1					
2					
3					
4					
5					

Total - column (e). Enter here and on page 1, Part I, line 3 . . . .

Total - column (f). Enter total (or prorated amount) here and in Part II, column (c), below . . . .

Part II Summary of Tax Liability of Foundation Managers and Proration of Payments

(a) Names of foundation managers liable for tax	(b) Investment no. from Part I, col. (a)	(c) Tax from Part I, col. (f), or prorated amount	(d) Manager's total tax liability (add amounts in col. (c)) (see page 6 of the instructions)

Form 4720 (2000)

Form 4720 (2000) Environmentalist Fund 77-7777777 Page 4

SCHEDULE E - Initial Taxes on Taxable Expenditures (Section 4945)

Part I Expenditures and Computation of Tax

(a) Item number	(b) Amount	(c) Date paid or incurred	(d) Name and address of recipient	(e) Description of expenditure and purposes for which made
1				
2	10,000	June 1, 20xx	Citizens Environmental Committee	Purchase of educational materials and website funding
3				
4				
5				

(f) Question number from Form 990-PF, Part VII-B, or Form 5227, Part VI-B, applicable to the expenditure	(g) Initial tax imposed on foundation (10% of col. (b))	(h) Initial tax imposed on foundation managers (if applicable)-(lesser of $5,000 or 2 1/2 % of col. (b))
5(c)	See attached request for abatement	
Total - column (g). Enter here and on page 1, Part I, line 4		
Total - column (h). Enter total (or prorated amount) here and in Part II, column (c), below . . .		

Part II Summary of Tax Liability of Foundation Managers and Proration of Payments

(a) Names of foundation managers liable for tax	(b) Item no. from Part I, col. (a)	(c) Tax from Part I, col. (h), or prorated amount	(d) Manager's total tax liability (add amounts in col. (c)) (see page 7 of the instructions)

SCHEDULE F - Initial Taxes on Political Expenditures (Section 4955)

Part I Expenditures and Computation of Tax

(a) Item number	(b) Amount	(c) Date paid or incurred	(d) Description of political expenditure	(e) Initial tax imposed on organization or foundation (10% of col. (b))	(f) Initial tax imposed on managers (if applicable) (lesser of $5,000 or 2 1/2% of col. (b))
1					
2					
3					
4					
5					
Total - column (e). Enter here and on page 1, Part I, line 5					
Total - column (f). Enter total (or prorated amount) here and in Part II, column (c), below . . .					

Part II Summary of Tax Liability of Organization Managers or Foundation Managers and Proration of Payments

(a) Names of organization managers or foundation managers liable for tax	(b) Item no. from Part I, col. (a)	(c) Tax from Part I, col. (f), or prorated amount	(d) Manager's total tax liability (add amounts in col. (c)) (see page 7 of the instructions)

Form 4720 (2000)

Form 4720 (2000) Environmentalist Fund 77-7777777 Page 5

SCHEDULE G - Tax on Excess Lobbying Expenditures (Section 4911)

1	Excess of grassroots expenditures over grassroots nontaxable amount (from Schedule A (Form 990), Part VI-A, column (b), line 43). (See page 7 of the instructions before making entry.)	1	
2	Excess of lobbying expenditures over lobbying nontaxable amount (from Schedule A (Form 990), Part VI-A, column (b), line 44). (See page 7 of the instructions before making entry.)	2	
3	Taxable lobbying expenditures - enter the larger of line 1 or line 2	3	
4	Tax - Enter 25% of line 3 here and on page 1, Part I, line 6	4	

SCHEDULE H - Taxes on Disqualifying Lobbying Expenditures (Section 4912)

Part I Expenditures and Computation of Tax

(a) Item number	(b) Amount	(c) Date paid or incurred	(d) Description of lobbying expenditures	(e) Tax imposed on organization (5% of col. (b))	(f) Tax imposed on organization managers (if applicable) - (5% of col. (b))
1					
2					
3					
4					
5					
Total - column (e). Enter here and on page 1, Part I, line 7					
Total - column (f). Enter total (or prorated amount) here and in Part II, column (c), below					

Part II Summary of Tax Liability of Organization Managers and Proration of Payments

(a) Names of organization managers liable for tax	(b) Item no. from Part I, col. (a)	(c) Tax from Part I, col. (f), or prorated amount	(d) Manager's total tax liability (add amounts in col. (c)) (see page 8 of the instructions)

SCHEDULE I - Initial Taxes on Excess Benefit Transactions (Section 4958)

Part I Excess Benefit Transactions and Tax Computation

(a) Transaction number	(b) Date of transaction	(c) Description of transaction
1		
2		
3		
4		
5		

(d) Amount of excess benefit	(e) Initial tax on disqualified persons (25% of col. (d))	(f) Tax on organization managers (if applicable) (lesser of $10,000 or 10% of col (d))

Form 4720 (2000)

Form 4720 (2000) Environmentalist Fund 77-7777777 Page 6

SCHEDULE I - Initial Taxes on Excess Benefit Transactions (Section 4958) Continued

Part II Summary of Tax Liability of Disqualified Persons and Proration of Payments

(a) Names of disqualified persons liable for tax	(b) Trans. no. from Part I, col. (a)	(c) Tax from Part I, col. (e), or prorated amount	(d) Disqualified person's total tax liability (add amounts in col. (c)) (see page 8 of the instructions)

Part III Summary of Tax Liability of 501(c)(3) and (4) Organization Managers and Proration of Payments

(a) Names of 501(c)(3) and (4) organization managers liable for tax	(b) Trans. no. from Part I, col. (a)	(c) Tax from Part I, col. (f), or prorated amount	(d) Manager's total tax liability (add amounts in col. (c)) (see page 8 of the instructions)

Under penalties of perjury, I declare that I have examined this return, including accompanying schedules and statements, and to the best of my knowledge and belief it is true, correct, and complete. Declaration of preparer (other than taxpayer) is based on all information of which preparer has any knowledge.

Jane D. Environmentalist President 5/1/01

Signature of officer or trustee Title Date

Signature (and organization name if applicable) of self-dealer, disqualified person, foundation manager, or organization manager Date

Signature (and organization name if applicable) of self-dealer, disqualified person, foundation manager, or organization manager Date

Signature (and organization name if applicable) of self-dealer, disqualified person, foundation manager, or organization manager Date

Signature (and organization name if applicable) of self-dealer, disqualified person, foundation manager, or organization manager Date

A. Good, C.P.A. 4/29/01

Signature of individual or firm preparing the return Date

A Qualified CPA Firm, 1001 Main Street, Hometown, Texas 77777 (444) 422-2222

Address of preparer Phone no. of preparer

Form 4720 (2000)

ENVIRONMENTALIST FUND **# 77-7777777**

ATTACHMENT TO FORM 4720
for the year ending December 31, 2000

STATEMENT regarding CORRECTION OF TAXABLE EXPENDITURE

In submitting its 1999 Form 990-PF, the Environmentalist Fund inadvertently failed to submit an expenditure responsibility grant report. This failure is corrected in this return by making a complete report of the required items properly included as an attachment to Part VII-B, *Statement Regarding Activities for which Form 4720 may be Required,* of this year's Form 990-PF.

The Environmentalist Fund, during its calendar year ending December 31, 1999, made a grant to the Citizens Environmental Committee (CEC), an unincorporated nonprofit, non tax-exempt, association. A pre-grant inquiry was conducted and an expenditure responsibility agreement was executed in a timely fashion. The grant information was reported on the 1999 Form 990-PF in Part XV, but a separate expenditure responsibility report was not submitted with the return.

A taxable expenditure occurred when the Environmentalist Fund failed to include detailed information about the grant in its 1999 Form 990-PF. The Fund had not previously made an expenditure responsibility grant that required separate reporting. The Fund's accountant failed to include the report. The Fund's officers engaged their lawyers to prepare the agreement regarding the grant. A copy of their letter stipulating the separate report was not furnished to the accountant. He thought the lawyers had satisfied all the requirements.

Pursuant to Internal Revenue Code §4962, Environmentalist Fund respectfully requests that the first tier §4945 penalty for failure to report, or initial tax of $1,500, be abated because the failure was due to reasonable causes and without willful neglect. I discovered a mistake had been made when I was reviewing the 2000 Form 990-PF prior to submitting it to the IRS. The inclusion of the proper report in the 2000 return effectively corrects the failure to report. Therefore Environmentalist Fund submits it is entitled to an abatement of the tax because it meets the requirements of §4962 and the instructions to Form 4720.

I swear that this information is true and correct and that the foundation's failure to make the expenditure responsibility report was inadvertent, accidental, and without intention or knowledge on my part or on the part of any of Environmentalist Fund's other officers.

5-1-01 Jane D. Environmentalist

Jane D. Environmentalist, President

Environmentalist Fund **77-7777777**
2000 Form 990-PF

Attachment to Form 4720
In reference to Form 990-PF, Part VII-B, Question 5c on page 5

Expenditure Responsibility Statement for the year 20xx

Pursuant to IRC Regulation §53.4945-5(d)(2), the ENVIRONMENTALIST FUND provides the following information:

(i) Grantee:	Citizens Environmental Committee 1444 Smith Terrace Hometown, Texas 77777	
(ii) Amount of Grant:	December 28, 1999	$10,000
(iii) Purpose of Grant:	The Citizens Environmental Committee (CEC) is an unincorporated nonprofit association operated by Hometown citizens unrelated to the fund's disqualified persons. This grant was for the purchase of educational materials and creation of a website. CEC had not sought recognition of its tax-exempt status in 1999 when the Fund made this grant in support of CEC's educational programs so that an expenditure responsibility agreement was executed.	
(iv) & (vi) Reports:	The CEC submitted a full and complete report of its expenditures pursuant to the grant on May 1, 2000.	
(v) Diversions:	To the knowledge of the grantor, no funds have been diverted to any activity other than the activity for which the grant was originally made.	
(vii) Verification:	The grantor has no reason to doubt the accuracy or reliability of the report from the grantee; therefore, no independent verification of the report was made.	

Attachment to Form 4720
In reference to Form 990-PF, Part VII-B, Question 5c

CHAPTER FIVE

Form 990-T: Exempt Organization Business Income Tax Return

Proper preparation of Form 990-T is partly a matter of remembering that an exempt organization is a normal taxpayer subject to all of the federal income tax code provisions applicable to for-profit taxpayers when it earns income that is unrelated to the accomplishment of its exempt purposes. Careful attention to the rules defining taxable unrelated business income yields a labyrinth of exceptions and modifications that allow a wide range of unrelated income to be excluded from tax and not reported on Form 990-T.

Tax-exempt organizations receive two types of income: earned and unearned. Unearned income—income for which the organization gives nothing in return—comes from grants, membership fees, and voluntary donations. One can think of it as *one-way-street* money. The motivation for giving the money is gratuitous and/or of a nonprofit character with no expectation of gain on the part of the giver. Such gifts are made with intent to donate and are specifically excluded from income tax.[1]

In contrast, an organization furnishes services/goods or invests its capital in return for earned income: an opera is seen, classes are attended, hospital care is provided, or credit counseling is given, for example. The purchasers of the goods and services do intend to receive something in return; they expect the street to be *two-way*. An investment company holding the organization's money expects to have to pay reasonable return for using the funds. In these examples, the organization receives earned income. The important issue this chapter considers is how to report and calculate the tax when earned income, referred to as trade or business income, becomes taxable unrelated business income. The rules that govern how earned income becomes unrelated business income (UBI) are complex. The fact that the business profits are used to pay for programs that accomplish the exempt organization's mission, referred to as the destination of the income, does not create an exclusion from tax. The activity that produces revenue must be connected to the program to be treated as related income—students pay tuition to be educated or people buy tickets to concerts, for example. In understanding these rules, it is useful to remember that the rationale for the unrelated business income tax (UBIT) is to eliminate unfair competition that results if a nonprofit organization escapes tax when it conducts the same activity as a for-profit.

Tax planning of the sort practiced by a good businessperson is in order for organizations receiving UBI. The best method for reducing the tax is to keep good records. The accounting system must support the desired allocation of deductions for personnel and facilities with time records, expense usage reports, auto logs, documentation reports, and so on.[2] Minutes of meetings of the board of directors or trustees should reflect discussion of relatedness of any project claimed to accomplish an exempt purpose. Contracts and other documents concerning activities that the organization wants to prove are related to its exempt purposes should contain appropriate language to reflect the project's exempt purposes. An organization's original purposes can be expanded and redefined to broaden the scope of potential activities or to justify some proposed activity as related. Such evolved or expanded purposes can be reported to the IRS to justify the relatedness of a new activity. If loss of exemption[3] is a strong possibility because of the extent and amount of unrelated business activity planned, a separate for-profit organization[4] can be formed to shield the exempt organization from a possible loss of exemption due to excessive business activity.

5.1 WHAT IS UNRELATED BUSINESS INCOME?

Unrelated business taxable income is defined as the gross income derived from any *unrelated trade or business regularly carried on*, less the *deductions connected* with the carrying on of such trade or business, computed with *modifications and exceptions*.[5] The italicized terms are key to identifying UBI.

A *trade or business* is any activity carried on for the production of income from selling goods or performing services. Accounting theory refers to trade or business income earned by a nonprofit organization as *exchange revenue:* The street is two-way—money is paid, and the organization gives something in return. To identify a trade or business, a "sweat test" can be applied. Purchasing a share of stock or a certificate of deposit to reap a return by then allowing someone else to use its assets is not considered to be a trade or business; interest and dividend income is not treated as business income. The concepts identifying income that is taxed as capital gain versus ordinary income to for-profit taxpayers are somewhat analogous. If the nonprofit uses personnel (including volunteers), buys inventory and supplies, and otherwise gets its hands dirty performing services and handling products, a business exists.

An *unrelated trade or business* is defined by the tax code to include any trade or business, the conduct of which is not substantially related (aside from the need of such organization for income or funds or the use it makes of the profits derived) to the exercise or performance by such organization of its charitable, educational, or other purpose or function constituting the basis for its exemption.[6] The most important question is whether the income-producing activity contributes importantly to, aids in accomplishing, or has a nexus to the organization's mission.[7] There are countless examples of activities generating unrelated business income that nonprofit organizations conduct, which are deemed to benefit society and thereby are suitable for a tax-exempt organization. Identifying related activity is not always simple, however, because some nonprofit organizations conduct activities similar to those of for-profit organizations, such as schools, hospitals, theaters, and bookstores. The following list of revenue-producing activities that the IRS has found are related to a nonprofit mission illustrate the concept of relatedness:

- Sale of products made by handicapped workers or trainees[8]
- Sale of educational materials[9]
- Fees for use of college golf course by students and faculty[10]
- Monthly charges for secretarial and telephone answering service that is a training program for indigent and homeless persons[11]
- Revenue from operation of diagnostic health devices, such as computed tomographic scans or magnetic resonance imaging machines by a hospital or health care organization[12]
- Sale of online bibliographic data from central databases[13]

(a) The Fragmentation Rule

Sometimes, a nonprofit has facilities that are dually used—for activities that embody both an exempt purpose as well as those that are nonexempt or unrelated. Revenue received in an activity that *combines* related and unrelated aspects must be identified, or fragmented, into the respective parts. An activity does not lose its identity as a trade or business merely because it is carried on within a larger group of similar activities that may or may not be related to the exempt purposes of the organization. If dual-use facilities are partly debt financed and partly paid for, the debt-financed income rules might also apply.[14]

Take, for example, a museum shop. The shop itself is clearly a trade or business, often established with a profit motive and operated in a commercial manner. Items sold in such shops, however, often include both educational items, such as books and reproductions of art works, and souvenirs. The fragmentation rule requires that all items sold be analyzed to identify:

- The educational, or related, items (the profit from which is not taxable)
- The unrelated souvenir items that do produce taxable income

The standards applied to identify museum objects as related or unrelated are well documented in IRS rulings.[15]

(b) Consequences of Receiving Unrelated Income

There are several potentially unpleasant consequences of earning unrelated business income.

(i) *Payment of Unrelated Income Tax.* Unrelated net income may be taxed at corporate or trust rates with estimated tax payments required as discussed later in this chapter. Social clubs, homeowner associations, and political organizations also pay the UBI tax on certain passive investment income in addition to the unrelated business income.

(ii) *Exempt Status Revocation.* A nonprofit organization can run a business as a substantial part of its activities, but not as its primary purpose.[16] Thus, its tax-exempt status could be revoked and all of its net income taxed, if the unrelated business activity is found to be its primary activity. As a rule, the tax code requires a nonprofit organization to be both organized and operated exclusively for an exempt purpose, although *exclusively* does not mean 100 percent.[17] In evaluating the amount of unrelated business activity that is permissible, not only the amount of gross revenue, but other factors as well, may be taken into consideration. Nonrevenue aspects of the activity, such as staff time devoted or value of donated services, are factors that might be determinative.

The basic issue is whether the operation of the business subsumes, or is inconsistent with, the organization's exempt activities.

A complex of nonexempt activity caused the IRS to revoke the exemption of the Orange County Agricultural Society.[18] Its UBI averaged between 29 and 34% of its gross revenue. Private inurement was also found because the Society was doing business with its board of directors. In another context, the IRS privately ruled that a 50–50 ratio of related to unrelated income was permitted for a day care center raising funds from travel tours.[19] An organization with unrelated income in excess of 15 to 20% of its gross revenue must be prepared to defend its exempt status.

(iii) *Excess Business Holdings.* A private foundation may not operate a business and is limited in the ownership percentage it can hold in a separate business entity.[20]

5.2 EXCEPTIONS AND MODIFICATIONS FROM TAX

The concepts of UBI are vague and contain many exceptions that have been carved out by special interest groups to allow nonprofit organizations to generate revenue free of tax. The exceptions and modifications are outlined below.

(a) The Irregular Exception

Profits from a business conducted irregularly is excluded from tax. A business is *regularly carried on* if it is operated with a frequency and continuity comparable to for-profit entities that conduct the same trade or business. Operation of a sandwich stand at the annual county fair is an example of a periodic and discontinuous business. A cafe that is open daily, by comparison, is a regular activity. A five-day antique show is an irregular business when compared to an antique store open five days each week. Taxpayers and the IRS argue about whether the preparation time involved in conducting a revenue-raising activity must be counted in measuring the irregular factor. Year-round sales efforts for ads in a labor organization's yearbook, in the IRS's eyes, meant the activity was regularly carried on. The facts indicated that the yearbook had relevance to the members throughout the year and "the vast majority of advertisements carried a definitely commercial message."[21]

(b) The Volunteer Exception

Any business in which substantially all the work is performed without compensation is excluded from UBI. *Substantially,* for this purpose, means at least 80 to 85% of the total work performed, measured normally by the total hours worked. A paid manager or executive, administrative personnel, and all sorts of support staff can manage the business if most of the work is performed by volunteers. This rule is the reason that the countless boxes of candy, coupon books, and other items sold by school children to raise funds for parent–teacher organizations do not result in unrelated business income to the school or PTA.

In most cases, the number of hours worked, rather than relative value of the work, is used to measure the percent test. This means that the value of volunteer time need not necessarily be quantified for comparison to monetary compensation paid. In the case of a group of volunteer singing doctors, the value of the doctors' time was considered. Because the doctors were the stars of the records producing the income, their time was counted by the court at a premium, which offset administrative personnel whose time was compensated modestly.[22] Having 77 percent of its labor donated by volunteers, however, was not enough to allow a bingo operation to avail itself of this exception. The 23 percent compensated workforce ratio was substantial enough to cause the Elks Lodge to pay tax on its bingo profits.[23]

Expense reimbursements, in-kind benefits, and prizes are treated as compensation if they are compensatory in nature. In the case that expense reimbursements enable the volunteers to work longer hours and serve the convenience of the organization, the payments need not be counted in measuring this exception. However, solicitors for a religious organization that traveled in vans and lived a "very Spartan life" were not unpaid volunteers, as the organization had claimed, because their livelihood was provided for by the organization. Similarly, when food, lodging, and other living expenses were furnished to sustain members of a religious group, the members working for the group's businesses were not treated as volunteers.[24]

(c) The Donated Goods Exception

The selling of merchandise, substantially all of which is received by the nonprofit as donations, is not treated as a taxable activity. Thrift and resale shops selling donated goods are afforded a special exception from UBI for donated goods they sell. A shop selling goods on consignment as well as donated goods must distinguish between the two types of goods. Under the fragmentation rules,[25] the consigned good sales would be separated, or fragmented, from the donated goods and any net profit from those sales included in UBI. Consignment sales by volunteer-run resale shops would be excluded under the volunteer exception.

(d) The Convenience Exception

For §501(c)(3) organizations only, a cafeteria, bookstore, residence, or similar facility used in the organization's programs and operated for the convenience of patients, visitors, employees, or students is specifically excepted from UBI.[26] The rationale for this exception says recovery of patients is hastened when family and friends visit or stay with them in the hospital, and the cafeteria facilitates the visits. Museum visitors can spend more time viewing art if they can stop to rest their feet and have a cup of coffee. When the cafe, shop, dorm, or parking lot is also open to the general public, the revenue produced by public use is unrelated income. It is thought by some that the whole facility becomes subject to UBIT if the facility's entrance is on a public street. At best, the income from a facility used by both qualified visitors and the disinterested public off the street is fragmented. The taxable and nontaxable revenue is identified and tabulated, and the net taxable portion is calculated under the dual-use rules.[27]

(e) The Passive Income Modification

For all §501(c) organizations other than social clubs (7), voluntary employee benefit associations (9), supplemental unemployment plans (17), and group legal service plans (20), specified types of investment income are modified, or excluded, from UBI unless the underlying property is subject to debt. IRC §512(b) excludes "all dividends, interest, royalties, rents, payments with respect to security loans, and annuities, and all deductions connected with such income." Passive income of a sort not specifically listed is not necessarily modified or excluded from UBI. Amounts distributed to a tax-exempt organization from a partnership retain their character as either nontaxable passive or active business taxable income. Distributions from a subchapter S corporation, however, are fully taxed with no modifications available.

Dividends and interest paid on amounts invested in savings accounts, certificates of deposit, money market accounts, bonds, loans, preferred or common stocks, payments in respect to security loans, annuities, and the net of any allocable deductions are excluded from UBI.

Rental income is considered a passive type of investment income that is modified (excluded) from unrelated business income, except:

- Personal property rentals are taxable unless they are rented incidentally (not more than 10 percent of rent) with real property.
- A fluctuating rental agreement that calculates the rent based on net profits from the property is unrelated income (however, rent based upon gross revenue is *not* UBI).
- When substantial services are rendered in connection with rentals, such as a theater complete with staff or a hotel room complete with room service, the rental is not considered passive.[28]

Royalties, whether measured by production or by the gross or taxable income from a property, are modified.[29] The fact that the term *royalties* is not defined under the code or regulations pertaining to unrelated income has caused significant controversy. The IRS insisted that a royalty must be received in an activity that is passive in order to qualify. The Tax Court instead found that a royalty paid for the use of intangible property rights can be modified, or not taxed. The battle focused on licensing of mailing lists, exempt organization logos, and associated issuance of affinity cards; the IRS conceded defeat in December 1999.[30] Income from an oil and gas working interest, for which the exempt organization is responsible for its share of development costs, is not modified or excluded from UBI.[31]

Research income is generally excluded from UBI unless the work is performed for private for-profit purposes, such as drug testing for a pharmaceutical company. Research conducted for the federal government and its agencies, states, municipalities, and their subdivisions, is excluded from UBI. Fundamental research (and in practice applied research), the results of which are made available to the general public, are also excluded.[32] Research of all types conducted by a college, university, or hospital is excluded.

Gains from the sale, exchange, or other disposition of property is classified as UBI dependent upon the character of the property sold. Generally, the normal income tax rules of §§1221 and 1231 for identifying capital versus ordinary income property apply to identify property covered by this exception. Sales of stock in trade or other inventory-type property, or of property held for sale to customers in the ordinary course of a trade or business, produces UBI. Net capital loss from the sale or other disposition of assets used in an unrelated trade, business, or debt-financed property, is not allowed to offset other UBI reported by a tax-exempt corporation. An exempt trust, however, can deduct a $3,000 net capital loss. Form 4797 is attached to Form 990-T to report sales of business property.

Social clubs can possibly achieve a tax-free sale of club property if another site is acquired within one year before, or three years after, a sale.[33] There is an exception to the general rule that a club is taxed on all of its investment income: Some clubs choose *not* to seek tax-exempt status in order to offset club activity losses against investment income. Care must be exercised in converting a club from tax-exempt to for-profit status. Appreciation inherent in the club's assets—often substantial—is taxed upon conversion to a for-profit status.[34]

For-profit subsidiary payments in the form of rent, interest, royalties, or other deductible expenses are not eligible to be modified and are instead taxable to a tax-exempt parent that owns more than 50 percent (by vote or value) of the subsidiary stock, partnership, or other beneficial interest.

Other special exceptions to classification as an unrelated business are provided in the tax code for public fairs and conventions, bingo games permitted under state law, certain low-cost articles distributed in connection with a fund-raising campaign, and exchanges of certain mailing lists.

5.3 UNRELATED DEBT-FINANCED INCOME

The modifications exempting passive investment income, such as dividends and interest, from the UBIT do not apply to the extent that the investment is made with borrowed funds, called *acquisition indebtedness*. Debt-financed property is defined as including property held for the production of income that was acquired or improved with borrowed funds and has a balance of acquisition indebtedness attributable to it during the year.[35] The classic examples are a margin account held against the nonprofit's endowment funds or a mortgage financing the purchase of a rental building.

(a) Properties Subject to Debt-Financed Rules

Real or other tangible or intangible property used 85 percent or more of the time it is actually devoted to and actually used directly in the organization's exempt or related activities is exempt from these rules.[36] Assume that a university borrows money and builds an office tower for its projected staff needs over a 20-year period. If less than 85 percent of the building is used by its staff and a net profit is earned, the non–university-use portion of the building income is unrelated business income.

Income included in UBI for some other reason, such as hotel room rentals or a 100 percent owned subsidiary's royalties, is specifically excluded by the code and is not counted twice because the property is debt financed.[37] Conversely, an indebted property used in an unrelated activity that is excluded from UBI because it is managed by volunteers, is for the convenience of members, or is a facility for sale of donated goods is not treated as unrelated debt-financed property.[38] Research property producing income otherwise excluded from the UBIT is not subject to the acquisition indebtedness taint.

Future-use land (not including buildings) acquired and held by a nonprofit for use within 10 years (churches get 15 years) from the date it is acquired, and located in the *neighborhood* in which the organization conducts a program, is exempt from this provision. This exception applies until the plans are abandoned; after five years, the organization's plans for use must be "reasonably certain."[39]

The tax status of the tenant or user is not determinative. Rental of an indebted medical office building used by staff physicians can be related to a hospital's purposes.[40] Although their restoration served a charitable purpose, the rental of restored historic properties to private tenants was deemed not to serve an exempt purpose where the properties were not open to the public.[41] Regulations suggest that all facts and circumstances of property usage will be considered.

Although investment of a pension fund is admittedly inherent in its exempt purposes, debt-financed investments made by such a fund (or most other exempt organizations) are not inherent in a fund's purposes.[42] For that reason, the Southwest Texas Electric Cooperative's purchase of Treasury notes with Rural Electrification Administration (REA) loan proceeds represented a debt-financed investment. Though the loan proceeds had to be used to pay construction costs, the cooperative's cash flow allowed it to pay part of the construction costs with operating funds. To take advantage of a more than 4 percent spread in the REA loan and prevailing Treasury note rates, the cooperative deliberately "drew down" on the REA loan. The Tax Court agreed with the IRS that the interest income was taxable debt-financed income.[43]

Indebted property producing no recurrent annual income, but held to produce appreciation in underlying value, or capital gain, is subject to this rule.[44] A look-back rule prevents deliberate payoff prior to sale to avoid the tax. The portion of the taxable gain is calculated using the highest amount of indebtedness during the 12 months preceding the sale as the numerator.[45]

Schools and their supporting organizations, certain pension trusts, and §501(c)(25) title holding companies may have a special exception for indebted real property. If the property is purchased in a partnership with for-profit investors, profit-and-loss–sharing ratios must have substantial economic effect and not violate the disproportionate allocation rules.[46]

(b) Acquisition Indebtedness

Acquisition indebtedness is the unpaid amount of any debt incurred to purchase or improve property or any debt "reasonably foreseen" at the time of acquisition that would not have been incurred otherwise.[47] Securities purchased on margin are debt financed; payments on loans of securities already owned are not. The formula for calculation of income subject to tax is:

$$\frac{\text{Income from property} \times \text{Average acquisition indebtedness}}{\text{Average adjusted basis}}$$

The average acquisition indebtedness equals the arithmetic average of each month or partial month of the tax year. The average adjusted basis is similarly calculated, and only straight-line depreciation is allowed. The proportion-of-use test applied to identify property used for exempt and nonexempt purposes can be based on a comparison of the number of days used for exempt purposes with the total time the property is used, on the basis of square footage used for each, or on relative costs.[48]

Debt placed on property by a donor (prior to donating) will be attributed to the organization only when the exempt organization agrees to pay all or part of the debt or makes any payments on the equity.[49] Property that is encumbered and subject to existing debt at the time it is received by bequest is not treated as acquisition indebted-property for 10 years from its acquisition if there is no assumption or obligation to pay the debt by the organization. Gifted property subject to debt is similarly excluded, if the donor placed the mortgage on the property over five years prior to gift and had owned the property over five years, unless there is an assumption or payment on the mortgage by the nonprofit. A life estate does not constitute a debt. When some other individual or organization is entitled to income from the property for life or another period of time, a remainder interest in the property is not considered to be indebted.[50]

Federal funding provided or insured by the Federal Housing Administration, if used to finance purchase, construction, or rehabilitation of residential property for low-income persons, is excluded.

Charitable gift annuities issued as the sole consideration in exchange for property worth more than 90 percent of the value of the annuity is not considered acquisition indebtedness. The annuity must be payable over the life (not for a minimum or maximum number of payments) of one or two persons alive at the time. The annuity must not be measured by the property's (or any other property's) income.

(c) Calculation of Taxable Portion

Only that portion of the net income of debt-financed property attributable to the debt is classified as UBI.[51] Each property subject to debt is calculated separately, with the resulting income or loss netted to arrive at the portion to include in UBI. A planning opportunity arises for an organization that intends to buy a dual-use building. The nontaxable exempt function portion of the property could purposefully be purchased with debt and the unrelated part of the facility purchased with cash available. Or, separate notes could be executed, with the taxable and unrelated property's debt being paid off first. Expenses directly connected with the property are deducted from gross revenue in the same proportion. The formula for calculating capital gain or loss is different in one respect than in the one used above: The highest amount of indebtedness during the year preceding sales is used as the numerator. The formula can be better understood by studying Schedule E of Form 990-T illustrated in Appendix 5A.

5.4 WHO FILES FORM 990-T?

All domestic and foreign nonprofits, including churches, state colleges and universities, trusts, individual retirement accounts, medical savings plans, and other tax-exempt organizations not required to file Forms 990, must file Form 990-T illustrated in Appendix 5A. This Exempt Organization Business Income Tax Return,[52] is filed to report gross income from UBI over $1,000 that is not excluded for one of the reasons outlined in §5.2.[53] Gross income for this purpose means gross receipts less cost of goods sold but before reduction for selling and administrative expenses. The tax on UBI applies to all organizations exempt from tax under §501(c) other than corporations created by an act of Congress and municipalities of the government. It also applies to:

- Tax-exempt employee trusts described in IRC §401, including individual retirement accounts

- State and municipal colleges and universities and the corporations they own
- Qualified state tuition programs described in IRC §529
- Education individual retirement accounts described in IRC §530 and medical savings accounts described in IRC §220(d)

In 1989, the IRS expanded the Form 990 to report details of revenue sources on page 6 in Part VII. Unrelated business income that is subject to tax is reported in column B, giving the IRS a red flag indicating that Form 990-T must be filed. Consequently, it is important to coordinate amounts reported on the 990-T with Part VII of Form 990 discussed in Chapter 2.8.

5.5 DUE DATES, TAX RATES, AND OTHER FILING ISSUES

(a) Due Date

Most Forms 990-T are due to be filed on the same day as the other Forms 990—the 15th day of the fifth month following the close of the organization's fiscal year (it used to be the third month). Trusts, employee trusts, and IRAs file by the 15th day of the fourth month following the close of the organization's fiscal year. Nonprofits that are corporations may obtain an automatic six-month extension of this time to file by submitting Form 7004, Application for Automatic Extension of Time to File Corporate Income Tax Return. Others use Form 2758, Application for Extension of Time to File Certain Excise, Income, Information, and Other Returns, to obtain a two- to three-month extension. The extension of time to file does not allow an extension of time to pay any tax due.

(b) Payment of Tax

The tax liability is paid in advance through the quarterly estimated tax system if the annual tax is in excess of $500. Estimated tax deposits are due the 15th day of the fifth, sixth, ninth, and twelfth months of the tax year. Payments are either made using Form 8109-B, Federal Tax Deposit Coupons, or through electronic funds transfer.[54] Exempt organization taxpayers with taxable income of $1 million or more must use the actual method and pay tax for its second through fourth quarter based on actual income earned for the year, rather than basing the payment on the prior year. The tax rates applicable to nonexempt corporations and trusts are applied to calculate the tax.

Although the impact may be reduced by the charitable deduction (using §170 individual limitations), the significantly higher tax rate imposed on trusts reflects a need for good planning by a tax-exempt trust. For this reason, such a trust would create a for-profit subsidiary from which to conduct unrelated business activity. Affiliated exempt organizations that are commonly controlled must combine their incomes. The 15 percent bracket applies only to the first $50,000 of their combined income; the 25 percent applies to the next $25,000, and so on. The affiliates can apportion the tax brackets among themselves as they please, or they can share the lower brackets equally.[55] An apportionment plan must be signed by all members and attached to their Form 990-T.

(c) Credits and Alternative Minimum Tax

Because an exempt organization earning UBI is taxed just like for-profit corporations and trusts, the general business and foreign tax credits and alternative minimum taxes (AMT) may apply.[56] The AMT was repealed (effective 1998) for corporations with average gross receipts of $5 million for the past three years. A discussion of these tax rules is beyond the scope of this book; a prudent organization should seek the help of competent consultants in this regard.

(d) Proxy Tax

Expenses of attempts to influence legislation—lobbying–are not deductible in arriving at taxable income. A civic association, labor union, or business league that has lobbying activity has a choice of either informing its members of the portion of their dues so expended or paying a tax of 35 percent of its lobbying expenses.[57] The amount of the proxy tax is reported on a single line in the tax calculation on Part III of Form 990-T. The taxable amount is also reported on page 5 of Form 990 in Part VI, question 85(f), so that the IRS is alerted as to when to expect the tax to be paid.

(e) Interest and Penalties

Several different charges are imposed when a return is filed late. The failure-to-file penalty of 5 percent of the tax due per month the return is late (up to a maximum of 25 percent) is imposed,[58] unless the organization can show reasonable cause for the delay. In the author's experience, the Ogden Service Center is often lenient toward first-time filers who voluntarily submit Forms 990-T and pay the tax. For the late filing and paying penalties to be abated, the failure to file cannot be due to willful neglect; ordinary business care and prudence must have been used to ascertain the requirement.[59] An explanation seeking abatement should be attached to the return requesting relief and explaining why the return was filed late, particularly if the organization regularly engages independent accountants who failed to advise it of its obligation to do so. Next, a penalty of 0.5 percent of the unpaid tax may be assessed for failure to pay (i.e., an annual rate of 6 percent up to a maximum of 25 percent of the amount due). Additionally, a penalty may be due for failure to pay the tax in advance through the estimated tax system described above. Form 2220 is used to calculate this penalty, which is assessed on a daily basis at the prevailing federal rate.

(f) Statute of Limitations

The statute of limitations for assessment of the unrelated business income tax on Form 990-T is three years and begins when the 990 contains sufficient facts (shown in Part VII) from which the UBIT can be determined.[60] Say, for example, an organization lists an amount for shop sales on its year 2000 Form 990, Part VII, column D, identifying it with the #2 exclusion code as being run by volunteers. Assume the IRS examines the organization in 2003 and finds, in their opinion, that less than the requisite 85 percent of labor was provided by volunteers. If the organization acted in good faith without intent to defraud the IRS or evade tax, tax cannot be assessed for returns filed before 2000. Note that substantial underpayment penalties might be assessed for the open years.[61]

(g) Why File to Report Losses

Form 990-T is due to be filed when gross income exceeds $1,000, even when the deductions an organization is entitled to claim result in a loss from the unrelated business activity. The statute of limitations for IRS examination of the issue begins to toll, and net operating losses can be carried over for up to 20 years to offset net unrelated income in subsequent years. An operating loss may also be carried back by filing an amended Form 990-T for the two immediately preceding tax years if income tax was paid.

(h) Consolidated Returns

As a rule, each nonprofit organization is required to file its own separate Form 990, except for subordinate members included in a group return.[62] A consolidated Form 990-T can be filed if (1) the 80 percent control requirements of IRC §1504 are satisfied, (2) all members are tax exempt under §501(a), (3) at least one member of the group is a title-holding company, and (4) all other members of the group are entitled to receive income from the title-holding company.

(i) Refund Claim

Payers of dividends, interest, and other types of income must do back-up withholding of income tax if Form W-9 is not furnished in order to indicate that no tax withholding is required by them. A tax-exempt organization files Form 990-T to claim a refund for any such tax. A tax-exempt organization investing in a regulated investment company might also have had some taxes paid by the company on its behalf for which it can claim a tax credit on Form 990-T.

5.6 NORMAL INCOME TAX RULES APPLY

(a) Accounting Methods and Periods

Taxable income is calculated using the method of accounting regularly used in keeping the exempt organization's books and records.[63] Organizations with more than $5 million of annual gross receipts must use the accrual method.[64] Also, an organization selling merchandise or goods that are accounted for piece by piece must maintain inventory records and also use the accrual method.[65] Any change in method results in *§481 adjustments*. Form 3115 is filed to seek permission for the change and to spread the effect of the change over five years (from the effective date of the change).[66]

(b) "Ordinary and Necessary" Criteria

Deductions claimed against the unrelated income must be "ordinary and necessary" in conducting the activity and must meet the other standards of IRC §162 for business deductions. *Ordinary* means common and accepted for the type of business operated; *necessary* means helpful and appropriate, and not indispensable. Ordinary does not necessarily mean required, but can mean appropriate or customary. Thus, an organization can deduct expenses commonly claimed by commercial businesses operating similar businesses.

(c) Profit Motive

To be deductible, the motivation for making an expenditure must be the production of income. The activity must be operated for the purpose of making a profit to be considered a business.[67] IRC §183 specifically prohibits the deduction of hobby losses, or those activities losing money for more than two years out of every five. In the social club arena, the IRS and the clubs battled for several years over the deductibility of nonmember activity losses against investment income. Ultimately, the clubs lost. The exploitation rule disallows deduction of related activity expenses against UBI, partly because exempt activities are not conducted with a profit motive.

(d) Depreciation

Equipment, buildings, vehicles, furniture, and other properties that are used in the business are deductible over their useful lives through the depreciation system. As a simple example, one third of the cost of a computer that is expected to become obsolete within three years is deductible each year for three years. Unfortunately, Congress uses these calculation rates and methods as political and economic tools, and the revenue code prescribes rates and methods that are not simple. IRC §§167, 168, and 179 apply and must be studied to properly calculate allowable deductions for depreciation.

(e) Inventory

If the organization keeps an inventory of items for sale, such as books, drugs, or merchandise of any sort, it must use an inventory method to deduct the cost of such goods. The concept is one of matching the cost of the item sold with its sales proceeds. If the organization buys 10 widgets for sale and at the end of a year only five have been sold, the cost of the five is deductible and the remaining five are capitalized as an asset to be deducted when in fact they are sold. Again, the system is far more complicated than this simple example, and an accountant should be consulted to ensure use of proper reporting and tabulation methods. IRC §§263A and 471 through 474 apply.

(f) Capital and Nondeductibles

A host of nondeductible items contained in §§261 through 280H might apply to disallow deductions either by total disallowance or required capitalization of permanent assets. Again, all the rules applicable to for-profit businesses apply, such as the luxury automobile limits, travel and entertainment substantiation requirements, and 50 percent disallowance for meals.

(g) Dividend Deduction

The dividends-received deductions provided by §§243 through 245 for taxable nonexempt corporations are not allowed. Normal corporations are allowed to exclude 70 percent of their investment dividends; exempt organizations are not. Note that this rule presents a problem only for dividends received from investments that are debt financed and thereby taxable. Most dividends received by exempts are excluded from the UBI under the *Modifications* for passive income.[68] For certain thinly capitalized subsidiaries, IRC §163(j) can remove the passive income exception.

(h) Charitable Deduction

Up to 10 percent of an exempt corporation's and 20 to 50 percent of a trust's unrelated taxable income, before the deduction, is deductible for contributions paid to another charitable organization.[69] Note that the deduction is not allowed for an organization's internal project expenditures or gifts to a controlled subsidiary. Contributions in excess of allowable amounts are eligible for a five-year carryover. Social clubs, voluntary employee business associations, unemployment benefit trusts, and group legal service plans can take a 100 percent deduction for direct charitable gifts and qualified set-asides for charitable purposes.[70]

(i) Net Operating Losses

A net operating loss can be applied to offset income on which income tax was paid for the two tax years preceding the loss by filing a carryback claim. The preferable way to file a carryback claim is to amend Form 990-T for each prior year to which the loss can be carried to offset income previously reported. The instructions direct the preparer to consult IRS Publication 536, which pertains to individual NOLs. Apparently since both nonprofit corporations and trusts file the 990-T, there is no form prescribed particularly for nonprofit organizations. The IRS technical assistors in Cincinnati say there is no specific guidance on this issue. Any remaining losses can be carried forward to offset net income for 20 years following the loss year.[71] Thus, it can be important for an exempt to file Form 990-T to establish a loss potentially available to offset future income.

5.7 THE UNIQUE DESIGN OF THE 990-T

Form 990-T has evolved over the years to accommodate the unique fashion in which deductions against certain types of income are claimed. The sequence of lines is somewhat different from other tax forms with special schedules for rentals, debt-financed UBI, payments from controlled subsidiaries, exploited exempt activities, and advertising. The form is designed to enforce the general concept that no portion of the organization's underlying mission–related expenses are deductible.

(a) Part I

Part I was revised (in 1992) by adding a column to present the direct expenses alongside gross income, for which supporting schedules are completed. Previously, only the net income was carried to this part. This redesign was said to reflect an IRS intention to evaluate deductible expenses. However, for line 1 income, the direct expenses other than cost of goods sold are deducted in Part II and may cause some confusion, particularly in relation to lines called Excess Exempt and Excess Readership Expenses. The suggestions for this part will therefore be presented according to the various types of UBI, rather than line by line. Modest organizations whose gross unrelated income does not exceed $10,000 need not play the line game; the total UBI is entered on line 13. For Form 990 and 990-PF filers, line 13 should equal the total on line 15, column (b) of Form 990-T.

(b) Part II, Deductions Not Taken Elsewhere

On Form 990-T, expenses are deducted either in Part I or Part II, not due to the nature of particular types of expenses, but strictly according to the form's design and the type of income. As the title implies, allocable expenses not deducted in Part I are claimed here. The IRS instructions for this part contain guidance for preparation. Helpful schedules designed to apply the different limitations for certain types of deductions flow into both Parts I and II and serve the following functions:

- Schedule A reports cost of goods sold for those organizations required to maintain inventories. There is no Schedule B, D, or H.
- Schedule C calculates the portion of taxable personal property rentals.
- Schedule E calculates the taxable portion of revenue attributable to debt-financed income.
- Schedule F calculates the taxable portion of revenue from controlled subsidiaries.
- Schedule G calculates the taxable income of social clubs, voluntary employee benefit associations, and supplemental employee benefit trusts setting aside part of their income for charitable purposes.
- Schedule I applies a deduction limitation for unrelated income exploited from an exempt activity, such as green fees paid by nonstudents to play on a school's golf course or commissions for nonmember insurance.
- Schedule J applies the deduction limitations and income allocations necessary to arrive at taxable advertising revenue.
- Schedule K reports officer, director, and trustee compensation attributable to unrelated business income.

5.8 CATEGORIES OF DEDUCTIONS

The complexity of Form 990-T goes beyond the task of understanding the income tax system. Exempt organizations, in their efforts to raise funds, have devised creative methods to make money utilizing their tangible and intangible assets and their staff. In the words of the regulations, such money-making schemes "exploit" the exempt functions. People and things are mingled and used for both exempt and income-producing purposes. Whatever method is used to arrive at the deductible expenses, including overhead or general and administrative costs, the method must not permit the amalgamation of for-profit and nonprofit activities.[72] If followed consistently from year to year, an organization can apply the method it uses for financial statement purposes as a reasonable basis for claiming UBI deductions. Regarding joint costs, the accounting profession says, "The cost allocation methodology used should be rational and systematic, it should result in an allocation of joint costs that is reasonable, and it should be applied consistently given similar facts and circumstances."[73] The UBI sections of the code "do not specifically address how expenses are to be allocated when exempt organizations are computing their UBI."[74] The regulations provide three specific types of deductible expenses.[75]

- Type 1—Expenses attributable solely to unrelated business activities
- Type 2—Dual-use property or project expenses
- Type 3—Exploited activity expenses

(a) Type 1

Expenses attributable solely to unrelated business activities are fully deductible.[76] Such expenses are those reasonably allocable under good accounting theory consistently applied using a method that evidences their connection with the production of unrelated gross income.[77] Two classic business expense deduction concepts are applied:

1. A "proximate and primary relationship" between the expense and the activity is the standard for deduction.[78] Proximate means near, close, or immediate, such as the full-time personnel devoted solely to the business.
2. A "but for" test can be applied by asking the question, "Would the expense be incurred if the unrelated activity was not carried on?"

(b) Type 2

A portion of dual-use or shared employees, facilities, equipment, and other overhead expenses is also deductible. Shared costs are allocated between related and unrelated activities on a reasonable basis. The only example given in the IRS regulations allocates 10 percent of an organization president's salary to the business activity to which he devotes 10 percent of his time.[79] This type presents a classic chicken and egg or tail-wagging-the-dog situation. Is the UBI activity an afterthought, or was a facility built to be dually used? When the exempt activity would be carried on regardless of the UBI funds and essentially came first, the exploitation rule (type 3) rather than the dual-use type of expense allocation applies. A mailing list developed and maintained for a symphonic society's ticket sales instead might be dual-use property.

It is sometimes difficult to decide whether the type 2 or 3 category should apply. It is important to note in making this choice that the exploitation method often yields a higher level of expense deduction. Conceivably, 100 percent of an exploited activity's expenses are allocable to the unrelated income, but subject to an income limitation. As discussed in §5.9, to make cost allocations, the denominator of the formulas can significantly influence the result.

(c) Type 3

The third type is an allocated portion of a program-related or exempt function activity's expense that produces income from an unrelated aspect (such as the sale of advertising), and is said to exploit the exempt activity. Under specific conditions that depend on the character of the exploited activity, the deduction of exempt function cost is allowed but may be limited by the income generated. The general rule is expressed negatively and disallows such deductions because they are not considered to have a proximate and primary relationship to the revenue. Nonetheless, to the extent of the revenue earned, a portion of this type 3 expense is deductible. The deductible portion of a type 3 expense is calculated through a series of steps in Schedules I and J of Form 990-T that do not allow a loss from an exploited activity to be deducted. To compute UBI, no expense attributable to the conduct of the exempt activity is deductible, except in specified circumstances and with limitation.[80] To be deductible, all three conditions must be satisfied:

- *Condition 1:* The unrelated trade or business activity is of a kind carried on for profit by taxable organizations, and the exempt activity exploited by the business is a type of activity normally conducted by taxable organizations in pursuance of such business.
- *Condition 2:* Expenses, depreciation, and similar items attributable to the exempt activity exceed the income (if any) derived from or attributable to the exempt activity.
- *Condition 3:* The allocation of such expenses to the unrelated trade or business activity does not result in a loss from such unrelated trade or business activity.[81] Schedules I and J of Form 990-T illustrate this condition.

Fund-raising activity in pursuit of voluntary contributions is a good example of a revenue activity that is not normally considered businesslike.[82] Generally, the cost of maintaining an organization's contributor or member lists is not deductible against the proceeds of sales of the list. The IRS says the regulation "is somewhat helpful in trying to decide whether the sale of a mailing list is a dual related/unrelated use or an exploitation of an exempt function."[83] The IRS admits that there seems to be "a significant question of whether exempt function expenses that exceed exempt function income may be deducted."

Type 3 (exploitation) deductions can be financially valuable. Essentially, program service costs, also known as exempt function costs, of an inherently businesslike exempt activity can be deducted for UBI purposes, despite the general rule that they cannot be. When the allocation is permitted, the organization essentially earns tax-free income to cover its exempt function costs. Treating expenses as a type 3 may result in a higher deduction than a type 2 that allows for only a calculated portion of the exempt function costs. Type 2 (dual-use) expenses may be advantageous in some circumstances because the type 3 allocable expense must first be reduced by exempt function revenue. Also, a loss deductible against other UBI cannot result from type 3 expenses,[84] whereas a dual-use facility loss may be deducted against other types of UBI.

Publications are less troublesome. The rules anticipate that periodicals are businesslike, and the exploited activity costs can be deducted.[85] A framework for allocating exempt function, or readership, costs against the advertising revenue is reported on Schedule J. Reportable income is calculated in two parts. First, any advertising revenue is offset by the direct cost of producing, selling, and presenting the ads in the publication. Second, revenue from the direct sale of the publication plus an imputed portion of member dues, if any, is tallied and offset by other costs referred to as *readership costs*.

Advertising revenue produces UBI. An advertisement contains words printed or aired to recognize a sponsor that are "qualitative and quantitative."[86] Words like "XYZ is the best" or "buy XYZ products" taint the revenue. Recognition of business sponsors with a listing of their name, address (including Internet without a link) and logo is not treated as an advertisement. The standard is rather broad and has been established by sponsor recognition allowed on public television and radio by the Federal Communication Commission. The sponsorship regulations proposed in March 2000, however, create new types of advertising revenue. Revenue received for permitting exclusive distribution of a company's products to an organization's participants is also deemed to be taxed under the proposed regulations. The exploitation method is used to allocate and report expenses attributable to this sort of revenue, and in the author's opinion such revenue may be reported in either Part I or Part J of Form 990-T, dependent on whether a publication is involved.

Sales of merchandise or products, scientific research, health care service, and many other categories of revenue production are conducted by both tax-exempts and for-profit businesses. Some activities, such as education and cultural performances (dance and theater), are conducted primarily by exempts but also by businesses, and technically qualify under Condition 1.

5.9 COST ALLOCATIONS

The UBI code sections "do not specifically address how a dual-use or exploited expense is to be allocated when exempt organizations are computing UBI."[87] The IRS Manual instructs examining agents that any reasonable method resulting in identifying relationship of the expenses to revenue produced is acceptable.[88] Different allocation methods are available, but once a method is chosen it must be consistently followed from year to year and for all purposes.[89] The choice of method depends on the organization's complexity and the nature of its activities. The AICPA (American Institute of Certified Public Accountants) and the NACUBO (National Association of College and University Business Officers), in response to the time spent and controversies resulting from IRS examinations, suggest the adoption of standards of cost allocations for UBI purposes.

The IRS has prescribed the fashion in which a §501(c)(4), (5), or (6) organization allocates its expenses to compute the cost of its lobbying activity.[90] Two simplified methods—a direct gross-up of labor costs (take total salaries and add 175 percent for indirect costs) and a ratio method (take total costs and allocate them based on number of hours personnel spend on various functions)—are suggested in addition to the complex rules of IRC §263A. Those rules should be carefully studied as a harbinger of future IRS rules. The AICPA Tax Exempt Organizations Resource Panel and the NACUBO have suggested that this sort of guidance be issued. Whatever method an exempt organization chooses to follow to allocate costs, the method should clearly reflect the economic realities of the organization and the UBI it receives, and should be evidenced by suitable documentation. Actual time records must be maintained by all personnel and professional advisors to reflect the effort devoted to related versus unrelated activities. Absent time records, an allocation based on relative gross income produced might be used. Direct and indirect expenses must be distinguished.

Direct expenses are those that increase proportionately with the usage of a facility or the volume of activity, and are also called *variable expenses*. For example, the number of persons attending an event influences the number of ushers or security guards and represents a direct cost, or, in other words, a cost attributable to that specific use that would not have been incurred *but for* the particular event. *Indirect costs* are incurred without regard to usage or frequency of participation, and are also called *fixed expenses.* An organization's building acquisition costs or annual audit fees, for example, do not necessarily vary with usage. Management and general expenses are normally of this character.

A *gross income method* of cost allocation is sometimes used to calculate cost of goods sold when costs bear a relationship to the revenue produced from exempt and nonexempt factors. The regulations say, "Such allocations based on receipts from exempt activities may not be reasonable since such receipts are not normally reflective of cost."[91]

A proration based on the number of participants might be suitable in some circumstances. This type of formula is used in calculating allocations for social clubs charging different prices to members and nonmembers. The hours a facility is used might be applied. The proper denominator of the fraction used to calculate costs allocable to UBI is also significant in reducing or increasing allowable deductions. Arguably, no fixed costs of a property used for exempt purposes should be allocated to UBI, but to date the courts have allowed allocation among both the exempt and nonexempt functions that benefit from building use. In a football stadium case, for example, the court allowed the following:[92]

$$\frac{\text{Number of hours or days used for unrelated purposes}}{\text{Total number of house or days in use}}$$

The IRS argued that fixed costs were allocated (produces a much smaller number) by:

$$\frac{\text{Number of hours or days used for unrelated purposes}}{\text{Total number of hours or days in entire year}}$$

The United Cancer Council's (UCC) allocation system for identifying the public education, fund-raising, and generic content of its direct mail materials was reviewed by the Tax Court. The UCC failed the commensurate test[93] because less than 10 percent of its publication, measured by the linear and square inches of material, contained educational information. It was ultimately found to also provide private inurement to fund-raising managers.[94]

The IRS has said it prefers a system that allocates costs to all activities similar to a generally accepted accounting principles (GAAP) functional expense statement. One commentator suggests reference to the foreign tax credit allocation rules for guidance in allocating dual-use facility costs.[95] Take, for example, a hospital pharmacy. A portion of the revenue is generated from sales to patients and is considered as related income. The nonpatient sales are instead classified as unrelated income. The objective is to assign the expenses of the pharmacy operation to the appropriate category of revenue. The easy way is to apportion the expenses using the relative percentages of related and unrelated revenue. Revenue, however, can be dissected and leveled for market and other differences. If the patient sales, for example, are made at a 20 percent discount below that of the amount charged over the counter, patient sales would be grossed back up, or the nonpatient revenue discounted, before calculating the ratio. This example follows the fragmentation rules, which require that unrelated sales be segregated from related sales in an activity that embodies both. Readers should be alert to developments on this topic.

5.10 IN-KIND DONATIONS

Three different types of in-kind donations are quantified and reported as revenue and corresponding expense by tax-exempt nonprofits—donated services, facility use, and material goods. Statement of Financial Accounting Standard (SFAS) No. 116 contains specific standards for valuing and reporting such gifts.[96] Donations of the first two types are not reported for Form 990 purposes,[97] presumably to remind taxpayers that the donation of services and facilities are not deductible. Tangible goods, however, are reported and may be deductible.[98]

Donated services and use of facilities (as well as tangible goods), in the author's opinion, are reportable as deductions for UBI purposes. This tax planning opportunity can be significant. Booking the in-kind donations does not produce taxable gross income if they are voluntary gifts not subject to income tax.[99] The corresponding expense, to the extent that it is directly associated with or can be partly allocated to an unrelated business activity, can result in alleviating UBIT.

Appendix 5A

Form **990-T** — **Exempt Organization Business Income Tax Return** (and proxy tax under section 6033(e)) — OMB No 1545-0687 — **2000**

Department of the Treasury
Internal Revenue Service

For calendar year 2000 or other tax year beginning July 1st ending June 30th
See separate instructions.

A [ ] Check box if address changed

Name of organization ([ ] check box if name changed and see instructions): Hometown Chapter, Campaign to Clean Up America

D Employer identification number (Employees' trust, see instr. for Block D on p. 7.): 44-4444444

B Exempt under section: [X] 501 (c) (3) [ ] 408(e) [ ] 220(e) [ ] 408A [ ] 530(a) [ ] 529(a)

Number, street, and room or suite no. (If a P.O. box, see page 7 of instructions.): 1111 Any Street

E NEW unrelated business activity codes (see instructions for Block E on page 7.): 900002

City or town: Hometown State: Texas ZIP code: 77777

F Group exemption number (see instructions for Block F on page 7)

C Book value of all assets at end of year: 458,400

G Check organization type [X] 501(c) corporation [ ] 501(c) trust [ ] 401(a) trust [ ] Other trust

H Describe the organization's primary unrelated business activity. Rental of vans

I During the tax year, was the corporation a subsidiary in an affiliated group or a parent-subsidiary controlled group? [ ] Yes [X] No
If "Yes," enter the name and identifying number of the parent corporation.

J The books are in care of: Joan Controller Telephone number (444) 444-4444

Part I Unrelated Trade or Business Income

			(A) Income	(B) Expenses	(C) Net
1a	Gross receipts or sales				
b	Less returns and allowances c Balance	1c			
2	Cost of goods sold (Schedule A, line 7)	2			
3	Gross profit (subtract line 2 from line 1c)	3			
4a	Capital gain net income (attach Schedule D)	4a			
b	Net gain (loss) (Form 4797, Part II, line 18) (attach Form 4797)	4b			
c	Capital loss deduction for trusts	4c			
5	Income (loss) from partnerships and S corporations (attach statement)	5			
6	Rent income (Schedule C)	6	4,500	1,600	2,900
7	Unrelated debt-financed income (Schedule E)	7			
8	Interest, annuities, royalties, and rents from controlled organizations (Schedule F)	8			
9	Investment income of a section 501(c)(7), (9), or (17) organization (Schedule G)	9			
10	Exploited exempt activity income (Schedule I)	10			
11	Advertising income (Schedule J)	11			
12	Other income (see page 8 of the instructions - attach schedule)	12			
13	**TOTAL** (combine lines 3 through 12)	13	4,500	1,600	2,900

Part II Deductions Not Taken Elsewhere

(See page 9 of the instructions for limitations on deductions.)
(Except for contributions, deductions must be directly connected with the unrelated business income.)

			Line	Amount
14	Compensation of officers, directors, and trustees (Schedule K)		14	
15	Salaries and wages		15	500
16	Repairs and maintenance		16	
17	Bad debts		17	
18	Interest (attach schedule)		18	
19	Taxes and licenses		19	
20	Charitable contributions (see page 11 of the instructions for limitation rules)		20	
21	Depreciation (attach Form 4562)	21		
22	Less depreciation claimed on Schedule A and elsewhere on return	22a	22b	
23	Depletion		23	
24	Contributions to deferred compensation plans		24	
25	Employee benefit programs		25	
26	Excess exempt expenses (Schedule I)		26	
27	Excess readership costs (Schedule J)		27	
28	Other deductions (attach schedule)		28	
29	**Total deductions** (add lines 14 through 28)		29	500
30	Unrelated business taxable income before net operating loss deduction (subtract line 29 from line 13)		30	2,400
31	Net operating loss deduction		31	
32	Unrelated business taxable income before specific deduction (subtract line 31 from line 30)		32	2,400
33	Specific deduction (Generally $1,000, but see line 33 instructions for exceptions)		33	1,000
34	**Unrelated business taxable income** (subtract line 33 from line 32). If line 33 is greater than line 32, enter the smaller of zero or line 32		34	1,400

For Paperwork Reduction Act Notice, see instructions. (HTA) Form 990-T (2000)

Form 990-T (2000) Hometown Chapter, Campaign to Clean Up America 44-4444444 Page 2

Part III Tax Computation

35 Organizations Taxable as Corporations (see instructions for tax computation on page 12).
Controlled group members (sections 1561 and 1563) - check here ☐ See instructions and:
a Enter your share of the $50,000, $25,000, and $9,925,000 taxable income brackets (in that order):
(1) ____ (2) ____ (3) ____
b Enter organization's share of: (1) additional 5% tax (not more than $11,750)
(2) additional 3% tax (not more than $100,000)

Line	Description	No.	Amount
c	Income tax on the amount on line 34	35c	210
36	**Trusts Taxable at Trust Rates** (see instructions for tax computation on page 12) Income tax on the amount on line 34 from: ☐ Tax rate schedule ☐ or Schedule D (Form 1041)	36	
37	**Proxy tax** (see page 13 of the instructions)	37	
38	Alternative minimum tax	38	
39	**Total** (add lines 37 and 38 to line 35c or 36, whichever applies)	39	210

Part IV Tax and Payments

Line	Description	No.	Amount	No.	Amount
40a	Foreign tax credit (corporations attach Form 1118; trusts attach Form 1116)	40a			
b	Other credits. (See page 13 of the instructions)	40b			
c	General business credit - Check if from: ☐ Form 3800 or ☐ Form (specify)	40c			
d	Credit for prior year minimum tax (attach Form 8801 or 8827)	40d			
e	Total credits (add lines 40a through 40d)			40e	
41	Subtract line 40e from line 39			41	210
42	Recapture taxes. Check if from: ☐ Form 4255 ☐ Form 8611			42	
43	**Total tax** (add lines 41 and 42)			43	210
44	**Payments:** (a) 1999 overpayment credited to 2000	44a	300		
b	2000 estimated tax payments	44b			
c	Tax deposited with Form 8868	44c			
d	Foreign organizations - Tax paid or withheld at source (see instructions)	44d			
e	Backup withholding (see instructions)	44e			
f	Other credits and payments (see instructions)	44f			
45	**Total payments** (add lines 44a through 44f)			45	300
46	Estimated tax penalty (see page 4 of the instructions). Check ☐ if Form 2220 is attached			46	
47	**Tax due—** If line 45 is less than the total of lines 43 and 46, enter amount owed			47	
48	**Overpayment—** If line 45 is larger than the total of lines 43 and 46, enter amount overpaid			48	90
49	Enter the amount of line 48 you want: Credited to 2001 estimated tax 90	**Refunded**		49	

Part V Statements Regarding Certain Activities and Other Information (See instructions on page 14.)

	Question	Yes	No
1	At any time during the 2000 calendar year, did the organization have an interest in or a signature or other authority over a financial account in a foreign country (such as a bank account, securities account, or other financial account)? If "Yes," the organization may have to file Form TD F 90-22.1. If "Yes," enter the name of the foreign country here		X
2	During the tax year, did the organization receive a distribution from, or was it the grantor of, or transferor to, a foreign trust? If "Yes," see page 14 of the instructions for other forms the organization may have to file.		X
3	Enter the amount of tax-exempt interest received or accrued during the tax year $		

Schedule A—Cost of Goods Sold (See instructions on page 15.) Not Applicable

Method of inventory valuation (specify)

Line	Description	No.	Amount	Line	Description	No.	Amount
1	Inventory at beginning of year	1		6	Inventory at end of year	6	
2	Purchases	2		7	**Cost of goods sold.** Subtract line 6 from line 5. (Enter here and on line 2, Part I.)	7	
3	Cost of labor	3					
4a	Additional section 263A costs (attach schedule)	4a		8	Do the rules of section 263A (with respect to property produced or acquired for resale) apply to the organization?	Yes	No
b	Other costs (attach schedule)	4b					
5	TOTAL - Add lines 1 through 4b	5					

Please Sign Here
Under penalties of perjury, I declare that I have examined this return, including accompanying schedules and statements, and to the best of my knowledge and belief, it is true, correct, and complete. Declaration of preparer (other than taxpayer) is based on all information of which preparer has any knowledge.
Signature of officer or fiduciary: [signature] Date: 4/30/01 Title: President

Paid Preparer's Use Only

Preparer's signature	a. Good C.P.A	Date 4/28/01	Check if self-employed X	Preparer's SSN or PTIN P 000 72674
Firm's name (or yours, if self-employed), address, and ZIP code	A Qualified CPA Firm, 3101 Richmond Ave., Suite 220, Houston, TX. 77098-3013		EIN 76-0269860	Phone no. 713-523-5739

Form 990-T (2000) Hometown Chapter, Campaign to Clean Up Ame 44-4444444 Page 3

Schedule C—Rent Income (From Real Property and Personal Property Leased With Real Property)

(See instructions on page 16.)

1 Description of property

(1) Vans rented to other nonprofit organizations
(2)
(3)
(4)

	2 Rent received or accrued		
	(a) From personal property (if the percentage of rent for personal property is more than 10% but not more than 50%)	(b) From real and personal property (if the percentage of rent for personal property exceeds 50% or if the rent is based on profit or income)	3 Deductions directly connected with the income in columns 2(a) and 2(b) (attach schedule)
(1)		4,500	Repairs 1,100
(2)			Depreciation 500
(3)			
(4)			
Total		Total 4,500	**Total deductions.** Enter here and on line 6, column (B), Part I, page 1 1,600

Total income (Add totals of columns 2(a) and 2(b). Enter here and on line 6, column (A), Part I, page 1.) 4,500

Schedule E—Unrelated Debt-Financed Income

(See instructions on page 16.)

	1 Description of debt-financed property	2 Gross income from or allocable to debt-financed property	3 Deductions directly connected with or allocable to debt-financed property: (a) Straight line depreciation (attach schedule)	(b) Other deductions
(1)				
(2)				
(3)				
(4)				

	4 Amount of average acquisition debt on or allocable to debt-financed property (attach schedule)	5 Average adjusted basis of or allocable to debt-financed property (attach schedule)	6 Column 4 divided by column 5	7 Gross income reportable (col. 2 x col. 6)	8 Allocable deductions (column 6 x total of columns 3(a) and 3(b))
(1)					
(2)					
(3)					
(4)					
Totals				Enter here and on line 7, col. (A), Part I, page 1.	Enter here and on line 7, col. (B), Part I, page 1.

Total dividends - received deductions included in column 8 . . . . .

Schedule F—Interest, Annuities, Royalties, and Rents From Controlled Organizations

(See instructions on page 17.)

	1 Name of Controlled Organization	2 Employer Identification Number	Exempt controlled organizations: 3 Net unrelated income (loss) (see instructions)	4 Total of specified payments made	5 Part of column (4) that is included in the controlling organization's gross income	6 Deductions directly connected with income in col (5)
(1)						
(2)						
(3)						
(4)						

Nonexempt Controlled Organizations

	7 Taxable Income	8 Net unrelated income (loss) (see instructions)	9 Total of specified payments made	10 Part of column (9) that is included in the controlling organization's gross income	11 Deductions directly connected with income in column (10)
(1)					
(2)					
(3)					
(4)					
12 Totals				Add columns 5 and 10. Enter here and on line 8, Column (A), Part I, page 1.	Add columns 6 and 11. Enter here and on line 8, Column (B), Part I, page 1.

Form 990-T (2000)

Form 990-T (2000) Hometown Chapter, Campaign to Clean Up Ame 44-4444444 Page 4

Schedule G—Investment Income of a Section 501(c)(7), (9), or (17) Organization
(See instructions on page 17.)

1 Description of income	2 Amount of income	3 Deductions directly connected (attach schedule)	4 Set-asides (attach schedule)	5 Total deductions and set-asides (col. 3 plus col. 4)
(1)				
(2)				
(3)				
(4)				
Totals	Enter here and on line 9, col. (A), Part I, p. 1.			Enter here and on line 9, column (B), Part I, page 1.

Schedule I—Exploited Exempt Activity Income, Other Than Advertising Income
(See instructions on page 18.)

1 Description of exploited activity	2 Gross unrelated business income from trade or business	3 Expenses directly connected with production of unrelated business income	4 Net income (loss) from unrelated trade or business (col. 2 minus col. 3). If a gain, compute cols. 5 through 7.	5 Gross income from activity that is not unrelated business income	6 Expenses attributable to column 5	7 Excess exempt expenses (column 6 minus column 5, but not more than column 4).
(1)						
(2)						
(3)						
(4)						
Column totals	Enter here and on line 10, col. (A), Part I, p. 1.	Enter here and on line 10, col. (B), Part I, p. 1.				Enter here and on line 26, Part II, page 1.

Schedule J—Advertising Income (See instructions on page 18.)

Part I Income From Periodicals Reported on a Consolidated Basis

1 Name of periodical	2 Gross advertising income	3 Direct advertising costs	4 Advertising gain or (loss) (column 2 minus column 3). If a gain, compute columns 5 through 7.	5 Circulation income	6 Readership costs	7 Excess readership costs (col. 6 minus col. 5, but not more than col. 4).
(1)						
(2)						
(3)						
(4)						
Column totals (carry to Part II, line (5))						

Part II Income From Periodicals Reported on a Separate Basis
(For each periodical listed in Part II, fill in columns 2 through 7 on a line-by-line basis.)

(1)						
(2)						
(3)						
(4)						
(5) Totals from Part I						
Column totals, Part II	Enter here and on line 11, col. (A), Part I, p. 1.	Enter here and on line 11, col. (B), Part I, p. 1.				Enter here and on line 27, Part II, page 1.

Schedule K—Compensation of Officers, Directors, and Trustees (See instructions on page 18.)

1 Name	2 Title	3 Percent of time devoted to business	4 Compensation attributable to unrelated business
Total - Enter here and on line 14, Part II, page 1			

Form 990-T (2000)

Form **4562**

Department of the Treasury
Internal Revenue Service (99)

Depreciation and Amortization

(Including Information on Listed Property)

See separate instructions. Attach this form to your return.

OMB No. 1545-0172

2000

Attachment Seq. No. 67

Name(s) shown on return	Business or activity to which this form relates	Identifying number
Hometown Chapter, Campaign to Clean Up America	Rental of vans	44-4444444

Part I Election To Expense Certain Tangible Property (Section 179)

NOTE: If you have any "listed property," complete Part V before you complete Part I.

1	Maximum dollar limitation. If an enterprise zone business, see page 2 of the instructions	1	20,000
2	Total cost of section 179 property placed in service. See page 2 of the instructions	2	
3	Threshold cost of section 179 property before reduction in limitation	3	200,000
4	Reduction in limitation. Subtract line 3 from line 2. If zero or less, enter -0-	4	
5	Dollar limitation for tax year. Subtract line 4 from line 1. If zero or less, enter -0-. If married filing separately, see page 2 of the instructions	5	20,000

	(a) Description of property	(b) Cost (business use only)	(c) Elected cost
6			
7	Listed property. Enter amount from line 27	7	

8	Total elected cost of section 179 property. Add amounts in column (c), lines 6 and 7	8	
9	Tentative deduction. Enter the smaller of line 5 or line 8	9	
10	Carryover of disallowed deduction from 1999. See page 3 of the instructions	10	
11	Business income limitation. Enter the smaller of business income (not less than zero) or line 5	11	
12	Section 179 expense deduction. Add lines 9 and 10, but do not enter more than line 11	12	
13	Carryover of disallowed deduction to 2001. Add lines 9 and 10, less line 12	13	

Note: Do not use Part II or Part III below for listed property (automobiles, certain other vehicles, cellular telephones, certain computers, or property used for entertainment, recreation, or amusement). Instead, use Part V for listed property.

Part II MACRS Depreciation for Assets Placed in Service Only During Your 2000 Tax Year (Do not include listed property.)

Section A - General Asset Account Election

14 If you are making the election under section 168(i)(4) to group any assets placed in service during the tax year into one or more general asset accounts, check this box. See page 3 of the instructions ☐

Section B - General Depreciation System (GDS) (See page 3 of the instructions.)

(a) Classification of property	(b) Month and year placed in service	(c) Basis for depreciation (business/investment)	(d) Recovery period (in years)	(e) Convention	(f) Method	(g) Depreciation deduction
15a 3-year property						
b 5-year property						
c 7-year property						
d 10-year property						
e 15-year property						
f 20-year property						
g 25-year property			25 yrs.		S/L	
h Residential rental property			27.5 yrs.	MM	S/L	
			27.5 yrs.	MM	S/L	
i Nonresidential real property			39 yrs.	MM	S/L	
				MM	S/L	

Section C - Alternative Depreciation System (ADS) (See page 5 of the instructions.)

(a) Classification of property	(b)	(c)	(d)	(e)	(f)	(g)
16a Class life					S/L	
b 12-year			12 yrs.		S/L	
c 40-year			40 yrs.	MM	S/L	

Part III Other Depreciation (Do not include listed property.) (See page 5 of the instructions.)

17	GDS and ADS deductions for assets placed in service in tax years beginning before 2000	17	500
18	Property subject to section 168(f)(1) election	18	
19	ACRS and other depreciation	19	

Part IV Summary (See page 6 of the instructions.)

20	Listed property. Enter amount from line 26	20	
21	Total. Add deductions on line 12, lines 15 and 16 in column (g), and lines 17 through 20. Enter here and on the appropriate lines of your return. Partnerships and S corporations - see instructions	21	500
22	For assets shown above and placed in service during the current year, enter the portion of the basis attributable to section 263A costs	22	

For Paperwork Reduction Act Notice, see the separate instructions. (HTA) Form 4562 (2000)

CHAPTER SIX

Successful IRS Communication

The IRS is an important player throughout the life of an exempt organization (EO). The qualification for receipt of tax-deductible donations and member dues; the privilege of receiving tax-free contributions, member dues, investment income, and exempt function income; and other special advantages granted by federal, state, and local governments are of significant economic value to EOs. Personnel in the IRS Exempt Organization group are well trained, cooperative, and knowledgeable. The attitude is normally supportive and the customary approach is to be helpful and to explain. Division personnel seem to assume that most nonprofits and their advisors operate in good faith as they are supposed to—to benefit the public and/or their members.

The IRS (along with most people) has entered the electronic age, providing guidance and information on the Internet. The central IRS Web site address is *www.irs.ustreas.gov*. The exempt organization division is only a slash away (*www.irs.ustreas.gov/bus-info/eo/index.html*), where readers can find forms and instructions, educational publications, Internal Revenue Bulletins, and Publication 78—the master list of §501(c)(3) organizations. The IRS plans to redesign its computer capabilities and to require electronic filing of Forms 990 by the year 2007. A CD-ROM containing all 990s filed each month has been available since the summer of 1999. The Urban Institute and Philanthropic Resources are taking advantage of this step by posting 990s for §501(c)(3) organizations—both private and public—on a charity information Web site called Guidestar.org.

Educational publications and handbooks are well written and, with the creation of a separate education department within the EO division, will only get better. Good telephone assistance (as a rule) is provided toll-free at 1-877-829-5500. Topping the list of resource materials in the bibliography is the *IRS Exempt Organizations Technical Instruction Program*. This training manual is a particularly important source of information regarding IRS thinking and policy direction. Due to personnel levels, there is a serious lack of published revenue rulings. Readers will notice that the revenue rulings cited in IRS publications have 1960, 1970, and sometimes 1950 dates. Though seemingly outdated, these rulings reflect the precedential IRS view on the particular issue involved.[1] Their age reflects IRS policy, beginning in the late 1970s due to staff limitations, to issue private letter rulings that eventually lead to almost no published rulings. IRS guidance, therefore, is mostly issued in its educational publications and instructions to the forms.

6.1 UNDERSTANDING THE IRS EXEMPT ORGANIZATION DIVISION

As a result of the Internal Revenue Service Restructuring and Reform Act of 1998, the IRS division previously known as EP/EO was divided into three parts: exempt organizations, employee plans, and government taxpayers. This division is expected to enhance direct accountability within each program, as well as enhanced technical excellence and interactive customer service efforts. The goal of the restructuring was simplification of the IRS hierarchy and elimination of regions and districts and their directors and assistant commissioner positions. Concurrent with (and one of the causes of) the reorganization were significant cuts in IRS funding during the 1990s. Meanwhile, the number of exempt organizations doubled. Positions of departing personnel were unfilled due to a hiring freeze, placing burdens on those remaining. Additionally, legal and accounting firms recruited senior personnel away from the IRS in significant numbers, causing a serious knowledge and experience drain in the IRS Washington office.

Until 1996, nine key district offices were responsible for tax issues for EOs in their respective assigned area under the guidance of a national office in Washington, D.C. As of October 2000, the EO division functions are centralized and divided as follows:

- Forms 1023, Application for Recognition of Exemption, are filed with the Ohio Key District Office (Kentucky address).

  For regular mail:

  Internal Revenue Service
  P.O. Box 192
  Covington, KY 41012-0192

  For express mail or a delivery service:

  Internal Revenue Service
  201 West Rivercenter Blvd.
  Attn: Extracting Stop 312
  Covington, KY 41011

- Annual information returns (Forms 990, 990PF, 990EZ, 990-T, and 5227) are all filed with the Utah Service Center.

  Internal Revenue Service Center
  Ogden, UT 84201-0027

- Field audit responsibility is assigned to the Key District Offices for the four regions.
- Technical guidance, training, and overall supervision of the exempt organization matters directed from a national office in Washington, D.C.

Because the U.S. tax system is based on voluntary compliance and funds allocated by Congress to provide oversight are limited, the IRS examines a very small portion of the hundreds of thousands of Forms 990 filed by tax-exempt organizations each year. They do, however, pay very close attention and closely scrutinize each and every Form 1023 and 1024. Centralization of the determination function in Cincinnati has been a positive move due to a concentration of knowledgeable agents. The information submitted must evidence that the new nonprofit is both organized and will be operated strictly for the benefit of its exempt constituents and not its founders, funders, or insiders.[2] Fund-raising plans, rate schedules for fees-for-service, detailed projections of revenue and expenses, membership privileges, rental agreements, salary contracts, and all other relevant information is reviewed with a fine-tooth comb before recognition of qualification for exemption is made by the IRS. Very careful attention must be paid to preparing Form 1023.

The Utah Service Center got off to a rocky start, because EO returns were initially processed by personnel unfamiliar with the exigencies of EO matters. These problems were solved by creation of personnel specifically assigned to 990-related returns. The Cincinnati office experienced a similar problem in connection with centralization of the determination process. A plan to recruit EO technicians experienced with Form 1023 and relocate them to Ohio was unsuccessful. As a result, the Ohio office has been understaffed since its creation.

After initial screening for completeness in Ohio, many applications are forwarded to other Key District Offices for review—adding at least a month to the process in the author's experience. Readers can only hope that the new hires that have been added for the past three years in a row will ease the Ohio office workload and streamline the application process in the future.

6.2 REPORTING ORGANIZATIONAL/PROGRAM CHANGES TO THE IRS

As an exempt organization grows and evolves over the years, it faces the question of how to report changes in its organizational documents—the bylaws and sometimes the charter—to the IRS. How does it inform the IRS of new and changing programs? How can it change its mission? Annually on Form 990, the organization is asked the following questions regarding changes:

- Did the organization engage in any activity not previously reported to the IRS? If "yes," attach a statement.
- Were any changes made in the organizing or governing documents but not reported to the IRS?

The procedure for reporting changes is to simply furnish the information and leave it up to the IRS to decide whether or not the change is acceptable. Commonly, no communication—acceptance or rejection—is issued in response to "yes" answers that include the appropriate accompanying attachments.

(a) Changes in Structure and/or Activities

An EO may choose to report changes in its organizational documents and/or activities to the Cincinnati Office with a letter requesting that they determine whether the changes have any impact on the organization's exempt status. This method of informing the IRS brings a response—the documents and plans are actually read and written approval is issued or questions asked. This submission is not treated as a formal ruling request; no user fee is charged unless a new Form 1023 is required. The dilemma faced by an EO making changes is therefore partly where to report them and sometimes whether advance approval for the change should be sought. As discussed below, the decision can be influenced by the managers' desire for written approval of the organizational change(s). The fact that Form 990 attachments are not necessarily scrutinized may also sway the decision.

The Ohio Key District Office is first and foremost assigned the responsibility for determining initial qualification for exemption.[3] As a part of that job, the office can also make determinations that fall short of formal ruling requests. In addition to responding to submission of changes in operations and organizing documents as discussed above, the Ohio office can also act on the following matters[4]:

- Classification of private foundation status
- Recognition of unusual grants[5]
- Advance approval of a private foundation's grant-making procedures[6]
- Classification as an exempt operating foundation[7]
- Advance approval of voter registration activities[8]

(b) When to Request a Ruling

In terms of IRS procedures, it is important to distinguish between gaining approval in advance of a change and risking a sanction for a *fait accompli.* Once a change has occurred in the form of reorganization, or if a major new activity is undertaken, the organization should choose the best method to inform the IRS, based on the succeeding discussion. Such action is taken when the relevant tax laws are clear and established precedents exist, and when there is little or no doubt that the change is acceptable.

However, there may be proposed changes for which the organization wishes to gain advance approval because of a lack of published rulings or other authoritative opinions on the subject. The procedure for obtaining sanction for prospective changes is to request a ruling from the Exempt Organizations Division in the IRS National Office. When significant funds are involved or if disapproval of the change would mean that the organization could lose its exemption, filing of a ruling request may be warranted.

A decision to request a ruling must be made in view of the cost and time involved in the process. The engagement of a professional who is experienced in representing clients with the IRS Exempt Organization division is a prudent investment when advance approval is desired. Even with the best of qualified assistance, National Office approval normally takes at least a year. The IRS issues a series of revenue procedures each spring to update procedures for seeking guidance in the form of private letter rulings, determination letters, and technical advice. A schedule of fees charged and addresses for submitting requests is provided. The most recent pronouncements set the user fee for a letter ruling at $2,100 ($600 for organizations whose gross receipts are under $150,000).[9]

6.3 CHANGING FISCAL YEAR

A common change that might occur during the life of an EO is a change in its tax accounting year. Although some commercial, tax-paying businesses must secure advance IRS approval to change their tax year,[10] a streamlined system is available for EOs. The EO simply files a "timely filed short period" Form 990 (or 990-EZ, 990-PF, or 990-T).[11] If a short-period return is filed by the 15th day of the fifth month following the end of the new year end, approval for the change is not required and it is not necessary to submit Form 1128 to the Washington, D.C., office.

Say, for example, a calendar-year EO wishes to change its tax year to a fiscal year spanning July 1 to June 30. By November 15, a six-month return is filed to report the financial transactions for the short-period year (the six months ending June 30 of the year of change). If the organization has not changed its year within the past 10 years (counting backward to include the prior short-period return as a full year), the change is automatic. The words *Change of Accounting Period* are simply written across the top of the front page. A private foundation that changes its tax year must prorate certain calculations and accelerate its payment of mandatory annual distributions.[12]

Form 1128, Application to Adopt, Change, or Retain a Tax Year, must be filed in two situations: (1) if the organization has changed its year end within the past 10 years, or (2) if the return for the short period is not timely filed.

When the organization has previously changed its year, the automatic procedure is still followed if the return is filed within 5½ months of the new year end. In that case, Form 1128 is attached to the short-period return.

When the filing is late, the organization must first file Form 1128 with the IRS Service Center in Ogden, Utah, to request permission to change its year. If the request is filed within 90 days of the new filing deadline (February 15 in the above example), the organization can request that the IRS consider it timely filed. If possible, the organization should explain that it acted reasonably and in good faith.[13] A filing fee of $130 (as of January 1, 1998)[14] is due to be paid. The appropriate Form 990 is not filed using the new tax year until IRS approval is received. Affiliated organizations holding a group exemption must follow Rev. Proc. 79-3 to effect a change.

6.4 CHANGING ACCOUNTING METHOD

Generally accepted accounting principles (GAAP) recommend that the accrual method of accounting be used for financial statement reporting; thus, a certified public accountant (CPA) cannot issue a "clean" or "unqualified" opinion on financial statements prepared on a cash receipts and disbursements basis. Because it is more simple, many organizations in their early years use the cash method, which is perfectly acceptable for filing Form 990 and (possibly) for reporting to boards and contributors. Maturing organizations commonly face the need to change to the accrual method, in order to secure an audited statement or to satisfy the requirements of its grantors and fiduciaries.

Before 1996, many nonprofits followed what was essentially a hybrid method of accounting. Although they used the accrual method for disbursements and fee-for-service revenue, the cash method was used to report donation revenue because pledges of donative support are not enforceable in most cases. Such organizations, therefore, chose not to record pledges as assets with a corresponding showing of income. The Financial Accounting Standards Board in Statement of Financial Accounting Standard (SFAS) No. 116, effective beginning in December 1995, began to require that such donations be reflected as revenue.[15] A large number of nonprofits were affected by this (and other) change of reporting. For 1996 and 1997 Form 990s, the IRS excused those organizations that adopted SFAS No.116 from filing Form 3115.[16] The IRS instructions still allow organizations that change their accounting method to reflect SFAS No. 116 to make the change without seeking permission. The impact of the change is reported on line 20, Part I, of Form 990, or line 3 or 5, Part III, of Form 990-PF.

As a rule, Form 3115 is filed to obtain IRS approval for a change in accounting method. Because an EO does not commonly pay tax, it is deemed to have IRS approval for such a change if it falls into one of the "automatic change procedures" categories outlined in the IRS instructions to the form. To essentially receive automatic approval, Form 3115 must be timely filed in duplicate as outlined below:[17]

- Form 3115 is filed within 270 days after the start of the year in which the change is effective. No response or approval for the change is returned to the EO. A Copy Form 3115 is filed (effective January 1, 2000) with:

  Internal Revenue Service
  Assistant Commissioner of Employee Plans and Exempt Organizations
  Attention E:EO, Box 120, Ben Franklin Station
  Washington, DC 20044

- No user fee is due.
- The *original* Form 3115 is attached directly behind the return filed for the year of accounting method change.

Late applications can be filed, but will be considered only upon a showing of "good cause"[18] and if it can be shown to the satisfaction of the Commissioner that granting the extension will not jeopardize the government's interests. Because EOs typically do not pay tax, the possibilities for such approval are good. A user fee of $130 must accompany late forms.

A change of accounting method necessitates reporting deferred or accelerated income or expenses that would have been reportable in the past if the new method had been used. Items "necessary to prevent amounts from being duplicated or omitted must be taken into account" over a period of years. The impact of the tax changes to a taxpaying entity are calculated to mitigate its burden.[19] In most cases, the change has no tax consequence for an EO filing its Form 990 or 990-PF; as a practical matter, the income or expense adjustments for an EO can be made instead in one year. There is no published guidance on this point, but IRS representatives agree with this suggestion, absent tax distortion. An EO whose unrelated business income is affected by an accounting method change should, however, reflect the adjustments. Tax may be due on the retroactive impact of the change in tax liability previously reported on Form 990-T. Careful study is appropriate for any EO making such a change that affects tax liability.

Since there is often no tax consequence of making such a change, an EO may be tempted to forgo formal approval for a change in its accounting method. Because the procedure is simple and no fee is due, it is advisable to seek approval. The period of limitation for examining Form 990 might remain open, if the change is significant. Particularly if unrelated business income tax (UBIT) is involved, the time for payment of any tax involved in the change might be accelerated, if approval has not been secured.

6.5 WHEN TO AMEND A FORM 990

If a mistake is discovered after Form 990 has been filed, the question arises whether an amended return should be filed or whether the change can simply be reflected in the return for the year in which the problem comes to light. When there is no tax consequence involved, or in accountants' language the change is not *material*, the correction can be reflected in the fund balance section on line 20 of Part I for Form 990 or 990-EZ as a prior-period adjustment. The extra efforts involved in preparing an amended return may not be necessary. This question has a new dimension in the electronic age. Presumably, Guidestar.org will replace the original return with its amendment. If so, this fact may influence the decision to amend a return available for all to see on the Internet.

Amendment is certainly appropriate when correction would cause a change in public charity status or when unrelated business income[20] would increase or decrease, causing an impact on the tax liability. As a rule, for an insignificant correction with no effect on retention of exempt status or tax liability, complete disclosure on the following year's return, along with inclusion of the omitted amounts, is acceptable. Importantly for certain public charities, the correction to revenue should not only be reported on line 20, Parts I, IV-A, and IV-B of Form 990, but also in Part IV of Schedule A where the correction can usually be made to the proper year amounts.

6.6 CHANGING PUBLIC CHARITY CLASS

(a) IRC §509(a)(1) to (a)(2) or Vice Versa

Exempt organizations classified as publicly supported organizations under IRC §509(a)(1) or (a)(2) can often qualify for both categories. Sometimes, changes in an organization's sources of support and exempt function revenue cause it to change its qualification from one subsection to another. The distinctions between qualification for one category or another are described in detail in Chapter 3§7. For purposes of this discussion, the issue is what the organization must do if it experiences such a change. In order to be classified as a publicly supported organization and not as a private foundation, passage of either test suffices. In one narrow circumstance, it is preferable to be classified as a §509(a)(1) organization: Only (a)(1)s qualify to receive terminating distributions from private foundations.

Qualification is based on percentage levels of public support calculated using a four-year moving average of financial support received annually. The calculation is made annually when the organization completes Schedule A of Form 990.[21] Checking the (a)(1) blank rather than the (a)(2) blank has not, in the past, prompted a response or notice from the Service Center that processes Forms 990. The organization must decide whether, in addition to informing the Utah Service Center, to report the change to the Ohio Office to request recognition or written approval. The question is whether the determination letter should be updated. Sometimes, it is a matter of the organization's officers and directors being tolerant of uncertainty. In some situations, support might change from year to year. The factors to consider in making the choice include:

- The IRS does not issue amended or new determination letters when Form 990, Schedule A, indicates that a change has occurred.
- Private foundations need not exercise expenditure responsibility[22] in making a grant to either category, so a new determination letter is not critical.
- IRS Publication 78 makes no distinction in its labeling of public charities, so the information is not entered into that IRS record.
- As of November 2000, the Key District Office does not charge a user fee for submission of the information.

(b) Ceasing to Qualify as a §509(a)(3) Organization

Failure to maintain qualification under IRC §509(a)(3) as a supporting organization[23] could occur for either of two reasons:

1. The organizational documents are altered in a manner that removes the requisite relationship with one or more public charities, and the organization becomes a private foundation supporting grantees of its choice.
2. A sufficient level of public support is obtained to allow the organization to convert to a §509(a)(1) or (2) organization.

In the first case, conversion to a private foundation requires no IRS approval, though most would favor overt sanction for the change. Preferably, the conversion is timed to occur at the end of the fiscal year. If not, a short-period final Form 990 would be filed through the conversion date. A short-period Form 990-PF would then be filed beginning with the date of the change. Required minimum distributions, excise tax on investment income,[24] and other private foundation sanctions would apply as if the organization were newly created on the date of conversion.[25] Full disclosure of the changes would be furnished to the IRS in filing both returns.

In the second case, the organization would continue to file Form 990 and the change would again be fully disclosed with the return for the year the change occurred. The dilemma previously discussed regarding a change from (a)(1) to (a)(2) or vice versa also applies in this case. No new determination letter is issued in response to the 990 filing. The EO should analyze its need to furnish evidence of its new status to potential supporters. This situation is rather unusual, and prudence would dictate reporting to the Ohio Office to assure approval of the new category of public status.

(c) Ceasing to Qualify as a Public Charity

An organization classified as a public charity may become reclassified as a private foundation for one of two reasons:

1. Its sources of support might fall below requisite amount of public support needed to qualify under IRC §509(a)(1) and (2).
2. It ceases to conduct the activity qualifying it as a public charity.

For an organization of which the public status is based on revenue, the calculation is made at the end of each year and affects the following year. Say, for example, the Form 990 for 2000 shows an EO's public support fell to 25 percent of its total support (based on revenue received from 1996 through 1999). Unless the facts and circumstances test applies,[26] beginning in the year 2001, the EO would be reclassified as a private foundation. Similar to a 509(a)(3) organization converting to private, all of the special rules applicable to private foundations would become applicable on the first day of 2001.

A church, school, or hospital qualifies as a public charity because of the activity it conducts without regard to its sources of revenue. When such an EO ceases to operate, it potentially becomes a private foundation on the date the change occurs. As the health care industry reformed itself during the 1990s, the assets of tax-exempt hospitals were purchased by for-profit hospitals. Typically, the proceeds of the asset sale were then invested to produce income to conduct a charitable grant-making program. For up to two years following the sale, it is conceivable for the hospital to reclassify itself as a public charity based on its sources of support during the time it operated the hospital. Subsequently, it would become a private foundation unless it reformed its organizational structure to qualify as a supporting organization.

6.7 WHEN THE IRS EXAMINES

After securing recognition of its qualification for tax exemption from the IRS Key District Office and filing Forms 990 annually with the Internal Revenue Service Center, a call may be received from the IRS Exempt Organization Office in the EO's area. The EO's ongoing qualification as an exempt organization may be questioned by the specialist who want to look at the organization's financial books and records. The knock on the EO's door comes in the form of a phone call from the IRS agent assigned to the case to the person at the organization identified as the "contact person" on Form 990. The agent will request to arrange an appointment to examine a particular year's return. Many EOs will refer such a call to their professional advisors, usually the accountant who prepared the Forms 990.[27]

The manner in which the IRS chooses EOs to examine varies from year to year and is always a matter of speculation. In past years, the IRS has looked at business leagues, at unrelated business activity, at bingo operations, at universities, at hospitals and their related clinics and doctors, and at private foundations. In the early 1990s, the IRS conducted a program to examine overclaimed deductions for fund-raising events, with companion examinations of the income tax returns of EO supporters of such events. Readers may be aware that work resulted in the new *quid pro quo* and other donor disclosure rules imposed by Congress beginning in 1995. In the mid-1990s, the IRS initiated a Coordinated Examination Program (CEP) to bring together a pool of experts to work on complicated cases involving significant charitable institutions. As a part of a *large case initiative,* conglomerate EOs with subsidiaries and for-profit and nonprofit related entities, particularly colleges and hospitals, were targeted. Lawyers, accountants, IRS income tax agents, and other specialists joined the EO representatives in conducting such examinations. As of November 2000, the CEP program continues and should be expected to be a significant part of the IRS's work plan for years to come.

Notes

CHAPTER 1

1. In the author's experience, some organizations are inexplicably omitted.
2. See Chapter 2§2(d) and Chapter 20 of *Tax Planning and Compliance* for discussion of factors indicating an organization is operated to benefit its founders, funders, fund-raisers, or other private individuals rather than its exempt beneficiaries.
3. Chapter 21 of *Tax Planning and Compliance* discusses the complicated array of definitions, exceptions, and modifications that cause certain types of business income to be taxed even when the nonprofit is essentially operating a business in competition with for-profit businesses.
4. Chapter 20 of *Tax Planning and Compliance* discusses sanctions called *intermediate sanctions* imposed on public charities that pay excessive benefits to its insiders. The similar rules applicable to private foundations, called self-dealing, are discussed in Chapter 14 of *Tax Planning and Compliance.*
5. Lobbying by public charities is limited by two different tests outlined in Chapter 23§5 of *Tax Planning and Compliance.* Private foundations are prohibited from making any expenditures for lobbying efforts but can support public charities that lobby so long as their grant is not designated for that purpose as discussed in Chapters 17§1 of *Tax Planning and Compliance.*
6. Chapter 3§3 contains a brief description of the labyrinth of rules applied to determine classification under the three very different types of public charities.
7. See Chapter 24 of *Tax Planning and Compliance* entitled "Deductibility and Disclosures."
8. Chapters 2 through 10 of *Tax Planning and Compliance* contain over 150 pages that discuss the requirements for the most common types, compare the categories, explain the attributes that distinguish them from each other, and consider instances in which they overlap.
9. Chapter 18 of *Tax Planning and Compliance* thoroughly outlines the determination process.

10. Explained in Chapter 2§8.
11. There is often talk of raising these levels—watch for new developments.
12. IRC §511(a)(2)(B).
13. Discussed in Chapter 3§5.
14. Penalties are imposed for failure to withhold and pay federal taxes from employees and failure to file other types of compensation reports. Chapter 25 of *Tax Planning and Compliance* contains checklists and guidance regarding this very important subject.
15. Chapter 3§2 discusses the criteria applied to define organizations qualifying as churches and their affiliates.
16. IRC §6033(a)(2) and (3).
17. Defined in Rev. Proc. 95-48, 1995-47 I.R.B. 13.
18. IRC §301.7701.
19. Discussed in Chapter 18§2 of *Tax Planning and Compliance.*
20. IRC §102.
21. *Colombo Club, Inc.*, 71-2 USTC ¶ 9674, 447 F.2d 1406 (9th Cir. 1971).
22. Rev. Rul. 60-144, 1960-1 C.B. 636.
23. Rev. Rul. 69-247, 1969-1 C.B. 303, modifying Rev. Rul. 62-10, 1962-1 C.B. 305 and reflecting the Tax Court decision in *California Thoroughbred Breeders Ass'n*, 47 T.C. 335, Dec. 28,225 (acq).
24. See Chapter 21§20(d).
25. IRC §6662.
26. IRC §6652(c)(1)(A) as amended by the Taxpayer Bill of Rights 2, §1314.
27. For rules pertaining to inclusion in a group exemption, see Chapter 18§1(f) of *Tax Planning and Compliance.*
28. Rev. Proc. 96-40, 1996-32 I.R.B. 8.
29. Effective June 8, 1999; Taxpayer Bill of Rights 2, §1313, amending IRC §6104(e).
30. IRC §6652 amended by Taxpayer Bill of Rights 2, §1313.
31. IRC §6104(d).
32. Chapter 6 of the author's book, *Financial Planning for Nonprofit Organizations* (New York: John Wiley & Sons, 1996) contains a concise outline of basic accounting principles that apply to nonprofits.
33. See Chapter 5§8.
34. Dennis P. Tishlian, "Reasonable Joint Cost Allocations in Nonprofits," *Journal of Accountancy*, November 1992, p. 66.
35. Discussed in Chapter 5.
36. In accordance with IRC §446(a).
37. IRS Notice 96-30, I.R.B. 1996-20; still cited in Form 990 instructions.
38. Discussed in Chapter 3§2.
39. Discussed in Chapter 4§17.
40. The following discussion is based on the guide issued as of May 1, 2000.

CHAPTER 2

1. Deductibility information must be disclosed by many nonprofits. See discussion about answers to questions 83 and 84 of Part VI later in this chapter.
2. Form 990-T is the subject of Chapter 5.
3. See following discussion of line 9.
4. A sponsorship is treated as a contribution when the words used to recognize the sponsor in print and by broadcast contain no quantitative or qualitative words promoting the sponsor according to IRC §513-(i). A thank you displaying the sponsor's name and logo is permitted. Saying the sponsor sells the best product in the world is an advertisement. These rules were evolving under regulations proposed in March 2000, as this manuscript was being prepared.
5. The estate tax rules of Reg. §20.2031 prescribe valuation methods; also see IRS Publication 56, *Determining the Value of Donated Property*.
6. Under rules discussed in Chapter 1§2, the author's CPA firm provides clients a public inspection copy of the Form 990 that omits donor information.
7. Rev. Proc. 90-12 (updated by Rev. Proc. 2001-13) defines a token item as one costing the organization less than $7.60 (during the year 2001) and provided to a donor of more than $38.00. The amounts were originally $5.00 and $25.00 and are adjusted annually for inflation.
8. Regs. §1.170A-9(e)(8) and §1.509(a)-3(g). Note that the definitions are somewhat different under these regulations so that a nonprofit should study the one pertaining to its category of public charity.
9. Reg. §1.170-13(f)(8); the IRS evidences the complication of these rules with three full pages in the Form 990 general instructions about contributions. Chapter 24 of *Tax Planning and Compliance*, entitled "Deductibility and Disclosures," contains 21 pages on this very important subject. Also see IRS Publication 1391, *Deductibility of Payments Made to Charities Conducting Fund-Raising Events*.
10. IRC§501(c)(9).
11. The public support tests are outlined in Chapter 3.
12. Reg. §1.509(a)-3(h).
13. *Miller v. Commissioner*, 34 T.C.M. 1207 (1975).
14. Rev. Proc. 90-12, 1990-1, C.B. 471. See Chapter 24§3(c) of *Tax Planning and Compliance*, for definition of the terms.
15. IRC §6115; Part VI, line 83b asks whether the nonprofit has made this disclosure.
16. For guidance on valuation issues, see preceding note 9.
17. Discussed in Chapter 1§3(b) and 6§2(c).
18. See discussion in Chapter 6.
19. An officer or key employee can themselves be penalized and the money must be returned if they receive unreasonable compensation according to IRC §4958. This important subject is discussed in Chapter 20 of *Tax Planning and Compliance* and should be consulted by organizations paying individuals total compensation in excess of $80,000 each, the threshold for application of the penalties.

20. See explanation of Statement of Position 98-2 in Chapter 1§4.
21. Discussed in Chapter 1§3.
22. IRC §170(e).
23. Chapter 20 of *Tax Planning and Compliance* explains the intermediate sanctions and provides suggestions for required documentation.
24. Ward L. Thomas and James Bloom, *Exempt Organizations Continuing Professional Education Technical Instruction Program Textbook*, 1995 (for 1996) edition, Chapter 1, "Reporting Compensation on Form 990"; also see IRS Publication 525, *Taxable and Nontaxable Income.*
25. IRC §482, discussed by the IRS in the 1996 CPE text at page 208.
26. Reg. §1.6043-3.
27. Chapter 22 of *Tax Planning and Compliance*, "Relationships with Other Organizations and Businesses," discusses the consequence of such relationships and the constraints within which they are permitted.
28. IRC §4955.
29. Chapter 6§4 of *Tax Planning and Compliance* considers the disclosure rules applicable to non–(c)(3) organizations.
30. Chapter 9 of *Tax Planning and Compliance* discusses the unique rules applicable to social clubs. Readers will also find useful information at www.clubtax.com, the Web site of Mitch Stamp, a Florida CPA who focuses on clubs.
31. See discussion in Chapter 1§1.
32. The Portland Golf Club decision discussed in Chapter 9§5(a) of *Tax Planning and Compliance* can be studied regarding limitations on a social club's nonmember activities treated as not entered into to produce a profit.
33. See also IRS Publication 598, *Tax on Unrelated Business Income of Exempt Organizations.*
34. IRC §512(a)(3)(B); see Chapter 5.
35. Priv. Ltr. Rul. 8515061.
36. See new §23.3(d) of *Tax Planning and Compliance*, 2001 Supplement.
37. Despite the presumed exemption, a non–§501(c)(3) organization that files Form 990 with the Ogden Service Center is asked to submit Form 1024. Such recognition is granted retroactively to date of formation (if activity and organizational documents were suitable for exemption from inception); the new political organization only receives recognition prospectively from the notice date.
38. IRC §162(e) denies a deduction for political campaign expenses.
39. IRS Announcement 2000-54 and 2000-72 was released August 9, 2000, stating an intention to issue a revenue ruling addressing questions concerning the new rules. In a question and answer format, the IRS considered 34 different issues and requested comments. Readers should look for further development.
40. Under the Federal Election Campaign Act of 1971.
41. Such organizations file Form 990 that contains the type of disclosures no imposed on §527 organizations.
42. P. L. 106-230 amending IRC §527 and adding §527(i) and (j).
43. Is completed directly on the IRS Web site at www.irs.gov/bus-info/eo/pol-file.html and physically mailed to Internal Revenue Service Center, Ogden, Utah 84201.

44. Described in Chapter 1§3.
45. IRC §6104(b) and (d); the rules are the same as those for Form 990 discussed in Chapter 1§3.

CHAPTER 3

1. Chapter 20 of *Tax Planning and Compliance* considers this important issue, and provides standards for measuring reasonable compensation and other types of transactions with insiders, such as rental of a building or sale of property as well as discussing the Intermediate Sanction rules.
2. *American Campaign Academy v. Commissioner*, 92 TC 1053 (1989).
3. Andrew Megosh, Larry Scollick, Mary Jo Salins, and Cheryl Chasin, *IRS Technical Instruction Program for FY 2001*, Chapter H, "Private Benefit Under IRS 501(c)(3)."
4. IRC §4958, added to the code in 1995; controversial proposed regulations were issued and final rules have yet to be issued as of October 2000.
5. Chapter 11 of *Tax Planning and Compliance* presents a detailed discussion of these rules.
6. Reg. §1.170A-9 contains over 35 pages in the author's tax service volume evidencing the complexity of these rules.
7. See discussion in 3§4.
8. Chapter 3 of *Tax Planning and Compliance* is devoted to these distinctions.
9. Chapter 5 of *Tax Planning and Compliance* explores the complex definitions of the various types of educational organizations.
10. Reg. §1170A-9(c)(2).
11. Chapter 10 of *Tax Planning and Compliance* describes the criteria for this classification.
12. Reg. §1.170A-9(e)(7).
13. IRC §170(e).
14. Reg. §1.170A-9(e)(7)(ii).
15. Rev. Rul. 75-435. 1975-2 C. B. 215.
16. As discussed in Chapter 1§4 according to SFAS 136.
17. Reg. §1.170A-9(e)(6)(i) and (v).
18. IRS Priv. Ltr. Rul. 9203040.
19. See Chapter 6§6.
20. Chapter 11 of *Tax Planning and Compliance* has an overview of the complex tests that have to be satisfied for an organization to gain the SO classification. One of three very different types of relationship—each with different criteria for board positions and reporting—must exist between the supporting organization and the organization(s) it supports.
21. Reg. §1.509(a)-3(h).
22. Rev. Rul. 83-153, 1983-2 C. B. 48; Rev. Rul. 75-387, 1975-2 C. B. 216.
23. Regs. §1.170A-9(e)(5)(iii) and §1.509(a)-3(c)(iii).

24. The process of terminating private foundation status is discussed in Chapter 12§4 of *Tax Planning and Compliance.*
25. Regs. §1.170A-9(e)(4) and §1.509(a)-3(c); see also discussion in Chapter 6§6.
26. Rules discussed in Chapter 1§4.
27. IRC §4946.
28. Rev. Proc. 75-50, 1975-2 C. B. 587.

CHAPTER 4

1. The technical aspects of the sanctions applied to PFs, found in IRC §4940-4946, are far reaching. *Tax Planning and Compliance* contains 135 pages presented in Chapters 12 through 17, on the complex rules that can be studied along with the following suggestions for completion of the form. For further study consult *Private Foundations: Tax Law* and *Compliance,* Blazek and Hopkins (New York: John Wiley & Sons, 1998).
2. Chapter 14 of *Tax Planning and Compliance* contains 24 pages of discussion of these rules.
3. Chapter 17 of *Tax Planning and Compliance* contains 31 pages of discussion on these rules.
4. Chapter 16 of *Tax Planning and Compliance* contains 8 pages of discussion on these rules.
5. Chapter 16 of *Tax Planning and Compliance* contains 7 pages of discussion on these rules.
6. The instructions for the 1990 form contained 22 pages—proof that this form is not getting simpler.
7. IRC §4946(a)(2).
8. § Reg. §1.4940-1.
9. Discussed in Chapters 1§4 and 5§8.
10. IRC §§162 and 212.
11. Discussed in Chapter 5.
12. Discussed in Chapter 1§4.
13. Chapter 13§4 of *Tax Planning and Compliance* considers several tax reduction ideas in depth.
14. IRC §§1011, 1012, 1014, 1015, and 1016 apply in completing this part. IRC §4940(c)(3)(B).
15. Reg.§ 53.4940-1(f)(2)(i)(B), which refers to IRC §1015.
16. Reg.§ 53.4940-1(f)(3).
17. The returns are being displayed on Guidestar.org.
18. See Chapter 13 of *Tax Planning and Compliance* for illustrations of this important tax savings opportunity.
19. Chapter 13 of *Private Foundations: Tax Law and Compliance* explains the circumstances under which a private foundation can go out of existence either by converting itself to a public charity or distributing its assets to other charitable or-

ganizations. Model forms and instructions on this complicated matter are provided.

20. IRC § 6655.
21. Discussed in Chapter 3§9.
22. Process and propriety of seeking approval discussed in Chapter 6.
23. IRC §513. Chapter 5 defines unrelated income and the many exceptions to taxation for certain types of unrelated income, including indebted investment properties.
24. IRC §507(a); see note 19 above.
25. Supra note 1.
26. The order in which qualifying distributions are applied is illustrated in Chapter 15§6 of *Tax Planning and Compliance.*
27. See Chapter 15§5 of *Tax Planning and Compliance.*

CHAPTER 5

1. Internal Revenue Code §102.
2. Discussed in Chapter 1§3.
3. Discussed in §5.1(b).
4. See Chapter 22 of *Tax Planning and Compliance,* "Relationships with Other Organizations and Businesses."
5. IRC §512(a)(1).
6. IRC §513(a); Reg. §1.513-1(b). The term is defined in reference to IRC §162.
7. See Chapter 1§1 regarding reasons tax exemption is granted.
8. Rev. Rul. 73-128, 1973-1, C.B. 222; Priv. Ltr. Rul. 9152039.
9. See Chapter 21§15 of *Tax Planning and Compliance* for a compendium of factors to use in determining when a publication program will be considered a business.
10. Usage by spouses, alumni, and donors was not considered as related in Priv. Ltr. Rul. 9645004.
11. IRS Priv. Ltr. Rul. 9009038.
12. IRS Tech. Adv. Mem. 8932004.
13. IRS Priv. Ltr. Rul. 9017028.
14. Discussed in §5.3.
15. Rev. Rul. 73-104 and 105, 1973-1 C.B. 258-265; Priv. Ltr. Ruls. 8303013, 8326003, 8236008, and 8328009 and Tech. Adv. Memo. 9550003.
16. Reg. §1.501(c)(3)-1(e)(1).
17. See Chapter 2.
18. *Orange County Agricultural Society Inc. v. Commissioner*, 90.1 USTC ¶50.076 (2d Cir. 1990), *aff'g* 55 T.C.M. 1602 (1988).
19. IRS Priv. Ltr. Rul. 9521004.
20. See Chapter 16 of *Tax Planning and Compliance* for rules defining impermissible excess business holdings for private foundations.
21. IRS Priv. Ltr. Rul. 9304001; see also Priv. Ltr. Rul. 9417003; *Suffolk County Patrolmen's Benevolent Association Inc. v. Commissioner*, 77 T.C. 1314 (1981), *acq.* 1984-1

C.B. 2; and *National College Athletic Association v. Commissioner*, 914 F.2d 1417(10th Cir. 1990).

22. *Greene County Medical Society Foundation v. U.S.*, 345 F. Supp. 900 (W. D. Mo. 1972).
23. Waco Lodge No. 166, Benevolent & Protective Order of Elks v. Commissioner, T. C. Memo. 1981-546, aff'd per curiam, 696 F.2d 372 (5th Cir. 1983).
24. *Shiloh Youth Revival Centers v. Commissioner*, 88 T. C. 579 (1987).
25. Discussed in §5.1(a).
26. IRC §513(a)(2).
27. Discussed in §5.9.
28. While agreeing there was some educational benefit from the site, a museum renting its exhibition halls for private receptions provided substantial services to its tenants that caused the usage fees to be unrelated income in Priv. Ltr. Rul. 9702003.
29. IRC §512(b)(2).
30. *Sierra Club v. Commissioner*, T. C. Memo. 1999-86 on remand from the 9th Circuit Court; *Planned Parenthood Federation of America v. Commissioner*, T. C. Memo. 1999-206 (June 1999); *Texas Farm Bureau v. U.S.*, 53 F.3rd 120 (5th Cir. 1995).
31. Reg. §1.512(b)-1(b).
32. IRC §512(b)(7); Priv. Ltr. Rul. 7924009.
33. Chapter 21§10(b) of *Tax Planning and Compliance* considers the special rules attributable to sales of social club properties.
34. Reg. §1.337(d)-4.
35. IRC §514.
36. Reg.§1.514(b)-1.
37. Reg.§1.514(b)-1(b)(2)(ii).
38. IRC §514(b)(1)(B) and (C).
39. IRC §514(b)(3)(A)-(E).
40. Reg. §1.514(b)-1(c)(1); Rev. Rul. 69-464, 19969-2 C. B. 132; Tech. Adv. Memo. 8906003.
41. Rev. Rul. 77-47, 1977-1 C. B. 156; Tech. Adv. Memo. 9017003.
42. §514(c)(4); *Elliot Knitwear Profit Sharing Plan v. Commissioner*, 71 T. C. 765 (1979), *aff'd* 614 F.2d 347 (3d Cir. 1980).
43. *Southwest Texas Electric Cooperative, Inc. v. Commmissioner*, 68 T. C. M. Dec. 50,008(M), T. C. Memo. 1994-363.
44. Reg. §1.514(b)-1(a).
45. Reg. §1.514(a)-1(a)(1)(v).
46. IRC §§168(h)(6), 514(c)(9), and 704(b)(2); Reg. §1.514(c)-2.
47. IRC §514(c).
48. Reg. §1.514(b)-1(b)(ii), §1.512(b)-1(b)(iii), Example 2; Priv. Ltr. Ruls. 8030105 and 8145087.
49. Reg. §1.514(c)-1(b).
50. Reg. §1.514(b)-1(c)(3).
51. IRC §514(a)(1).

52. See Appendix 5A.
53. Reg. §1.6012-2(e); Reg. §1.61-3.
54. The depositing method used is the same as the organization's payroll tax payment method.
55. Reg. §1.1561-3(b).
56. IRC §§27, 28, 29, 38–44, 51, 55–59, and 59A.
57. IRC §6033(e)(2); Chapter 6§4 of *Tax Planning and Compliance* discusses alternative methods of allocating an organization's administrative costs to lobbying activities.
58. IRC §6651. When the return is delinquent over 60 days, the minimum tax for failure to file is the smaller of the actual tax or $100.
59. Reg. §301.6651-1(c) explains the acceptable excuses.
60. Rev. Rul. 69-247,1969-1 C. B. 303, modifying Rev. Rul. 62-10,1962-1 C. B. 305 and reflecting the Tax Court decision in *California Thoroughbred Breeders Ass'n*, 47 T. C. 335, Dec. 28, 225 (acq).
61. IRC §6662.
62. Discussed in Chapter 1§2(e).
63. IRC §446(a).
64. IRC §448(c).
65. IRC §§263A and 471.
66. Rules pertaining to seeking approval for a change in method are presented in Chapter 6§4.
67. IRC §162; Reg. §1.512(a)-1(b); *Iowa State University of Science & Technology v. U.S., infra* n. 51; *Commissioner v. Groetzinger*, 480 U.S. 23 (1987); Reg. §1.513-1(4)(d)(iii); *Portland Golf Club v. Commissioner*, 110 S. Ct. 2780 (1990).
68. IRC §512(b).
69. IRC §512(b)(10 and 11).
70. IRC §§170(b)(2), 512(a)(3)(B)(i), and 642(c).
71. IRC §172(b).
72. *Iowa State University of Science and Technology v. U.S.*, 500 F.2d 508 (Ct.Cl. 1974).
73. Statement of Position 98-2, *Accounting for Costs of Activities of Not-for-Profit Organizations and State and Local Governmental Entities That Include Fund Raising*, issued March 11, 1998, as an amendment to the AICPA Audit and Accounting Guide.
74. 1991 *Exempt Organizations Continuing Professional Education Technical Instruction Program*, at page 20.
75. Reg. 1.512(a)-1.
76. 121 IRC §512(a)(1); Reg. §1.512(a)-1(b).
77. *Iowa State University of Science and Technology v. U.S.*, 500 F.2d 508 (Ct.Cl. 1974).
78. Reg. §1.512(a)-1(a).
79. Reg. §1.512(a)-1(c).
80. Reg. §1.512(a)-1(d)(1).
81. Reg. §1.512(a)-1(d)(2).
82. Reg. §1.513-1(c)(iii) says, "Income derived from the conduct of an annual dance or similar fund-raising event for charity would not be income from trade or business

regularly carried on." In *U.S. v. American Bar Endowment*, 477 U.S. 105 (1986), an insurance sales program, the profit (which reportedly was dependent on member generosity), was determined to be a taxable business, not a fund-raising effort. The "donated" portion of the member premium was not voluntary, and the program was conducted with the intention of producing a profit. Note that because of this decision, the ABA's total cost in relation to the insurance program would be deductible.

83. 1992 *Exempt Organizations Continuing Professional Education Technical Instruction Program* (published annually and ordered from the IRS Reading Room in Washington, DC, or the IRS Web site), at 74, in discussion of the example found in Reg. §1.512(a)-1(e).
84. Reg. §1.512(a)-1(d)(1); *West Virginia Medical Association v. Commissioner*, 882 F.2d 123 (4th Cir. 1989).
85. Reg. §1.512(a)-1(f).
86. Prop. Reg. §513-4(c)(1) and (2); readers should be alert for new developments.
87. 1991 *Exempt Organizations Continuing Professional Education Technical Instruction Program*, at page 20.
88. *Exempt Organizations Examination Guidelines Handbook*, Internal Revenue Manual, §720(7).
89. *Portland Golf Club, supra* n.112.
90. Reg. §1.162-28.
91. Reg. §1.512(a)-1(f)(6).
92. *Rensselaer Polytechnic Institute v. Commissioner*, 732 F.2d 1058 (2d Cir. 1984), *aff'g* 79 T. C. 967 (1982).
93. See Chapter 2§2 of *Tax Planning and Compliance*.
94. *United Cancer Council, Inc. v. Commissioner*, 109 T. C. 326 (December 12, 1997).
95. Special report of Laura Kalish entitled "Allocation of Expenses—Foreign Solution," *The Exempt Organization Tax Review*, February 1995, p. 283.
96. See §27.3(b).
97. There is no published precedent for this position. An IRS exempt organization specialist's informal opinion was that there could be no deduction because no cash changed hands. There are several precedents in the tax code for imputed income. Under IRC §482, income can be allocated between related companies, essentially on paper. Interest income is imputed to certain below-market rate loans under IRC §7872. Although the analogy is not perfect (because it is not an exchange transaction in which the exempt organization earns its side of the donated services), the value of goods or services received in a barter transaction are reportable income as outlined in IRS Publication 525, *Taxable and Nontaxable Income*.
98. IRC §170(e).
99. IRC §102.

CHAPTER 6

1. Chapters 1 through 17 of *Tax Planning and Compliance* contain 342 pages chock full of citations to the published rulings and more recent technical advice memoranda.
2. See discussion of qualifications for tax-exempt status in Chapter 1§1.
3. Chapter 18 of *Tax Planning and Compliance* has 123 pages of detailed, line-by-line instructions for this important process.
4. Rev. Proc. 98-4, 1998-1 IRB 113.
5. Discussed in Chapter 11§2.
6. See Chapter 17§3(e).
7. See Chapter 13§ 7.
8. See Chapter 17§1.
9. Rev. Procs. 98-1, 98-2, 98-3, 98-4, 98-5, 98-8, 1998-1 IRB 7-255.
10. IRC §446(e); IRS Publication 538, *Accounting Periods and Methods*, contains detailed instructions and guidance.
11. Rev. Proc. 85-58, 1985-2 C. B. 740.
12. See Chapter 15§§1 and 2(b) of *Tax Planning and Compliance*.
13. Under Reg. §301.9100-1.
14. Rev. Proc. 98-8, 1998-1 IRB 225; this procedure lists user fees for exempt organization filings and is updated annually.
15. See Chapter 1§4(a) for more discussion of the impact of the accounting rules tax reporting.
16. Notice 96-13, 1996-1 C. B. 378.
17. Rev. Proc. 85-37, 1985-2 C. B. 438, modified by 97-37, 1997-33 IRB 18.
18. The guidelines for showing good cause are found in IRC §6110.
19. IRC §481.
20. See Chapter 5.
21. On page 3 of Schedule A illustrated in Appendix 4A.
22. Chapter 17§5 of *Tax Planning and Compliance* addresses this special private foundation issue.
23. Defined in Chapter 3§5.
24. Chapters 13 and 15 of *Tax Planning and Compliance* address these issues.
25. See Chapter 15 of *Tax Planning and Compliance*.
26. See Chapter 3§3.
27. Chapter 28 of *Tax Planning and Compliance* contains detailed suggestions and model IRS documents used in connection with an examination.

Index